I0902638

blessed to bless

blessed to bless

AN INTRODUCTION TO THE BIBLE

Tim Sean Youmans

CHURCH PUBLISHING INCORPORATED

Church Publishing
19 East 34th Street
New York, NY 10016
www.churchpublishing.org

Cover design by Jennifer Kopec, 2Pug Design
Typeset by Rose Design

Library of Congress Cataloging-in-Publication Data

Names: Youmans, Tim Sean, author.
Title: Blessed to bless : an introduction to the Bible / Tim Sean Youmans.
Identifiers: LCCN 2019048944 (print) | LCCN 2019048945 (ebook) | ISBN 9781640652460 (paperback) | ISBN 9781640652477 (epub)
Subjects: LCSH: Bible--Introductions.
Classification: LCC BS475.3 .Y68 2020 (print) | LCC BS475.3 (ebook) | DDC 220.6/1--dc23
LC record available at https://lccn.loc.gov/2019048944
LC ebook record available at https://lccn.loc.gov/2019048945

for Succor Hill

Contents

SECTION TWO

EXODUS, WILDERNESS, CONQUEST, AND THE JUDGES / 53

Unit One: The Exodus: Forty Years in the Wilderness and the Halacha / 55

Unit Two: Joshua and the Conquest of Canaan, the Dark Period of the Judges, and the Call of Samuel / 95

“. . . all the families of the earth will be blessed because of you.” (Gen. 12:3)

“Therefore, go and make disciples of all nations, baptizing them in the name of the Father and of the Son and of the Holy Spirit, teaching them to obey everything I have commanded you. Look, I myself with be with you every day until the end of this present age.” (Matt. 28:19–20)

Introduction

Many people revere and respect the Bible, but very few people have actually read it. This is because the Bible can be very intimidating. It's a gargantuan collection of books, written long ago by over forty different authors. People disagree about how it should be read and what the stories mean. *Blessed to Bless* is a basic introduction to the Bible and those complexities.

What you read here is the result of an invitation given to the parents of fifth through eighth graders at Casady School in Oklahoma City, a pre-K through twelfth grade Episcopal preparatory day school. Middle school students at Casady move through a four-year survey of the Bible, studying the Hebrew Scriptures (what Christians call the Old Testament) in the first three years and then they do an introduction of the Christian Scriptures (or the New Testament) in the fourth year. Parents are invited to read through the Bible during the school year following the same pace as their child. When we began, I expected fifteen or so to be interested. I was surprised when over ninety parents showed interest! A website was set up in which I posted the same reading assignments the students were given in class along with commentary. These have become the chapters of this book.

I often tell my students that religion (and in this case the Bible) is like baseball. It can be as complicated as you want it to be (with all the variables of pitcher and batter statistics, superstitions, and the like) or it can be simple (a bunch of folks playing catch). This introduction tries to be simple and basic, but at times will point out the potential complexities of certain stories and ideas within the Bible. It is far from a comprehensive explanation of the Bible, but it will serve you as a foundation for deeper study.

Does this book have a religious agenda? Yes and no. Casady School, like many Episcopal day schools, has students from a wide range of religious backgrounds. The school's population is comprised of Evangelical, Catholic, and Orthodox Christian families, as well as Hindu, Jewish,

Muslim, and Buddhist families. We also have a number of nonreligious families, including intentionally science-driven secular families. Our school loves and respects these families; we do not aggressively attempt to proselytize our students.

On the other hand, because we respect our students and families, I'm honest about my own faith and understanding of the scriptures. I am an Episcopal priest who was raised in a Baptist, evangelical home. I do think God is at work in the world, present in the day-to-day lives of people, and that the essence of those interactions and hopes are expressed within the Bible. That is why I've entitled this book, *Blessed to Bless*. God blesses the entire world through the life of Jesus Christ and then invites us to join in this relational equation. Ultimately, I will be pointing this out to you as you move through the Bible, but it is done with respect for my diverse audience. I share Jesus, but I do so in the same way I sense Jesus shared himself: honestly, generously, and nonanxiously. As I walk you through the Hebrew and Christian Scriptures, it is my hope that you will sense this at work.

This book is for people like these students and their parents. If you are a Christian and you want a basic introduction to the Bible, this book is for you. If you are not religious but you want to have a sense of what the Bible contains and what it means to Christians, this book is also for you. It can be read together as parent and child; it can be used with a group of parents reading the Bible together with their children, and it can be used for a Sunday school class for teens or adults. It's for all types of beginners as well as those who want a refresher of the scope of our salvation story.

How to Use This Book

Each chapter begins with a reading assignment from the Bible. Do not skip this. I write the commentary assuming you have read that particular text of scripture. If you skip it, the chapter's content might seem to have a stranger rhythm than if you did read the biblical passage first. In order to get the most out of this survey, read the biblical text first, usually three to five Bible chapters (about the length of three to five normal pages), then read the guide here. Each chapter ends with a few questions for you to consider and discuss.

If you decide to read two chapters of this book each week, you will complete this survey of the Bible in about one year's time, depending on your consistency. Keep in mind that you will not be reading the Bible in its entirety. This book is a survey, which introduces you to the larger framework of the Bible, not every word. Even so, if you read everything that is assigned, you will have read more of the Bible than the majority of the population, even most practicing Christians. And you will have a foundation upon which to read and study further.

Written on an eighth-grade reading level, there are times when I wanted to get into more complexity but chose not to do so. This is written for approximately the same age as those classroom students who inspired it, namely ten- to fifteen-year-olds. But there is no reason why it cannot be used for older teens and adults, especially ones who have no previous knowledge of the scriptures whatsoever. It is a basic introduction. You'll also notice places set aside in the text called BVC. This is short for *Bible Vocabulary Concept* and will help define important concepts along the way as we read the Bible. They will also be listed alphabetically by book of the Bible in the appendix on page 313.

One of the resources I will refer to throughout this book that will help you is called *The Bible Project*. This group of theologians and artists have created short overview videos for each book of the Bible, as well as videos about various themes and word studies in the scriptures. These videos are wonderfully helpful to understanding your reading and for small group discussion. Visit www.thebibleproject.com.

It is important to mention that some stories in the Bible are rated "R" for violent or sexually charged content. These are difficult stories and some young adult readers may not have the critical thinking skills and sensitivity to understand them. If you are using this in a small group or classroom setting, it will require some discretion of the leader or teacher. Such warnings will be found in the *Blessed to Bless Leader's Guide*, which is available online as a free download at *www.blessedtobless.us* or *www.churchpublishing.org/blessedtobless*. Some of those stories are mentioned in this book, but more generally (and vaguely) than if we dealt with them in their entirety.

What kind of Bible should you use? If you are new to the Bible, there are a couple of things you need to know. One, there are a wide variety of translations. The scriptures were written in three languages: Hebrew, Aramaic, and Greek. Translating from one language to another requires making decisions on what those words meant by those who wrote them. Sometimes this is straightforward and sometimes it is a puzzle with a variety of possibilities. Some Bibles tend to be more direct translations, which means they chose as close to the equivalent words in English as possible. When this is done, something may get lost in translation. Other Bibles tend to be a paraphrase, which means the translator shaped the English to capture the meaning intended by the author in ways a reader of English can understand. Most Bibles are somewhere in the middle of these two extremes. This book draws quotes from the Common English Bible (CEB), which is a combination of both approaches, depending on the passage.

Second, Bibles have what are commonly referred to as "chapter" and "verse." The Bible was not written with these in place, but they were added later (circa fifteenth century) to help the reader locate places in the books.

Having said all of that, are you ready? Let's start reading the Bible.

SECTION ONE

The Book of Genesis

Unit One

The Creation and the Fall

Genesis 1–11

1
The Creation Story(s)

Read Genesis chapters 1–2.

There isn't one creation story, but two. The original stories in Hebrew were not written with chapters and verses; those were added around the fifteenth century BCE (before the Common Era) so people could locate the stories. Sometimes those chapters and verses are mislocated and change the meaning of the story. This is one of those times.

Story One: Genesis 1:1–2:4
Story Two: Genesis 2:5–24

Go look again at the first two chapters and notice where one story ends and the second one starts.

Why does this matter? Notice how they differ. We are not the least bit interested in playing "gotcha" with ancient Hebrew stories and proving them "wrong." The ways in which they are different doesn't lessen their value, but asks you, as the reader, to wonder why.

The first story is mostly about the natural world. It is presented with a certain amount of order and in many ways reads like a list. It emphasizes God's organization of nature, things having "kinds" and categories. It suggests God created with intention and purpose. It repeatedly calls what is created "good." Pay close attention when any literary text repeats itself (including the Bible); it is trying to underscore that idea. The order and goodness of creation is an important Hebrew idea: creation is intrinsically good because God declared it so. That's the good news. The bad news will, however, be just around the corner in Genesis, chapter 3.

In the first story, man and woman are created at the same time as the crowning achievement of creation. (In the second story, the man is created first, by himself. Then the woman is created later on, after he becomes lonely.) The first story conveys an engaging idea: human beings are created in the image of God (Latin: *imago Dei*). What it does not do, however, is spell out specifically what that means. What do you think it means? That we "look" like God? Wait, does God have white skin? Dark skin? Curly hair? Green eyes? What do you think being created with the imprint of God might mean? This question lead us to the intangible (hard to measure) aspects we might share: love, compassion, creativity, logic, humor, relationships.

▸***Imago Dei*** is the Latin phrasing for the "image of God," often used to describe the larger Hebrew concept of human beings sharing aspects of God's nature.

The first story is like a prescientific approximation of a human scientific impulse, more primitive certainly, but the basic form of scientific thinking is embedded there. It is set up like a list that puts things into categories. Story number one is sort of "left brain."

Story number two is less like an ordered observation and more like a situational drama. While story one is like a documentary, this one is like a sitcom. The man is created first, becomes lonely, and God creates a partner for him. The two stories speak to two different parts of human nature: the desire to catalogue and organize, and the desire for relationship. It is right and left brain thinking, side-by-side.

▸**Young earth** is the idea that the biblical creation accounts are literal descriptions of the earth's origins, and if you track human history using this primeval text, the earth is approximately 6,000 years old.

Questions for Reflection or Discussion

1. If you were to write a story about the creation of the earth, would it be more like story number one or story number two?
2. The Hebrew tradition believes that human beings share the image of God. What do you think that could mean?

2
The Second Creation Story

Read Genesis 2:4–25 again.

It is this second creation story that most people associate with the Bible's creation account. God creates a garden and then Adam is created and is asked to subdue the garden, to tend it and take care of it. This was God's original intention for humanity: to care for the earth. The name *Adam* comes from a Hebrew word *adtham,* for dirt or soil. He is created from soil, and then he will grow food from the soil, so there is this profound connection with the earth. Even if you read this story symbolically, human beings, like soil, are made of minerals. We share that in common.

▸**The Garden** (or *edenic*) often refers to a perfect world or a utopia before the "The Fall." We need to "get back to *the Garden.*"

Adam becomes lonely. Though God is with him in a special way, God is perhaps too different from Adam. God decides to create a helper for Adam, so God creates animals to keep him company. But this wasn't suitable. He puts Adam to sleep and takes a rib from his side and forms a woman. Here, the story uses a different word for Adam, *ish*, which translates *man*. The woman is called *isha*, or *from man*. Later Adam gives her the name *Havah*, which means "life," and that name eventually was pronounced Eve.

The number seven, after the seven days of creation, comes to represent a complete cycle, or perfection, and in time becomes designated as the "number of God." The number six often represents humanity, because in the first creation story human beings were created on the sixth day.

God resting on the seventh day becomes the foundation for the larger concept of the need to rest. Thousands of years later, when God is giving the Hebrew tribe laws to shape their life, he commands they take the seventh day and rest.

The Hebrew word used for breath, *ruach*, is also used for spirit and wind. So the idea of God breathing into the nostrils of "Soil (or *adtham*)" eventually was expanded into a double layer of meaning. God's breath is Spirit.

Lastly, there is some disagreement about the exact nature of the creation accounts. Are they literal historical descriptions or symbolic stories? If you try to track the general chronology of the history back to the time of Adam and Eve (you cannot track it precisely because it is prehistoric, or before written histories), then the earth is approximately 6,000 years old. Scientific method has observed the age of the earth to be about 3.4 billion years old. Which is it?

We will discuss these issues further when reading chapter 4 of Genesis. So put a pin in this topic and we will circle back around.

Questions for Reflection or Discussion

1. In the creation account God rests on the seventh day. Do you or your family take a day of rest? If so, how? If not, why not?
2. Adam is tasked with tilling the garden and caring for the earth. Can you name some ways that you and your family help care for the earth?

3

The Fall of Humanity

Read Genesis 3:1–24.

This story is often referred to as the "fall of man" or the "fall of humanity." The man and the woman are allowed to eat the fruit from any tree in the garden except one—the *Tree of the Knowledge of Good and Evil*. The fruit, by the way, was not an apple. The story does not specify, so I wonder, "What fruit would possibly tempt you to disobey God?" When asking this question a few years ago, after a moment of serious thought a student very earnestly said, "Fried chicken." It has thus been named in my class ever since.

Here is one way to illustrate this: You are at a family picnic. You hear a flutter of giggles behind you. You turn around and your three-year-old nephew is running naked in the sprinkler. Everyone laughs and giggles, snaps a few pictures to embarrass him in front of future girlfriends, but there is no real concern. Why? "Because the child is innocent and doesn't know what he's doing is inappropriate."

Same setting, an hour later. Except this time, you hear awkward murmurs and gasps. Uncle Ted, who is sixty years old, is running naked through the sprinklers! People are scrambling to cover him up with blankets and escort him into the house. A weird tension comes over the picnic. Why? "Because Uncle Ted ought to know better!"

Uncle Ted is supposed to know that what he is doing is inappropriate. One is innocent, the other is not. In the garden story, being naked has a symbolic meaning. When they lost their innocence by gaining knowledge they did not previously have, life became awkward and complicated.

Why wouldn't God want Adam and Eve to know good and evil?

There is pain involved when we lose innocence, especially when it is lost prematurely. The story suggests that God intended humanity to maintain innocence, at least for a while. Disobedience is defined, in this story, as jumping the gun on God. So a question for you: remaining within the "world" of this story, do you think God would have ever given the man and the woman the ability to know good and evil?

> ▸**Sin** and **original sin.** *Sin* is when human beings act or think against God's original intent. *Original sin* is the belief that Adam and Eve introduced sin into the human race and every human is subsequently born sinful.

When talking about this story, I often ask fifth graders, who are ten years old, "Do your parents let you watch PG-13 movies?" It's typically 50/50, but I press the ones who are not allowed. "Why not? What are your parents afraid of?"

And their answers are smart. "My parents don't want me to see something that is bad because I might copy what I see. Or it will confuse me."

"Why would it confuse you?" I ask.

"Because we aren't ready for it!"

Is the story suggesting the same idea? Adam and Eve would have eventually been ready for the knowledge of good and evil, but they acted too soon—all things in due season. I don't know if this is the answer or if it is even the right question to ask, but it seems important.

Apply this to other areas of life. Knowledge is a powerful commodity and ought to be used for the good of everyone around us. When we mishandle it, we betray the purpose of our creation. Christian theology calls this the "*fall of humanity*" or "*sin*."

> ▸**The snake** is a symbol for a dangerous temptation and later associated with the devil because of a story from Jewish mythology about Satan being a fallen *serpah.*

Questions for Reflection or Discussion

1. Does God want people to know the difference between good and evil? If so, when and how?

2. Should children watch PG-13 movies before age thirteen? R movies before age seventeen? Most parents are okay with kids seeing some things in these movies and not others. Discuss the distinctions.
3. A simple definition of sin is doing or thinking things that God would rather you did not do or think. What things in your life does God consider sin?

4

The Consequences of Sin

Symbolism. A symbol has two or more levels of meaning. One, it is the thing that it actually is, but it also conveys some other meaning. Religious culture tends to have a variety of symbols. The book of Genesis, especially the first eleven chapters, has quite a few:

- *soil*: represents humanity
- *apple* (*or fruit*): represents the knowledge of good and evil, and sometimes temptation
- *snake*: represents a dangerous temptation that can hurt you
- *garden*: represents a perfect world or Utopia

As you read Genesis 3 about the "fall of humanity," notice that when God is going to address these consequences, the literary structure changes to poetry. Poetry is highly figurative and full of symbolism. Often people will conclude that means it is "not true." That could be the case with figurative language, but not always. Poetic language can also mean it is more concentrated or more important than narrative (storytelling) forms. It is one way of saying, "Pay attention, this has particular meaning."

There is a poetic inset in Genesis 3:14–19 laying out the consequences of Adam and Eve's disobedience to God. Keep in mind that these things are *not* the Creator's intention for them:

- **Snake.** Will now crawl on its belly and there will be hatred between it and the woman and her offspring. One of her offspring will crush the serpent's head, and the serpent will strike his heel.
- **Woman**. She will have pain in childbearing and her desire will be focused on her husband and he will rule over her. Again, keep in mind this is not the relationship God intended but the broken version. This suggests that equality between spouses was God's original intention.

- **Man.** Work will now be hard. Notice the parallel. The poetic language emphasizes that the ground will become cursed and will not cooperate with the man. Remember, what did God use to make Adam? What was his essence? It was soil. Is this a play on words? Did Adam's disobedience place him at war with aspects of himself?

▸***Her offspring will crush your head and the serpent will strike his heel.*** Christians believe this to be a foreshadowing of the death of Jesus (the serpent will strike his heel) and Jesus' victory over that death in the resurrection (her offspring will crush your head).

God banishes Adam and Even from the Garden and places cherubim at the gate with flaming, flashing swords to keep them out. There are basically three kinds of celestial creatures described in the scriptures. The first type are called *malakim*, which means messenger, and are often referred to as *angels*. They appear in human form with some unmentioned aspect giving those around them a clue that they are celestial beings. (Sorry to disappoint you, but they never have wings.) Another type are *cherub* (singular) or *cherubim* (plural). They are a hybrid human/animal with wings. A third type are *seraphim*, which show up in various forms but generally are luminous serpent-like creatures with wings. Cherubim and seraphim are most associated with the worship of God.

Your next reading is Genesis 4. In the next few entries we will work through some of the modern concerns about these stories. Are they literal or figurative? Can they be both? Was the earth created 5,775 years ago or 4.5 billion years ago? Keep those questions in mind as you read the passages.

Questions for Reflection or Discussion

1. Some think that men ruling over their wives is the way God wants marriages to be. What do you think?
2. Most people are freaked out by snakes. Do you have any snake stories?
3. The punishment is set in a poetic form. Why do you think the writers presented it that way?

5
Cain and Abel

Read Genesis 4:1–25.

Is the earth 5,775 years old or is it 4.5 billion years old?

That first date is an approximate dating that backtracks to the time of Adam and Eve. It is an estimate because those stories are often called *primeval* (which means a "young us"), *prehistoric* (before written histories), and *primordial* because they deal with origins. The time is generally estimated at 6,000 years ago.

As you read chapter 4, I was hoping it would raise some questions for you as a modern reader:

1. Who was Cain afraid would come and harm him?
2. Who did Cain marry and have a child with?
3. For what group of people did Cain build a city?

As I said earlier, we're not trying to play "gotcha" with the Bible. The postscientific questions we might be inclined to ask of these stories were not even on the radar of the people who told these stories around the campfire. In this sense, the stories were mytho-poetic.

Myth? The Bible is a myth? It's very important to clarify what the prefix *mytho* means. It does not mean false. Rather, myths are the stories that frame a culture's sense of themselves and their values. So a mythos can be historically true or not. Veracity really isn't the point. The point is . . . well . . . the point of the story.

For stories like the Garden of Eden, it is about the role of God as creator and the tendency of human beings to disobey the Creator's directions. The story of Cain and Abel is about the quality of gifts to God, the attitude in which those gifts are given, and the tendency toward jealousy, anger, and violence. (For a peek of this at work in the New Testament, look at Matthew 5:21–26.)

▸**Mytho-poetic** are stories that show what is important to a group of people or a culture. These stories can be fiction, nonfiction, or a mixture of both.

There are three basic ways people tend to interpret these stories. Keep in mind this is a simple version:

1. **Literal.** The story means exactly what it says. God took six, twenty-four-hour days to create the earth, and all human beings came from two actual people.
2. **Symbolic.** Elements of the story are pointing to something else. Yes, it is a story about two people in a garden, but those two people represent something larger than just two people. Adam and Eve (soil and life) represent all of civilization and human beings inclination to misuse knowledge and disobey God.
3. **A mixture of literal and symbolic.** This is the position that I take and the one taken by most Episcopalians.

Darren Aronofsky's movie *Noah* did a beautiful sequence that shows the mixing of a literal and symbolic handling of the story.[1]

The trick is to not throw the baby out with the bathwater. People tend to gravitate toward binary thinking, which means something being all one thing or all the other. Sometimes you need to think this way, but sometimes it limits you. Remember the observation about the two creation stories: one is oriented to left brain and the other to the right brain? We need to come to the scriptures with this in mind.

As for Cain and Abel, here are a couple of the more important ideas: "Am I my brother's keeper?" We are responsible for each other in community. Genesis doesn't say specifically why God chose Abel's offering over Cain's, though it does suggest Cain already had a negative attitude. Later, writers in the New Testament suggest Abel had a higher quality of faith (Heb. 11:4).

▸**Am I my brother's keeper?** When God asked Cain where his brother was, he acted as if it wasn't his responsibility to take care of him. When used, this phrase implies that we are responsible for each other.

1. *https://www.youtube.com/watch?v=UR5z9zzYt3I.*

There is a more complex interpretation if you want to think about it on a higher level. Able is a rancher and herdsman; Cain, a farmer. Cain's livelihood requires that animal herds stay out of his crops, so he will need to build a fence. So the story speaks about the conflict that arose from the shift of a hunter-gatherer society to farming society. God prefers the first because it is more closely tied to a daily dependence on God, whereas farming tends toward a self-dependent act and human ownership, thus drawing the farmer away from dependence on God.

What do you think? Welcome to religious interpretation. Isn't it fun?

What can be seen more clearly is that the sin of Adam and Eve in the Garden led to an act of jealousy and violence when Cain killed Abel. His blood "crying to me from the ground" (Gen. 4:10), which is definitely symbolic.

▸**Mark of Cain.** This was a mark God put on Cain to protect him from others harming him after he was banished for killing Abel. No one knows what the mark looked like.

The mark that protected Cain? No one knows what that was supposed to be. Some racist movements have made a claim that the mark was dark skin, but that is nonsense.[2] And even if it were, the "mark" is one of grace and protection.

▸**East of Eden.** God punished Cain by sending him "east of Eden." This is used to refer to someone who has been banished by a group of people or society.

Adam and Eve have a third son named Seth.

Questions for Reflection or Discussion

1. Do you think the earth is around 6,000 years old, tracing back, as best Bible scholars can? Or do you think the earth is 4.5 billion years old based on dating developed by scientific method?

2. This is an interesting explanation on what the mark of Cain might have been: *https://www.gotquestions.org/mark-Cain.html.*

2. Do you think there is a way for both creation stories to have truth in them? Both the Hebrew version and the conclusions of science? What kinds of truth are in each kind of account?
3. Do you feel like you are "your brother's keeper"? What does this mean to you?

6
The Long Ages

Read Genesis 5:1–32.

What about those extended ages listed in Genesis 5? Anthropologists don't point to any evidence that human beings ever lived 969 years (Methuselah). In fact, evidence points to human life in the past being much shorter. Is something else going on here?

- Were they following a lunar calendar that explains the higher numbers?
- Are the numbers symbolic for certain ideas that the storytellers conveyed?
- A higher age suggests more respect, is that what is being exaggerated?

Enoch, mentioned in the genealogy, is described as one who "did not die" but was taken away by God. He is one of two named in the Hebrew Bible who did so. The other is Elijah, who we will read about in later chapters.

Now look at Genesis 6:1–4:

> When the number of people started to increase throughout the fertile land, daughters were born to them. The divine beings saw how beautiful these human women were, so they married the ones they chose. The LORD said, "My breath will not remain in humans forever, because they are flesh. They will live one hundred twenty years." In those days, giants lived on the earth and also afterward, when divine beings and human daughters had sexual relations and gave birth to children. These were the ancient heroes, famous men.

This is a peculiar passage that is describing something that cannot be clearly identified. "Divine Beings" in the Common English Bible (CEB) are translated as "Sons of God" in the New Revised Standard Version (NRSV). These names could mean a variety of things, but it has generally been interpreted as a kind of angelic being. We have read about cherubim and seraphim, and now they mention Nephilim. It seems in this case that angelic beings had children with human women, and their offspring were these super-human creatures. Over time, the ancient Hebrew culture wondered if people with extraordinary abilities, or those who were unusually tall, could be the descendants of the Nephilim. We will read about these descendants in the book of Numbers, chapter 13.

▸ **Dystopia.** The opposite of utopia, a world gone wrong and falling apart.

But God seems unhappy with all of this and the story pivots toward Noah and the Great Flood. Read the story in its entirety, Genesis 6–9. If you have never read the actual account, you may be surprised by a few things.

Questions for Reflection or Discussion

1. What about these long ages?
2. Do you think people lived that long back then or that the numbers have a hidden meaning?

7
Noah and the Great Flood

Read the entire story of Noah and the ark in one sitting. It is four chapters, or as I like to say, four pages. Don't read what follows here until you have done that first. It is Genesis chapters 6–9:17.

How is it that children are not completely freaked out by this story?

▸**Antediluvian.** Before the flood.

This is a story about God's wrath, with one exception—the grace given to one man and his family.

I always say, don't underestimate the ability of a boat, cute animals, and a rainbow to soften a story. Keep in mind that children tend to tacitly trust what grown-ups tell them. They assume that the people drowned by God must have been so completely corrupt to have deserved their demise. But I wonder, how many children are disturbed by the whole thing? Think about the premise for a child: do something bad, and God will drown you! That's rough.

▸**Deluge.** Another word for flood.

The earth was "corrupt" and "filled with violence." At the end of the story it establishes a foundational concept for those who commit violence—blood for blood, life for life. When you commit violence against a human that is created in the image of God, you are committing an act of violence against that image, and your life is to be taken in response. Look again at Genesis 9:5–6.

There is a kind of dark irony; God is heartbroken by comprehensive violence, so he commits comprehensive violence. That is a stark notion. It's sad, and the text says it makes God sad and regretful. Violence breaks God's heart.

▸This is the first time the measurement of a **cubit** is mentioned in the Bible. It was generally considered the length from a man's elbow to the tips of his fingers, about 18 inches.

God says that Noah will be the last patriarch who lives an extraordinarily long life (Gen. 6:3). After Noah a human being's years will not surpass 120 years. Noah lived 950 years.

Noah sends out a black raven before the dove. This could be a literary device, a black bird being a sign of foreboding. The white dove and the olive branch eventually have come to represent peace. Why? Because after the flood, in the wake of God ridding the earth of violence, peace can now exist.

▸**Olive branch.** When the dove returned with an olive branch, it was a sign that there was land. The earth had been washed of violence.

That's all for this chapter. We will consider what happens after Noah gets off the boat, particularly the rarely reported story of Noah getting drunk and cursing his grandson and descendants forever.

If you have time in the next couple of weeks, watch Darren Aronofsky's film *Noah*. Most of what he did was rooted in Jewish and Christian interpretations of the story and the practice of Jewish Midrash. Watching it will offer you a different perspective to consider.

▸**Apocalypse.** Typically associated with the end of the world, but actually means "to reveal" something. A story about the end of the world is an apocalypse in that God reveals the coming destruction to someone, like he did to Noah.

Questions for Reflection or Discussion

1. Most people were familiar with this story as a child. Was this story scary to you when you were younger? Why or why not?
2. Violence makes God sad in this story. Talk about the value of human life and discuss the different kinds of violence in the world today.

8
Sloppy Drunk Noah

Read Genesis 9:1–28 (some will be a repeat).

The narrative says that the first thing Noah does when the boat settles on dry land is build an altar and offer a sacrifice to God. Then he immediately plants a vineyard and gets drunk. Any vineyard owner knows it takes between five to seven years to yield grapes. A good amount of time transpired in that one sentence, between his planting a vineyard and getting drunk.

What happened during that time? Why does Noah curse his grandson Canaan and his descendants? The answer might be found in the five to seven years it took to grow the grapes.

Scholars aren't definitive about it, but what could very likely be implied in the story is that Noah's grandson attempted to overthrow the tribal headship of his grandfather because Noah was suffering from a posttraumatic reaction to the flood.

Wait. Where did you read that?

Admittedly, you have to read a great deal between the lines to get that interpretation, but that is part of the challenge and fun of interpreting ancient stories. If it's accurate, Noah's period of ineffectual leadership is conveyed symbolically in getting drunk, passing out naked, and embarrassing himself in front of the tribe.

So something sketchy happened between Noah and his grandson Canaan. As you read forward into the Bible, you will begin to notice that the Canaanites are not seen in the most positive light. The *shaming of Canaan* will resurface again and again as we move forward. *Canaanites* are significant players in the larger arc of the entire Bible. Pay attention. Make a mental note.

The story of Noah and the Great Flood is about God's judgment, tempered with grace toward one family and his desire to not completely give up on humanity. He makes a covenant with Noah that he will never again destroy the earth with water, and he "signs" that agreement by placing a rainbow in the sky. It is such a dark story, but there is a glimmer of God's care and hope for creation.

Questions for Reflection or Discussion

1. How do you feel when someone gets drunk? Why do they drink so much?
2. Noah curses his grandson. Why do you think he does this? What did Canaan do wrong?
3. The flood was a traumatic event and likely deeply affected Noah. What are other traumatic events that can profoundly change us? In what ways do they change us, good and bad?

9
Tower of Babel

Scan Genesis 10, then read Genesis 11:1–9.

Genesis chapters 1–11 are considered the mytho-poetic origin stories of the ancient Hebrew people. To reiterate from chapter 5, the word "myth" does not mean false. Rather, myths are the stories that hold a culture's understanding of itself. They can be fictional, historical, or a blending of both. It may be confusing to describe biblical stories to be a mixture of both; however religious stories speak to both sides of the human brain, the creative imaginative side and the logical rational side.

Genesis chapters 1–11 seek to answer a series of origin questions: Where did life come from? How did humanity begin? What is the source of evil? How did violence first emerge? Where did human language come from?

In Genesis chapter 10 Noah sends each of his three sons in different directions to repopulate the world. This is referred to as the *Table of Nations*. Shem goes east toward Mesopotamia; Ham is given Egypt, including the small bit of land given to his cursed son Canaan (modern-day Middle East, also known as the *Levant*); and Japheth goes north into what is now the nation of Turkey.

The final story in this collection of primordial, primeval, mytho-poetic stories is the *Tower of Babel* found in chapter 11. Can you see a similar theme in this story as the one in the Garden of Eden? When building Babel, they don't expressly say they are trying to be God, but striving for the heavens in order to make a name for themselves. They want to elevate their position. God confuses their language and frustrates their effort, scattering them across the region. (Make a mental note that this city is the forerunner of *Babylon*. This will become important later in our reading.)

Once again, the scientific point of view takes issue with the suggestion that the varied global languages originated in one location at one point in time. But knowing whether this story is literally true isn't important to what the story is trying to say about human nature. It may be important to you, but that is where the wide variety of interpretations come into play.

At the heart of all these stories is a common idea. God is God, human beings are not. We are created in the image of God and share certain aspects of God, but we are not God. When human beings attempt to rise to the level of God, they do damage to self and each other. Human beings have created a huge problem. How will God resolve that problem? The answer is a long process that begins in Genesis chapter 12.

Questions for Reflection or Discussion

1. At this point you may want to talk about what you think about these early Genesis stories in general. Which are your favorites? Why?
2. What story seems to be the truest of all of them? In what way? What are other theories about the origins of language?

10
Is All of This Literal?

The elephant in the room for many of you reading up to this point might be the relationship between these stories and the scientific understandings of the origins of life. I tend to read these scriptures with a right-brained, poetic, literary sensibility. So generally speaking, I am not all that interested in whether the stories written by ancient Hebrews are getting the science correct. It isn't because it is unimportant. Rather, these stories were a sincere attempt to address crucial issues in their lives.

The Garden of Eden is a picture of human beings living in harmony with God and what goes wrong when we reject that notion. Cain and Abel are a picture of our tendency toward using violence to deal with our disappointments and jealousies. The story of the Great Flood underscores this tendency, spiraling out of control and breaking the heart of God. The Tower of Babel is a brief but poignant picture of our inclination to abuse the unique nature that human beings possess. God created us "only slightly less than divine" (Ps. 8:5) with the image of God formed within us. These ancient stories depict a humanity unwilling to be satisfied with the wonder of that nature. It is not enough, it seems, to have the imprint of the *imago Dei*; we want to be gods ourselves. The first eleven chapters of Genesis are a poetic rendering of the beauty and tragedy of that reality.

Unit Two

God Conceives a Blessing Culture

Genesis 12–50

Scholars agree that the story of Abraham is its own section. Genesis chapters 1–11 are the mytho-poetic origin stories that include the fall of humanity. Genesis chapters 12–50 are in many ways the beginning of the answer to that human fall. Genesis 1–11 presents the problem; Genesis 12–50 begins God's response.

11

The Call of Abram and Sarai

Watch an overview of Genesis chapters 1–11 from The Bible Project. Then read Genesis chapters 12–13. This is known as the Call of Abraham.

God comes to a descendant of Noah and tells him that he will make him and his descendants a great nation. He will bless him, curse those who curse him, bless those who bless him, and his name will become great. But there is a caveat. Do you see it? *Through you all the nations of the earth will be blessed.*

Could this exchange between God and Abram be the thesis for the entire Bible? God blesses Abraham so that through his descendants all the nations of the earth will be blessed. Jesus, a descendent of Abram, ultimately fulfills this promise on the grandest of scales. In this way, the Bible is a unified story that leads to Jesus. But as you will see, it is a long and convoluted road getting there. For many Christians using this book to read through the Bible, this might be a frustrating journey. You might ask, "Can't we study Jesus from the beginning?" In some respects, that would be like reading the last chapter of a novel while you are reading the rest of it. There will be times we will look forward toward Christianity and point out the ways the Old Testament is leading to Jesus, but for the most part we are going to experience this history in a way similar to the people who then experienced it.

▸**Patriarch** and **matriarch.** The head father and mother of a family or tribe. Abraham and Sarah are the chief patriarch and matriarch of the Hebrew culture.

How do you feel about this idea that God tells a particular person that his family, and eventually the culture that emerges from them, are charged with a special purpose, that of blessing the entire world? What could that possibly mean? Was Abram interested in such a thing?

Think of it this way: let's say God told you he would make you the most celebrated person in your community. Everybody would know you, from the elementary students, through middle school up to high school, and all the way up through the administration. You would be respected and everyone would get excited whenever they saw you. But there is a catch: you have to use that influence and power to make sure everyone is doing okay. If someone was being bullied, you would have to step in. If someone was struggling with school, you would talk to them and make sure they had tutors or the help they needed. You would advocate for them among their peer groups, talk to the principal, their teachers, etc.

Would you want that gig?

Abram is considered a person of great faith because he leaves the security of his father's tribe land and starts his life over in the land of Canaan. (By the way, where have you heard the name *Canaan* before? Genesis 9:25?) However, read carefully; it isn't quite that simple. Immediately after Abram's great act of trust in God, he folds like a cheap accordion; escaping a famine he goes to Egypt and tells the Pharaoh that Sarai is his sister and not his wife, being afraid they would kill him in order to take her because she was so beautiful. But didn't God just tell him that he would protect him on this Vision Quest? God promised to "curse those who curse him." These two pictures of Abram and Sarah establish a pattern you should be looking for as you read on—faithful and faithless. Are Abram/Abraham and Sarai/Sarah people of great faith? Or are they not?

Questions for Reflection or Discussion

1. What has been the hardest change you have made as a family? Who did you trust the most in that situation? Each other? God?
2. When you get scared or anxious, how do you handle it? What or who helps you get through it?
3. If God offered you a position of privilege but it required that you "bless all the people around you," would you take that deal?
4. If you had to pick up and move away to a strange land, who would you take with you besides your immediate family and why?

12

Abram and Sarai's Undulating Faith

Look again at Genesis 12–13, then continue, reading chapters 14, 15, and 16.

Most folks think the scriptures are a collection of stories that each have a useful moral lesson about how to be a better person. Sometimes that is true, but more often the collection of stories are better understood as a whole. This is particularly true with Genesis. As I've pointed out earlier, Genesis is divided into two sections:

Genesis 1–11: The Creation and origin stories

Genesis 12–50: Abraham and Sarah and their descendants

The real thesis of Genesis is found in how these two sections are related. The first section presents the problem, and section two begins the resolution. If you want to review, take a few minutes and again watch *The Bible Project* video about Genesis 1–11.

We will be reading stories about Abraham and his brood in what will be an ever-expanding tribe. Located within those stories is the *Vision Quest* given to Abram and Sarai: to create a culture that will bless all the nations of the earth, and in that blessing repair the brokenness described in the origin stories.

Sometimes this quest will be messy. It is often a two-steps-forward-three-steps-back kind of existence. You saw this immediately in chapter 12 right after their initial call, as Abram and Sarai set off for Egypt and Abram lies about Sarai. You will read it again when Sarai gives up trying to conceive a baby and starts to think the way this culture will come into being is through one of her female slaves. This was not an uncommon practice at the time. Abram conceives a child with one of Sarai's slaves, an

Egyptian woman named Hagar. In that culture, the child would legally be Abram's and Sarai's baby. It causes all kinds of jealousy, and Sarai ends up trying to cast out the slave and her baby Ishmael. God intervenes and sends them back home.

A couple of notes of importance: Abram and his nephew must part ways because there isn't enough grazing land for all of their sheep. Lot chooses to go west of the Jordan River and settles south of the Dead Sea in the cities of Sodom and Gomorrah. Not too long after this Abram must go rescue Lot from some warring tribes.

▸**Sodom and Gomorrah.** The cities that Abram's nephew Lot moved to when they parted ways. God destroyed these cities for their inhospitality and wickedness. The term is used now to refer to a wicked place.

The king that Abram meets in Genesis 13 is a significant archetype. He was a king and priest from Salem (later what would become Jeru-Salem) named Melchizedek. He gives Abram a gift of bread and wine, and Abram gives him a gift, a tithe of his goods (or 10 percent of his profit). Though this occurs some two thousand years before the appearance of Jesus, Christians view Melchizedek as a prefiguring or allusion to the future Jesus. The hint is the bringing of bread and wine and that Abram gives him the same gift one would give God. Jump ahead and take a look at Hebrews 7 in the New Testament.

Questions for Reflection or Discussion

1. Do you ever find yourself making the same mistakes over and over again? What are they? Who gets the most frustrated with you regarding these mistakes?
2. How do you think God feels about Abram and Sarai's up-and-down trust in this adventure God has sent them on?
3. Do you think Melchizedek is a "pre-appearance" of Jesus or a mysterious king that has some symbols in common with Jesus? How so?

13
Circumcision and Three Visitors

Read Genesis chapters 17, 18, and 19:1–29.

God tells Abram that as a sign of the covenant between them, he needs to make a permanent physical mark on every male child. On the eighth day after a baby boy is born, Abram is to take a sharp flint knife and cut off the extra piece of skin that covers the tip of the infant's penis, then stitch it up, and let it heal. From that day forward, the boy's penis will look different than other men in the region. This will be a physical sign that he is part of Abram's tribe. It is called *circumcision*, and Abram seals the covenant by circumcising himself and all the boys and men in his camp, including his son, Ishmael.

▸**circumcision.** The physical mark Israelite boys would undergo to indicate they were a part of the Abrahamic tribe, ritualistically cutting off the foreskin of the penis, typically on the eighth day after birth (Gen. 17:10–13; Josh. 5:2–9).

Notice God makes a slight change to their names. Abram becomes Abraham. Sarai becomes Sarah. The slight change is the addition of their status in the tribe. Abram is now "Father Abraham" and Sarah is now the royalty, or princess.

Jewish and Muslim men continue the practice of circumcision for boys at birth; many Christians also practice this with their infants. Numerous medical sources have determined that circumcision is hygienic and lowers the chance for infection and cancer in the private area. Most hospitals ask the parents if they would like their infant son circumcised as an option. Some see the practice as barbaric and want to pass laws making it illegal. In the modern age, if you are not Jewish or Muslim, it has become a controversial procedure. But many nonreligious parents still have this done to their infant sons.

What happens next? Sarah laughs at God.

The exact tenor of her laughter is undetermined, but when three divine messengers arrive at her tent and tell her she will have a baby in the next year, she has apparently had enough of God's promises, and she laughs it off. And who can blame her? She is in her nineties at this point. If your family was all gathered around the Thanksgiving table and Grandpa tapped his wineglass to make a special announcement that Granny was going to have a baby, you might start laughing too.

When the three visitors confront her about it, she denies it. They tell her that when the baby comes they are to name him "laughter." Isaac is "laughter" in Hebrew.

Immediately after this encounter, God tells Abraham that he is going to destroy the cities of Sodom and Gomorrah for their wickedness. The problem here is that Abraham has family in Sodom. If you recall from your earlier reading in Genesis 13, Lot took his family and settled in Sodom. What ensues is a peculiar exchange between Abraham and God—an argument really. Abraham starts bartering with God, asking him to not destroy those cities. He sounds like a child trying to manipulate his parents for more video game time, starting with a wide target and then bargaining with God toward something narrower. He is trying to save Lot and his family.

Is this a presumptuous move on the part of Abraham? Is it faithlessness? Does Abraham not trust God's judgment? If God is all-knowing, then Abraham ought to trust him with the decision. It shows how their relationship is somewhat tenuous. If he really wants God to just spare Lot, then why not just ask God to do that? Why the manipulation?

On the other hand, the very fact that Abraham is having an argument with God shows that he trusts their relationship. You could argue that this challenge is an act of great faith. Which do you think it is?

Now it's about to get a little weird. Notice at the outset of chapter 19 that it says: "The two angels came to Sodom." Where did the third one go? Some Christians believe that the three visitors to Abraham and Sarah were actually a pre-appearance of the Triune God of Christianity (Father, Son, Holy Spirit). This is similar to the theory of a "pre-appearance" of Christ in Melchizedek in Genesis 14. Perhaps since only two of the three visitors went to Sodom, the third must have remained for the argument between God and Abraham. If that is the case, then as God argues with Abraham, Jesus Christ and the Holy Spirit go to Sodom to judge the city. This fits accordingly with the future understanding of Jesus as one who will "judge the living and the dead" in the early Christian creed. A stretch? Perhaps, but it is not an uncommon interpretation.

Keep in mind this view is superimposed upon the story that occurred some two thousand years before the appearance of Christ and any explicit notion of the Trinity. As we will stress later in this journey through the Bible, a distinction for Judaism among all the Mesopotamian religions was its insistence on monotheism (one god) as opposed to polytheism (many gods). In that sense, a safer reading of this story is that the three visitors were angels. I'll let you decide.

> ▸**Polytheism.** Worshiping of more than one god. **Monotheism.** Worship of one god. Abraham and Sarah were distinct from regional polytheistic practices. They followed one God, a foundational teaching for the Abrahamic faiths.

Now, Sodom and Gomorrah. The sins of the cities are multifaceted, but at the heart of them all is a self-centered crude and offensive behavior. The acts that the people in Sodom and Gomorrah wanted to commit with the angels are often held up as the worst of sins. That Lot would rather they attack his daughters than the two guests speaks to how special and beautiful these messengers must have been. Regardless, the terms *Sodom* and *Gomorrah* are now synonymous with selfish disregard for others, including senseless, meaningless attacks.

The controversial aspect of Sodom and Gomorrah is the desire of the townsmen wanting to have sex with the angels. What has been overemphasized is the apparent homosexual rape hinted at in the story, but the offense is more expansive than that. The people of Sodom and Gomorrah want to rape *divine beings*, which is a different thing than a human being. Don't get me wrong, the entire account is awful. Lot is so committed to protecting his guests he would rather the townspeople attack his daughters than the angels! This is a horrible situation all around.

The result? God destroys Sodom and Gomorrah. He tells Lot and his family to flee and to not look back. Lot's wife looks anyway and is turned into a pillar of salt for disobeying the instruction to not look at the destruction. As an aside, image-search the words "Dead Sea Pillars of Salt." Sodom and Gomorrah were located south of the Dead Sea near some spectacular salt formations, some of which rise up in a very statuesque manner. Students ask me if one of these pillars is Lot's wife. Perhaps. But it begs the question, did those salt formations help shape the story?

What happens next is one of the worst stories in the Bible, but keep in mind that the scriptures are not celebrating it. Lot flees from the area and lives in a cave with his daughters. Anxious they will not be able to find someone adequate to marry, Lot's daughters get their father drunk and trick him into impregnating them. The offspring of this horrific act becomes the ancestral origins of the Moabite people, a group with which Israel shares a contentious relationship for centuries to come. So make a mental note: we will see the Moabites again.

Questions for Reflection or Discussion

1. Sarah is ninety-nine years old. By laughing at the three visitors' news, was she being unfaithful to God? Why or why not?
2. Is arguing with God about whether or not to punish the righteous along with the wicked more an act of faith or faithlessness?
3. Do you think the three visitors are just messengers and angels? Or do you think they might be a pre-appearance of the Trinity: Father, Son, and Holy Spirit?

14
The Testing of Abraham

Read Genesis chapters 20, 21, and 22.

Abraham did it again! He lied again.

Abraham encounters a foreign king, and out of fear, tells them Sarah is not his wife but his sister. Déjà vu. This time it is with Abimelech, a tribal king in the Negeb, southwest of the Dead Sea. Apparently, Sarah (even in old age) was a pretty good-looking old lady.

Abraham tells Abimelech that Sarah is in fact his half-sister, that they have different mothers, but the same father. This is generally ignored by readers of the Bible, because we don't want to think that the patriarch of our faith married his half-sister. One safe interpretation of this story was that it was a continuation of his previous lie, and Abraham was still living out of his fear. In this era and culture it was very important to marry within your tribe, so marriage between cousins was common, and marriage between half-siblings was allowed under extreme circumstances, though it was later forbidden in the law of Moses. Regardless, it does not paint a picture of Abraham being a person of *consistent* faith, but rather one who's faith undulated, up and down, depending on the circumstances.

Sound like anybody you know? Are Abraham and Sarah people of great faith?

Sarah finally bears a son (Isaac) and the jealousy between her and Hagar flares up again. Now there are two firstborn sons in the household. She once again tells Abraham to cast Hagar and Ishmael out, this time to their pending death in the desert. God hears Ishmael crying (Ishmael means "God hears") and saves them. They live in the Sinai Peninsula, and God promises that a great nation will emerge from his descendants.

Islam does not emerge for some 2,700 years after Abraham. But when the prophet Mohammed has his vision in the seventh century CE, he is living in Arabia, the same region where Hagar and Ishmael settled.

In that sense, the Arabian people are considered descendants of Ishmael. Islam shares regional and cultural ties to Abraham. That is why Abraham is considered the father of three world religions. In chronological order they are:

Judaism 2,000 BCE (through Isaac)
Christianity 33 CE (through Isaac)
Islam 670 CE (through Ishmael)

The Testing of Abraham

If I heard a voice claiming to be God and telling me to take my son up a mountain and sacrifice him as an offering, I would reject it out of hand. In fact, I would check myself into a hospital. My sense of the character of God has no room for such a request. I would venture that most of you feel the same way.

This is a difficult story to digest. Here are four common interpretations:

1. God is putting, what has been up to this point, a contentious relationship to the test. Thus far, Abraham and Sarah's faith has been an up and down endeavor. Could the point of God's request be to see if Abraham finally fully trusts in God? If this is the primary interpretation, then notice that Abraham does not question God at all, but simply does what he is asked. This is in stark contrast to the other encounters we have read.
2. Some of the surrounding Mesopotamian religions practiced child sacrifice. This could be a literary device to draw a dramatic distinction between their gods and the God of Abraham.
3. This is a theological foreshadowing of the sacrifice that God will make of his own son for the sins of humanity. Just as Abraham and Sarah have an only son in Isaac, so God gave his only son for the sins of the world. Isaac asks his father where the animal they will be sacrificing will come from, and Abraham says, "God will provide the lamb." Christians see a fulfillment of this promise when Jesus offers himself as the "lamb of God."

4. A nonreligious reading takes severe issues with such a story, seeing it as child abuse, and would read it as a dark schizophrenic episode.

As I've said previously, religious notions and stories often have more in common with literary and artistic imagination than they do the rational, logical mind. In that sense, these encounters are a kind of dark poetry, full of highly charged symbols, that point to the bigger notions of sacrifice and trust. I don't discount the darkness, nor the difficulty of them.

Personally, I would have walked away from the relationship had it been me. A typical devotional rendering of the story is that God asks us to surrender everything to him, even the things that God himself promised to provide. This is what one might call "advanced spirituality." It would be similar to living into a certain vision for your vocation or family that you prayed and worked for decades to achieve, and then once you obtain it you begin to get the sense God wants you to walk away from it. It's dramatic, but not outside the realm of possibility. This story enlightens and underscores such journeys, but in a very dark way.

Note: In the Islamic telling of this story, it is not Isaac that God asks Abraham to sacrifice, but Ishmael.

Question for Reflection or Discussion

1. This is a very difficult story to understand. Which of these interpretations do you think is the best and why?

15

Isaac Marries His Cousin Rebekah

Read Genesis chapter 24.

Sarah dies. Notice that Abraham is very careful to offer money to the tribe occupying that territory for the spot where he will bury Sarah—Machpelah. This will come up again at future points.

It is from this point that you begin to notice an ever-increasing delineation of tribal lines. Abraham sends Isaac's servant to find him a wife, but *not* from the tribe of the Canaanites (Remember "Cursed be Canaan"? Noah cursed his grandson Canaan a few generations prior in Genesis 9:24–27). There obviously was some cultural tension between Abraham's descendants and Canaan's. Be looking for it. And notice Isaac is marrying his first cousin. That is how important it was at this point to marry within one's own culture.

Isaac's servant will choose a woman who not only offers *him* water but also offers water to his camels. It is a practical sign more than a mystical sign. He wants a woman who will help Isaac take care of his tribal responsibilities. You will see in future stories that going to the water well at the end of the day was a good time to meet the women of the tribe. Women were sent to the well at twilight to get enough water to last the evening. Back then, you went to the well to "meet girls."

Note: When making a covenant, they grasp under the thigh. Why? The most likely answer is this was a way of showing submission to one who had authority over you.

Question for Reflection or Discussion

1. Families sometimes have unspoken rules about who you are *allowed* to marry. Sometimes those attitudes are not unspoken. Do you sense

there are rules about that in your extended family? You might even pose the question to people in your family? Often these restrictions are soft (present but not overtly expressed), things like religion, ethnicity, geography, socioeconomic background, vocation. Sometimes it is even an assiciation with a sports team. To what degree are these distinctions important when choosing a spouse?

16

Jacob, Esau, and Tribal Leadership

Read Genesis chapters 25, 26, and 27.

After Sarah dies, Abraham married Keturah and has numerous children with her. Toward the end of his life, he gives his entire inheritance to Isaac and gives gifts to his other children and sends them away toward the east. When Abraham dies, Isaac and Ishmael together bury him in the cave at Machpelah with Sarah. Ishmael's tribe grows through twelve of his princely offspring. This becomes important later as Abraham's grandson Esau will marry one of Ishmael's daughters.

Isaac and Rebekah have trouble conceiving, a repeat of Sarah's difficulty. Isaac pleads with God, and she conceives, but it comes with an unusual prediction. The twins will fight with each other in her womb, and this will be a foreshadowing of the conflict between these two brothers and their offspring. The younger infant will usurp the older one. Do you see the pattern that is forming? Either the story is predicting the tribal conflict, or it is trying to explain it. Which came first, the chicken or the egg? Regardless, usurping will be a repeated theme through much of the Hebrew Bible.

Notice there is a third account of someone lying about their wife being their sister, except this time it is Isaac. This repeats the theme of that undulating up-and-down trust in God's provision and protection.

Rebekah finally has a baby, but from the beginning it is a contentious event. I love all of the undercurrents of the story of Jacob and Esau. Esau is strong, good at hunting, but anyone who would sell his inheritance and birthright (his position as the tribal head) for a bowl of lentil stew would be a weak leader. It's the subtext of the story. There was the divine premonition Rebekah had during her pregnancy, "the older will serve the younger." What ensues is a mother manipulating her son to do something to bring that to fruition.

Moms manipulating their children? *That* has never happened before!

Jacob steals his brother's familial blessing by deceiving his blind father Isaac. I wonder if Jacob and Rebekah had simply been patient and let circumstances unfold naturally, would God have arranged the transition to Jacob's tribal headship more smoothly? Does God use unethical or deceptive methods to achieve a greater good? The story never says one way or the other. It only suggests this was predicted by God while the babies were in the womb, and so it came to fruition.

Esau swears he will kill him in retaliation. Jacob flees and soon becomes associated with his act of betrayal. His name, Jacob, means "grasps the heel" but comes to be associated with *usurper and deceiver* or *a thief and a liar*. Jacob will be the tribal head, but his moral authority has been compromised. Is this what God wanted? There is a quote attributed to Napoleon that goes something like: "To obtain power one must be absolutely petty, but to exercise power, one must be absolutely great. Rarely do these two qualities ever coexist within the same person."

Questions for Reflection or Discussion

1. Who would make a better tribal chieftain, Esau or Jacob? Why?
2. If you were in a situation where you knew you would make a better leader than the one put in charge, would you trust God to make the opportunity for you or would you be more inclined to try and trick and maneuver your way into that position?

17
Rachel, Leah, Bilhah, and Zilpah

Read Genesis chapters 28, 29, and 30.

Notice how chapter 27 ends and chapter 28 begins. Rebekah said to Isaac, "I'm sick and tired of these local Hittite women! I would rather die than see Jacob marry one of them." It is that tribal mentality again, but with a strongly xenophobic (fear of people who are different) tone. Because of this, Jacob will marry cousins within their immediate tribe, and Esau will marry descendants of Ishmael (a Canaanite woman), further deepening the cultural division between the brothers. There is some sad irony later in chapter 28. His parents send Jacob off to find a wife, but they implore him to *not* marry a Canaanite. To ensure he does not, they send him to his Uncle Laban's house to marry someone within his tribe.

On the way to his Uncle Laban's land, Jacob has a dream where he sees a ladder from heaven (aka Jacob's Ladder), with angels ascending and descending. The promise to his grandparents is repeated to him in a dream: "And all people will be blessed through you." How can you dislike Canaanites and at the same time be charged with blessing all the people of the earth? It is setting up one of the *big* tensions in the entire Bible. It is a tension that I believe is eventually resolved, but not at this point.

Jacob arrives in Padam Arran and falls in love at first sight with his cousin Rachel (he weeps after their first kiss), but he is deceived by his Uncle Laban, a polytheist (many gods), into working for him double-time to marry both of his cousins: Rachel and Leah. There are some tense family dynamics between Jacob, his two cousin-wives, and their slave women. It is important to note that the only one he is truly in love with is Rachel, who has trouble conceiving children (just like her mother-in-law Rebekah and grandmother-in-law Sarah). Rachel eventually gets pregnant and gives birth to Joseph and Benjamin, who will be important in stories around the corner.

Through Rachel and Leah and their two slave women, Bilhah and Zilpah, Jacob ultimately has twelve sons: Reuben, Simeon, Levi, Judah, Dan, Naphtali, Gad, Asher, Issachar, Zebulun, Joseph, and Benjamin, and one daughter, Dinah. In addition, Jacob eventually adopts the two sons of Joseph, Manasseh and Ephraim, into the tribe, making them part of his inheritance. More on that in a later chapter.

> ▸**polygamy.** Having more than one wife, a practice not uncommon in the period of the biblical stories, especially in the Old Testament.

Jacob grows incredibly wealthy working for his Uncle Laban. (Did you read the peculiar genetic goat breeding he did by using color charts in 31:10–12? Weird "science.") Eventually he must go back and take over the tribal headship. Remember, he has a deep sense of responsibility to fulfill the Vision Quest of his grandparents—stars of the sky, grains of dust on the ground, a blessing to all the nations of the earth.

Questions for Reflection or Discussion

1. Does your family put pressure on you to succeed? Somebody else in your family? How or why?
2. Does your family have a mission or a Vision Quest?

18

Jacob Wrestles with a Man? an Angel? God?

Read Genesis chapters 31, 32, and 33.

We all want to be blessed, to feel significant, and that we matter to someone and to the world. It has been a driver in my own life. I am the middle child of divorced parents, an absent father, and a somewhat introverted mother. Has my need to achieve and succeed been driven by a desire for their blessing? To get affirmation?

Jacob was born into a family that had an extravagant promise hanging over their heads. Don't diminish how that *must* have impacted the culture of that family. Their family and descendants were to be great. God will bless them and make them great, and through them God will bless all the families of the earth. Talk about high family expectations!

Was that what drove Rebekah to push Jacob so hard, even to the point of deception? Was that why she was so anxious about tribal purity? Is that what drives Jacob to dream of heavenly stairways and have dreams of angelic visitations that repeat the family Vision Quest? They are haunted by the notion of *blessing*. My paraphrase of the account:

> Jacob learns that his brother Esau is coming to greet him with a garrison of 400 men. He sends Rachel, Leah, Bilhah, and Zilpah ahead, and flees the other direction, across the River Jabbok. He meets a man and they fight, wrestling all night, neither of them relenting. In the morning, the man gives up but not before he wounds Jacob, striking him in the hip.
>
> "You win." the man says.
>
> And Jacob's response is peculiar.
>
> "I will not let you go until you bless me."
>
> "What is your name?" the man asks.

> "Grabs-the-Heel," The name had become associated with something else entirely for the people of that region. They heard the stories. The name was now associated with usurpation and deception. When people heard the name Jacob, they thought, "Liar. Thief." Yes, he is the titular head of Abraham's tribe, but his leadership is tainted. His blessing is a lie. Jacob is desperate to fulfill the promise of the Blessing, but his reputation is tainted. How can he bless others when he is a phony?
>
> "I will not let you go until you bless me."
>
> The man gives him a new name. Isra-El. Because you "wrestled with God and human beings and won."
>
> And then he blessed him.

We all want to be blessed, to have a sense of significance, and hopefully we want to then share that blessing with others. But often that sense of worth is tainted with our poor attempts at gaining significance. This is at the heart of this story.

It's often called "Jacob wrestling the angel," and that is a reasonable rendering of the language, a messenger of God. But more is implied: Jacob is fighting with God for significance and forgiveness.

Israel. Not only does it change the nature of Jacob's identity, it will describe the nation that grows from this family, a people who wrestle with God.

Genesis 34–36

The rape of Dinah. The theme of tribal identity and loyalty is here again. A Shechem prince is enamored with Dinah and sleeps with her (forces himself on her?). Jacob is willing to let him marry Dinah if their entire tribe will convert to the practice of the Abrahamic tribe. The prince's father agrees and tells all the grown Shechemite men they must be circumcised. While they are recovering from their surgery, Dinah's brothers burst in and kill them all in revenge.

After a brief time being reunited with his brother Esau, the difference in their religious practice separates them. Esau marries into the Canaanite culture and is polytheistic. Jacob is monotheistic. Eventually the descendants of Esau settle in the region of Edom in the southeast portion of Canaan.

We will encounter the descendants of the Edomites down the road, as well as the descendants of the Moabites (remember Lot's daughters and their offspring?). So make a mental note. Edomites, Moabites.

Questions for Reflection or Discussion

1. Jacob demands a blessing from this divine visitor because deep down he knows his blessing is a phony. Do you feel blessed? Are you getting enough blessing from your family in order to succeed? Where are places outside of the family people attempt to get a blessing?
2. What do you think about being named "wrestles with God"? Is that a good name or not? Why?

19
Joseph and Promises Fulfilled

Read Genesis chapters 37–50. This is a longer reading than we have been doing, thirteen pages.

You have reached the end of the book of Genesis. These are the stories of the patriarchs and matriarchs of the Hebrew tribe. God created human beings morally free and through their own choices they alienate themselves from each other and from God. God plans to create a "blessing culture" through which healing and ultimate blessing will come to all the families of the earth.

The final story, fourteen chapters at the end of Genesis, demonstrates a common pattern that will be repeated in future stories: God blesses people, then these people break the relationship with God, and God repairs what was broken.

Joseph is the favorite child of Israel (Jacob) and Rachel, the wife that he is deeply in love with (the others are tribal obligations). This child is intelligent and gifted, and Israel (Jacob) and Rachel show him favoritism. The other half-brothers are resentful and sell him into slavery, telling their father the boy was killed by wild animals.

In a series of events, the talented Joseph rises up from slavery and imprisonment to become governor of Egypt, second only to Pharaoh. He rises to power by leading Egypt to store up grain for a coming famine. His brothers travel to Egypt to buy food during this famine and are reunited with the half-brother they betrayed. It is a story of forgiveness. One of the final statements of Joseph captures the larger theme of all these stories in Genesis:

You intended it for harm, but God intended it for good.

A note about tribal identity: Joseph unintentionally fulfills the promise of his great-grandfather Abraham: "Through you all the families of the earth will be blessed." Joseph blesses the people of Egypt and saves them from famine. This is the first time you see fruit of the Vision Quest.

Joseph marries Aseneth, the daughter of Potipherah, an Egyptian priest of On. Aseneth bore Joseph two sons, Manasseh and Ephraim. This is important, as both these grandsons of Israel will eventually become tribal heads for the Hebrews—cross-cultural leaders.

There is a repeat of the whole switch-a-roo blessing. It is done by, of all people, Israel (Jacob). When he adopts Joseph's Egyptian sons into the tribe and gives them a tribal portion, he crosses his hands for the younger to usurp the older. Joseph objects and tries to switch his father's hands back. But Israel insists. A precedent has been set; the traditional expected means of blessing will often be usurped for a greater good.

The story of Judah and Tamar (chapter 38) fits into this genre, that of an unlikely person becoming a main player in a story. Judah, a son of Jacob and Leah, must help his widowed daughter-in-law, Tamar, after her husband, Er, dies. Tribal law requires that the next oldest brother marry the widow and attempt to give her a child so she can have an heir and someone who will care for her in old age. Er's brother Onan is unwilling to fulfill this obligation (the term, Onanism, comes from this story of him spilling his seed, or sperm, on the ground). Tamar takes matters into her own hands by deceiving and seducing her father-in-law Judah in order to get the pregnancy she needs to survive. It is one hot mess. The twin children that are born of this union between Judah and Tamar are linked to the future Jesus. Perez is in the line of Judah that bears David, and Jesus was born in the line of David.

God takes the messiness of our convoluted choices and uses them for larger redemptive purposes.

You intended it for harm, but God intended it for good.

Questions for Reflection or Discussion

1. Can you think of an event in your life that when it was happening to you it was terrible, but later you saw the good that came from it, either for you or someone else?
2. Is there anything you are going through now that in the long run might be good for you and someone else?

20

Abraham's Family Is the Foundation

Watch both of The Bible Project videos on Genesis, part I and II.

The groundwork has been laid now for you to forge ahead into the heart of the Bible. What you will be reading now is the religious history of the descendants of Abraham and Sarah. The origin stories in Genesis 1–11 are in some ways a self-contained mini-drama that ends unresolved. The story of Abraham and Sarah begins what will be the eventual resolution of that conflict. The Christian tradition sees the Bible as a unified narrative that will eventually lead to a resolution. Keep in mind that the history of Abraham and Sarah's descendants is a process. They will grow, change, and develop in a similar manner that a person grows, changes, and develops. So with that in mind, let's keep reading.

SECTION TWO

Exodus, Wilderness, Conquest, and the Judges

The Books of Exodus, Leviticus, Numbers, Deuteronomy, Joshua, Judges, Ruth, Job, and 1 Samuel

Unit One

The Exodus: Forty Years in the Wilderness and the Halacha

Exodus 1–34; Leviticus 11, 17;
Numbers 11–13, 16–17, 2–22

21
Reviewing Genesis

The book of Genesis is divided into two sections. Chapters 1–11 are what are sometimes called the mytho-poetic stories. "Mythos" does not mean false or made up. Rather a myth is a story that conveys ideas that are important to a culture. So they can be fiction, history, or a mixture of genres. Genesis 1–11 are origin stories about the earth, human nature, sin, and include an ancient apocalyptic flood story. The first eleven chapters tell the story of the creation and the fall of humanity.

Chapters 12–50 tell the story of one particular family, Abraham and Sarah, and their offspring. God envisions that this family's descendants will be a means for the brokenness set into motion in Genesis 1–11 to be repaired. It won't happen immediately, but in the very distant future. This God *gives* Abraham and Sarah a Vision Quest: *through their descendants all the families of the earth will be blessed.* And so the second half of Genesis is setting the stage for that culture to grow and one day fulfill that purpose. They will be *blessed to bless.*

22
Escape from Egypt

Read Exodus chapters 1-14.

One way to cover these chapters is by watching Dreamwork's *Prince of Egypt*.[1] It is an animated film, geared toward children. These chapters have some interesting aspects that the film skips or changes.

Joseph is the bridge between Abraham's tribe in Canaan and the story of Moses in Egypt. You'll recall from Genesis 39–47, Joseph was a hero in Egypt, but eventually "a new king came to power in Egypt who didn't know Joseph" (Exod.1:8). The tribal people of Abraham were initially respected in this foreign settlement and in some sense were seduced by the affirmation they received in Egypt under Joseph. They were given a separate place to live, the region of Goshen, in order to maintain some cultural distinction. But they stayed too long and were eventually enslaved by a Pharaoh who didn't care about the past. Four hundred years transpire—a very long time.

The Name of God

The name Moses (mosh-ah) is a Hebrew word that sounds like the words "to draw out." When this Pharaoh's daughter found him, she took him as her son and named him Moses (Moshe), saying, "I pulled him out (*meshitihu*) of the water" (Exod. 2:10). This has a double layer of meaning, the first being the description of the Egyptian princess drawing him out of the water, and then secondarily, Moses rising to draw the people out of slavery.

1. *The Prince of Egypt*, directed by Brenda Chapman, Simon Wells, Steve Hickner (Universal City, CA: DreamWorks, 1998), film.

Notice the literary parallel here. Just as Pharaoh killed the firstborn sons of the Hebrew slaves, so now God will do the same to the Egyptians. The term for the intentional killing of infants is *infanticide* (infant-cide). Words created with the Latin root and the various prefixes may be familiar: homicide (killing of a man), fratricide (killing a brother), satricide (sister), suicide (killing oneself), regicide (killing of a king or queen). I hate that it is often these biblical stories that introduce these dark aspects of human nature to those fully reading the Bible the first time.

Moses married Zipporah, a Midianite shepherdess. Midian was a region associated with northwestern Arabia, and for this story it is assumed that Zipporah's family was from the Sinai Peninsula. Moses marries outside his tribe. He was a Hebrew who was raised culturally as an Egyptian and then marries the daughter of Jethro, a Midianite priest. Take note of what must have been some level of ethnic, religious, and cultural integration. This is important as we move forward in the story.

Moses asks God for the Lord's name. God responds with an obscure Hebrew word (*YHWH*) that had never been in use but that was similar in form to the verb "to be." It has been translated "I am," or "I am who I am." A more awkward but perhaps more accurate rendering would be "existing" or "existence." Regardless, it sets a precedent in Hebrew culture of God being nameless. To name something is to define it and, in a sense, control it. Have you ever met someone who controls their relationships by giving everybody nicknames? It may be disguised as cute and friendly, but on another level, it is patronizing. God cannot be defined and controlled. God is nameless and held in mystery. Hebrews thus have referred to God as "God of the name (*Elohim Hashem*)" or "He whose name may not be spoken." Over time, in the Hebrew tradition, God seems to have many names, but they are actually descriptions of God's behavior, much like a nickname is given to someone based on what they do or how they are perceived:

El Shaddai (Lord God Almighty)
El Elyon (The Most High God)
Adonai (Lord, Master)
Yahweh (Lord, Jehovah)

Jehovah Nissi (The Lord My Banner)
Jehovah-Raah (The Lord My Shepherd)
Jehovah Makeh (The Lord Who Strikes You)
Jehovah Rapha (The Lord That Heals)
Jehovah Shammah (The Lord Is There)
Jehovah Tsidkenu (The Lord Our Righteousness)
Jehovah Mekoddishkem (The Lord Who Sanctifies You)
El Olam (The Everlasting God)
Elohim (God)
Qanna (Jealous)
Jehovah Jireh (The Lord Will Provide)
Jehovah Shalom (The Lord Is Peace)
Jehovah Sabaoth (The Lord of Hosts)

Circumcision (Again)

Did you notice the strange story of God setting out to kill Moses as he headed back to Egypt to rescue the slaves in Exodus 4:24? These are the kinds of encounters I find fascinating, like puzzles that need solving. Moses's Midian wife Zipporah intercedes by circumcising their son Gershom and dousing Moses's big toe with the blood from the procedure. Interestingly, in Mesopotamian culture, the feet were sometimes a euphemism for the male private parts. So maybe she threw the foreskin at Moses's private areas in anger that he had refused to circumcise his son "down there." Regardless, Zipporah is depicted as a wife who is encouraging Moses to be faithful to his adopted Hebrew tradition. Midianites could have been monotheistic tribes that shared a common understanding of God with the Hebrews; they also descended from Abraham's son Midian.

So what does it mean? It may mean that Moses only had a vague knowledge of the rite of circumcision and had dismissed its necessity. He was not raised as a Hebrew slave, and as we will see in later readings, the Hebrew tribe was somewhat unclear about their ancient tribal obligations.

Remember, 400 years had passed. What sense of their Hebrew ritual and practice had been forgotten or muddled in those generations? Lodged in this story is the heroics of Zipporah, a non-Hebrew Midianite woman, who recognized what was needed—a firm commitment to the tribe's ancient God and covenant. She circumcises Gershom and throws the evidence at Moses's feet, and only then are they able to head toward Egypt committed to their new venture.

Plagues upon Egypt

Following YHWH's command, Moses returns to Egypt with the power that he has received. Ten plagues eventually fall upon the Egyptians by Moses's (and his brother Aaron's) command:

1. Water turns into blood (Exod. 7:14–24)
2. Frogs swarm the land (Exod. 7:25–8:15)
3. Lice come upon humans and animals (Exod. 8:16–19)
4. Swarms of flies fill the houses (Exod. 8:20–32)
5. A deadly disease attacks all the livestock (Exod. 9:1–7)
6. Boils fester upon humans and animals (Exod. 9:8–12)
7. A thunderstorm of hail and fire falls on the land (Exod. 9:13–35)
8. Locusts descend and eat all the vegetation (Exod. 10:1–20)
9. Dense darkness so that no one could see (Exod. 10:21–29)
10. The death of every firstborn child (Exod. 11:1–12:36)

The final plague is the source story of the Jewish Feast of Passover. For Christians, this is a festival that also symbolically points to the sacrifice and salvation of Jesus, as he celebrated the Passover meal as his last supper with his disciples before his blood was shed to save and protect his people from judgment and death (Matt. 26:17). These are called "typologies," ideas or symbols that repeat themselves in different forms across different stories into the New Testament. Passover is the "type" and Jesus' last supper and his sacrificial blood is called the "antitype." We will see more of these as we read ahead.

▸**Infanticide.** Killing infants to demoralize your enemy or to control their population. **Genocide.** Killing the entire population, or generation, to demoralize your enemy.

Questions for Reflection or Discussion

1. Moses comes to realize that his wonderful life as Egyptian royalty was at the expense of the Hebrew people. If you inherited a wealthy company and found out that the profits came from the suffering of other people, what would you do?
2. If God had asked you to go back and free enslaved people, what do you think, feel, and do?

23

"Hangry" and Scared

Read Exodus chapters 15–17. Watch The Bible Project video on Exodus chapters 1–18.

The first song in the Hebrew Bible is the Song of Moses in Exodus 15. The story of Moses crossing the Red Sea is also fairly well known. Notice that the pulling back of the waters did not happen in an instant, but rather took the winds blowing all night long. The movie *Exodus: Gods and Kings*[1] depicts this act as having been caused by a great earthquake that created a tsunami that pulled back the waters temporarily.

The story itself has some chronology and geography issues to sort out. The Hebrew slaves escaped Rameses, then fled, and crossed the Red Sea. If you look at a map, you see that the Red Sea is about 150 miles south and then east of the lower tip of the Sinai Peninsula. This would take a group of that size months to traverse. It isn't out of the question that it took Pharaoh that long to regret the loss of his cheap labor source and chase them down with his army, but the locations for water at Marah, Massah, and Meribah are back up north on the west side of the peninsula. Mount Sinai, where the commandments were given early on in their journey, is located in the south central region. So how did they cross the Red Sea and then get back over to get water and the Ten Commandments?

The most common solution is that it wasn't the traditional Red Sea they were crossing, but rather the Sea of Reeds, a body of water not too far from the city of Rameses, where they fled. The names may have been corrupted as the story was transmitted, or it is possible that what is now called that the Gulf of Suez was then considered part of the Red Sea. These are questions to ponder.

---

1. *Exodus: Gods and Kings*, directed by Ridley Scott (Century City, CA: 20th Century Fox, 2014), film.

After the crossing of the Red Sea there are a host of stories that are often overlooked because they are not so fantastic. Nearly every movie made about Moses stops at the crossing of the Red Sea. Someone needs to make the film *Moses: the Sequel*.

Remember, Moses was not raised as a Hebrew but an Egyptian. When he finally flees his upbringing, he marries into the family of a Midianite priest. Embedded in these stories is an idea that you should always keep in mind: Moses is being tutored in the ways of an old, almost dead, faith. Some of the ideas and practices of Abraham, Isaac, and Jacob surely remained with their Hebrew descendants, but perhaps they got muddled during those 400 years of slavery. What these stories do is give us a peek into the formation of a religious culture. God and Moses are going to recreate or expand formal Judaism.

It is hard for us to see how deeply we are affected and shaped by our culture, especially over time. Often we are so close to our context we are not even aware of how it shapes our thinking. The Israelites will be living out of a "slave mentality." You read it in these accounts. The people very quickly wanted to go back to Egypt, even if it meant slavery. Would you rather be adequately fed and be a slave, or anxious about food and shelter and live into freedom?

▸**Water from the rock**. A phrase that refers to the idea that God will provide out of nothing.

Have you ever heard the term "hangry"? This sometimes happens on long road trips with the family; you're trying to make it to a certain point before you stop to eat and the people in the car get increasingly cantankerous. My kids call that "hangry." You are angry because you are hungry. Finally you stop and get something to eat, and the demeanor of the car is transformed to sweetness and love, all because you now have a cheeseburger in your belly. Don't tell me the soul and body aren't intimately intertwined.

What-is-it?

God provided a flaky white substance that could be ground up into a sweet flour. It appeared in the morning like dew on the ground and burned off as the sun rose in the sky. The people see it and then ask, "What is it?" In Hebrew, the words are pronounced "Man-na?" And so that is what they end up naming it: what-is-it? Man-na, bread from heaven. There is a poignant devotional piece to this event. God tells Moses to instruct the people to only take enough for the day. If they try to save it up, it will stink and rot with maggots. God wanted them to depend on God on a daily basis, not on their own clever ability to manage their lives. YHWH was building a relationship that required their daily trust. Make yourself vulnerable to God; that is where you grow in intimacy with God.

A peek into the future: 1,500 years later, when Jesus multiplies the loaves and feeds thousands of people, he refers to this story and to himself as the bread from heaven. Jesus is *manna*. As a priest, when I give people the bread at communion, I often very quietly whisper, "Manna?" before I hand them the bread. "What-is-it?" I am asking. And then I answer my own question, "The body of Christ, the bread of heaven." It is another typology. Manna is the type; Jesus as bread from heaven is the antitype.

▸**Manna.** The name for the flaky bread was a similar sounding word for the question, "What-is-it?" The answer is *miraculous bread from heaven.*

Bitterness, questioning, testing, quarreling. The writer of the story is describing the atmosphere of these runaway Hebrew slaves. These are some conflicted folks, scared and full of doubt. The literary device of alliteration, and these four "m" sounds, are framing the events. It is good practice to read the scriptures with a literary sensibility. The writer of this story is "doing a thing" here.

Then there are the Amalekites. This is the first skirmish the Hebrews encounter. God comes to their aid when Moses has his staff raised in the air, but as he fatigues and the staff lowers, they begin to lose. Aaron and Hur find a rock for Moses to sit on and they hold up his arms for him. Make a mental note about the Amalekites. They show up again in the book of 1 Samuel in a very significant manner.

Questions for Reflection or Discussion

1. Do you get hangry? Would you rather be free and suffer for a while as you get established in your new life, or be a slave and have shelter, food, and water?
2. God told them only to take enough manna and quail for one day's worth. Do you think it is wrong to store up money or resources? Does it keep us from depending on God?

24

The Ten Commandments

Read Exodus chapters 18–21.

You might hear someone at some point in your life say something like, "The United States Constitution is based on the Bible." While I understand why people who love both the United States Constitution and the Bible would want to make a direct correlation between the two, it just isn't that simple. The Greeks had quite a bit to do with our modern democracy, and the theocratic form of government we see in Exodus is very different from the representative democracy we have in the United States. However, one thing the two do share is that both are systems of law interpreted by a series of district judges. All laws, whether rooted in a theocracy or a democracy, will need to be applied differently based on context, and that is what judges did for the Hebrews and what judges do in American democracy.

Jethro, Moses's Midian priest father-in-law, gives him some sage advice. He tells Moses he can't do everything himself; he needs to enlist some help. So he tells Moses to choose some wise leaders to help him: judges who will weigh in on decisions for groups of 1000, 100, 50, and 10. Moses will weigh in on the decisions in the concentrated echelon of ten; the other judges will weigh in for larger groups.

For the remaining chapters in this section, we are going to be working through the rest of the Torah in two ways. We will continue to follow the narrative of the Hebrews struggling in the wilderness and we will also look at selections from the laws they were developing.

Torah is the Hebrew word for "law" or "teachings" and is also typically the designation for the first five books of the Hebrew Bible, also called the Pentateuch (five). In the Hebrew tradition, the scriptures are divided into three collections:

Torah (*translated as teachings or instruction, sometimes called "The Law"*): Genesis, Exodus, Leviticus, Numbers, Deuteronomy

Nev'iim (*the prophets or the history books*): Joshua, Judges, Ruth, Samuel, Kings, Isaiah, Jeremiah, Ezekiel, Hosea, Joel, Amos, Obadiah, Jonah, Micah, Nahum, Habakkuk, Zephaniah, Haggai, Zechariah, Malachi

Ketuv'iim (*the writings*): Psalms, Proverbs, Job, Song of Songs, Ruth, Lamentations, Ecclesiastes, Esther, Daniel, Ezra-Nehemiah, Chronicles

If you make an acrostic of these three collections, it is TNK, which is then expanded with vowels and pronounced *Tanakh* (tah-knock). This is the way the Hebrew tradition refers to their scriptures, what Christians call the Old Testament or Hebrew Scriptures.

Torah is specifically those instructions that were given to Moses to guide the life of the Hebrews as they ventured into the wilderness and beyond. In this chapter's reading, you learned that God gave them a baseline of ten laws. As we read in chapters 21 and 22, there are many more. All total, there are 613 laws or guidelines, and these were called "the Pathway." In Hebrew it is pronounced *Hal-a-cha.* It was the way a Hebrew person was supposed to walk, and if they got off that path, it would be the reason for their demise.

When Jewish people refer to Torah, they mean the first five books (noted above); this is their main scripture. The other books in the Nev'iim and Ketuv'iim are important and seen as sacred, but not as sacred as the five of the Torah.

Receiving the Law

God assembles the people at the base of Mount Sinai, sets up a barrier, and forbids anyone to go any further. Only Moses can approach God on the dark mountain. Later Aaron may go with him. Anyone who crosses the barrier is to be put to death with stones or arrows. In this story Moses is like a second Adam, reentering the presence of God that was lost when Adam was banished from the Garden. While in his presence he is given the Ten Commandments and told this:

> . . . while Moses went up to God. The Lord called to him from the mountain, "This is what you should say to Jacob's household and declare to the Israelites: You saw what I did to the Egyptians, and how I lifted you up on eagles' wings and brought you to me. So now, if you faithfully obey me and stay true to my covenant, you will be my most precious possession out of all the peoples, since the whole earth belongs to me. You will be a kingdom of priests for me and a holy nation. These are the words you should say to the Israelites." (Exod. 19:3–6)

You will be a treasured people, out of all the nations, a *kingdom of priests*. A priest, in the Hebrew way of thinking, was someone who advocated for the people to God. So if their culture was going to be priests to the whole world (remember the call of Abraham, "You will be blessed to bless"?), they would need to be holy people. In order for this to happen, God is going to give them some guidelines to live by. These guidelines will form them into a priestly people. The Ten Commandments are the foundation of those guidelines.

▸**God's chosen people.** God chooses Israel for a specific task, to be advocates (priests) to God on behalf of the entire world. Sometimes Israel is also described as a *kingdom of priests* (advocates).

The Ten Commandments, sometimes referred to as the *Decalogue* (ten), are divided into two categories.

1. The first four are about a person's (or group's) *relationship to the God:*
    - You must have no other gods before me.
    - Do not make an idol for yourself.
    - Do not use the Lord your God's name as if it were of no significance.
    - Remember the Sabbath day, and treat it as holy.
2. The next six deal with *relationships between people:*
    - Honor your father and your mother.
    - Do not kill.

- Do not commit adultery.
- Do not steal.
- Do not testify falsely against your neighbor.
- Do not desire to try to take your neighbor's house.

Notice the last commandment is not a law to either do or not do something, based on actions, but rather is a command not to feel a certain way. That is hard. It is called *coveting*. And what is so bad about coveting is that wanting what others have can lead to worse sins, like lying, theft, and murder. It can cause neighbors to hate each other and lead to violence.

What is adultery? It is when a person who is married cheats on their spouse with someone else.

Lastly, there is a pretty stunning description of the seriousness of being in God's presence. God takes up residence in a unique manner on Mount Sinai. A strict boundary is set up on the perimeter, punishable by death if crossed by anyone other than Moses. God wants to be in their presence once again, but at this point it will only be through Moses. More on that as we move forward.

Reading chapter 21 offered you a sample of the other 603 instructions given in the Halacha.

The next reading, Exodus 32–34, jumps ahead a bit. If you want to quickly read chapters 23 through 31, go ahead. It is a listing of some of the additional laws Moses gave to the people and descriptions of some holy furniture and uniforms for the leaders. But we will come back to that topic. In fact, we will be jumping all over the Torah (or Pentateuch) in the next few chapters, looking at the instructions (laws), customs, and practices that God is instituting with Moses.

Questions for Reflection or Discussion

1. Describe an area of your life where you have tried to do everything yourself and found out it was a lot easier when you enlisted some help.

2. God calls Israel his "treasured possession," not because they were his favorite, but because he had a special task for them to complete and the laws were guidelines to help prepare them. Can you think of something you contribute to the world that is unique to you? What kinds of guidelines do you follow to prepare you?

25
The Golden Calf and the Presence of God

Read Exodus chapters 32–34.

Moses is on Mount Sinai in the presence of God a second time; while away the people get anxious and convince Aaron, Moses's brother, to create a golden calf to worship. When Moses returns and sees this, he does three things:

- He smashes the tablets in a fit of rage.
- He grinds up the golden calf, mixes it with water, and forces the people to drink it.
- He puts together a team of Levite assassins to hunt down the organizers of this event and kill them with the exception of Aaron. Was his hand forced under duress?

Did you find anything comical in Aaron's explanation? "So they gave it [gold] to me, I threw it into the fire, and out came this bull calf!" (Exod. 32:24). Really? Is Aaron three-years-old?

And then God has his own response, sending a plague to kill those guilty of idolatry.

Part of this story is Moses trying to convince God not to abandon them.

> Why should the Egyptians say, "He had an evil plan to take the people out and kill them in the mountains and so wipe them off the earth"? Calm down your fierce anger. Change your mind about doing terrible things to your own people. (Exod. 32:12)

This is a priestly act, advocating for the people, despite their guilt. And he makes an appeal to God's ego and reputation: "Lord, why does your fury burn against your own people, whom you brought out of the land of Egypt with great power and amazing force?" (Exod. 32:11).

Then Moses and God point them to their long-term destination. They will return to the land of Canaan with a promise that God will drive out those tribes that are living there. They are known collectively as the "Seven Canaanite Tribes." You might take some issue with this. What about those tribes? Doesn't God love them? This is a tension that we will be observing in these stories for the next one thousand years, but particularly in this period, what is called the *Wilderness* and *Conquest of Canaan*. Don't forget the first time we encountered the name Canaan. It was Noah's grandson who was banished for something shady that happened between Noah and Canaan. So there seems to be a history between the descendants of Noah and those of Canaan. More on that in a later chapter.

Moses creates a meeting place where he talks with God and calls it the *Tent of Meeting*. A pillar of cloud hovers near the entrance when God is there during the day, and at night it was a pillar of fire (Exod. 13). A firenado?

Tribal Identity

One of the larger themes in the Hebrew and Christian Scriptures to start tracking is *tribal identity*. The scriptures are a religious history of the Hebrew people. Earlier, in our reading in Genesis, we looked at the origin stories: Creation, Garden of Eden, the Flood. In some respects those earlier stories can be considered universal, or accounts that concern all of human civilization. It may be splitting hairs because those stories are within the Hebrew tradition, but even so, they are universal stories.

But when God calls Abraham and Sarah to begin a family-tribe-nation, the stories become more culturally specific. At this point, we are fully located in the history of one particular tribe among many, that of the descendants of Abraham, Isaac, and Jacob. (In the Episcopal Church we include the women, saying Abraham and Sarah; Isaac and Rebecca; Jacob, Rachel, and Leah. I often take it a step further and include the slave women of Jacob—Bilhah and Zilpah, since they had the children of what became tribal heads.)

The theme of tribal identity is important to revisit because Moses will be introducing laws, rituals, and cultural traditions that will shape that specific tribe. It is in part why the passage you read forbids them to intermarry with other tribes. It takes it to an even more extreme place, "You must tear down their altars, smash their sacred stone pillars, and cut down their sacred poles" (Exod. 34:13). God so vehemently wants to build a culture that is specific to one brand of monotheism that he takes a hardline against mixing cultures, even to the point of intolerance.

There is a dark side to this. As modern readers we ask, "Why can't these tribes learn to coexist?" Religious and cultural tolerance is such an important part of the American experience. We are a tapestry of a variety of faiths and cultures that all enjoy freedom of expression and religion. Why can't that be the message of fifteenth-century BCE Israel? God is trying to help them build a culture that will bless all the families of the earth. And so for a time they need to concentrate on the development of that blessing culture. Do you see the historical irony? In order to be a "blessing culture," there will be times that cultures are pitted against each other.

Try on this analogy: most parents want their children to be kind and decent to everybody, but it is safe to say that parents do not want their children to be friends with everyone, especially with those with high risk behaviors. For simplicity's sake, let's say the lion's share of the Canaanite tribes were to be avoided for the same reason. If you read these stories closely, you see that there are exceptions to this rule. Both attitudes coexist. We will revisit this topic throughout our reading of the Bible.

At this point in our reading together, trust the process. This is a tension that will play itself out, good and bad. We will be tracking it as we read. Make a mental note: tribes.

The Presence of God

Chapter 33 is a two-sided coin, capturing the complexity of the relationship between Moses and God. Moses is described as one who sees God *face-to-face*, as one speaks to a friend. But then he gets into an argument with God, asking him repeatedly if God will be present with him. Twice Moses asks and twice God says, "Yes." But then Moses asks for a sign, or said a different way, "Prove it." This changes their relationship. No longer will Moses see him *face-to-face*, but only out of the corner of his eye, and then Moses will only see God's backside. (An attempt at ancient humor?)

I like the honesty. How many times have I doubted God, and how has this changed our relationship? I shudder to think. Even so, God stays in the relationship. In chapter 34, we have a description of how Moses must veil his face after being in the presence of God. This raises some questions about what exactly Moses's status with God is at this point. Let's just say it is becoming complicated.

Next we will scan both Exodus chapters 25–31 and 35–40. God gives Moses instructions about building a box to carry the tablets, a portable worship space and tent to meet with God, and a uniform for the priests who will make the sacrifices. Bezalel, in chapter 37, is mentioned as the artist that God used to create these items.

Questions for Reflection or Discussion

1. God wants the people to only worship him and not a statue. What kinds of things do you think people today worship other than God? What are the "golden calves" in today's world?
2. Can you identify and talk about people in your life that you should be friendly toward but maybe not be friends with? Why?
3. Moses doubted God's presence even after all that he had seen God do. Why do you suppose he was so anxious? What caused him to doubt?

26

The Tabernacle, Ark, and Priesthood

Scan (or read if you are a hearty reader) Exodus chapters 25–31 and 35–40. Watch The Bible Project video on Exodus, part II.

If you are still reading at this point, then it may come as no surprise to you that there are portions of the scriptures that are hard to get through. Exodus chapters 25–31 give you a first taste of the laws. Leviticus gives even more.

These stories were written in a very different tone than we are accustomed to now, and compiled anywhere from 2,600 to 3,600 years ago, depending on the dating of the various books. So when someone mentions these laws in Exodus or in the book of Leviticus, what mostly comes to mind are obscure laws that don't have modern sensibilities. If you are one who has followed the recent religious discussions about human sexuality, then you might associate Leviticus as one of the places in the Bible that gives a prohibition against homosexual acts. The truth is that most readers of the Bible ignore the book of Leviticus, or they cherry-pick it for ideas that help build arguments for a given issue.

Rather than study all of these laws in detail, we will consider larger concepts that serve as an umbrella over all these laws:

- Moses, under the direction of God and with the help of appointed judges, formulated instruction that would help the people survive in the wilderness, strengthen their tribal life together, and give them a clear cultural identity as a kingdom of priests.
- Moses begins to creatively shape their religious life together with rituals, sacrifices, offerings to God, festivals of remembrance, celebrations, and the creation of sacred space where God will "live."

If you understand Torah (Genesis, Exodus, Leviticus, Numbers, Deuteronomy) as telling a larger story, these instructions and lists make a little more sense. They were a fragile and vulnerable people, and this gave them a strict framework that would help them survive.

Think of it this way: you have a similar dynamic to your life, whether you are particularly religious or not. You have rules you live by and rituals (religious or not) that affirm your values. You have clothing (outfits or costumes) you wear at different times and places for different purposes; you have holidays and anniversaries you keep to remember the events and people that have shaped who you are.

This can be especially true if you have been through some difficult times and you are now on the other side of that situation, living a healthier spiritual life. We shape our lives to maintain that health and wholeness. Thus Moses:

- created a portable tabernacle where the people focused their devotion to God, because they only stayed in one place for a certain amount of time;
- created a priesthood, a group who would speak to God on behalf of the people and make sacrifices for their mistakes;
- fashioned uniforms for the priests that were rich with symbols from their recent struggles and distant past;
- designed a beautiful box, the Ark of the Covenant, that would hold the laws given by God that would strengthen them and protect them; and
- established different kinds of sacrifices for the harms caused by the people against God and each other.

Some research has made a cultural connection of the design of these Hebrew artifacts with Egyptian ones. This makes sense, since Moses would have been highly influenced by his upbringing as a prince of Egypt.

Important Symbols to Remember

The **tabernacle** was a portable holy space that they would set up wherever they were camping. Within the grounds were two components: an area of preparation and an area to burn sacrifices to God. Different kinds of **sacrifices** were made. We mostly think of the ones that were for sins, but there were also "fellowship offerings" of either grain or animals that were a way of saying "thank you" and involved a community meal. So a spiritual barbeque? Sort of, yes.

They developed a more elaborate version of the Tent of Meeting. This would be called "the sanctuary." That space was composed of two rooms. The outer room held the **lampstand**, which had seven lights (and is different from the eight/nine lights of the menorah of Hanukkah). Seven is considered the perfect number from the seven days of creation and is thus the number of God. It also had a table with twelve pieces of bread called the **Bread of Presence** or the "Show Bread." This bread was for God only and represented the way he provided bread for the twelve tribes.

The priests burned **incense** 24/7 within the tent in the tabernacle as a visual representation of the prayers of the people rising to God. But it also masked the smell of the animal sacrifices.

The Inner Room was called the **Holy of Holies** and only the high priest was allowed in that room. The **Ark** (box) **of the Covenant** was kept in that room, a gold trimmed box that traditionally held three items: the tablets of the Ten Commandments, a bowl of manna, and the staff of Aaron's that sprouted almond buds (that story is found in Numbers 17 about God choosing Aaron to succeed Moses among all the tribal leaders). Atop this decorative box were two cherubim, bowing prostrate toward a small space between them. The Hebrews knew that God was everywhere, but this small space was believed to be a "hot-spot" where God dwelled intensely. It was called the **Mercy Seat**, because God is where you go to beg for mercy.

Moses had the priests establish a ritual bath called a *mikvah*, which sounds similar to the Hebrew word for *hope*. The priests would wash before going into the sanctuary, but there were also a

Note: In today's church, when a priest washes their hands before Holy Communion it is an echo of this practice. You can also see the seeds of Christian baptism in this ritual. We will talk about this in detail when we read the Gospels.

variety of mikvahs that people did. One was to reset spiritually, starting over after having done something that made them unclean.

Eventually, the Hebrews required any convert to Judaism to undergo a mikvah as the final act before becoming a Hebrew.

The priests kept two stones inside their vest, ***Urim*** (light) and ***Thummim*** (innocent) or *lights* and *perfections*. They used these somehow to read the will of God, but no one is sure exactly how. Were they used as dice? Reflecting light?

The priest's breastplate displayed twelve decorative stones, one for each of the tribes of Israel. Scholars cannot identify exactly which stone was associated with each tribe.

The altar for the burned sacrifices had four horns at each corner. These horns eventually became a place of safety from false accusation, similar to finding "sanctuary" in a medieval cathedral. A person accused of a crime could run into the tabernacle, grab hold of the horns on the altar, and be protected for the time being. Similarly, Moses named certain cities that would functioned in much the same way, an early form of "guilty until proven innocent." Golan, Ramoth, and Bosor on the east of the Jordan River and Kedesh, Shechem, and Hebron on the western side served as "cities of refuge" (Deut. 4; Num. 35).

Our next reading will be a hop, skip, and a jump around the book of Leviticus. Scan chapters 1–7, then read chapter 11, and watch *The Bible Project* video on Leviticus.

Questions for Reflection or Discussion

1. Can you name three guiding principles that you or your family hold that help define what is important to you?
2. What are some of the "costumes" worn by you or others during important times of your life?
3. Do you own any special or "holy items"? Why are they holy or special?

27
The Pathway of God: Halacha

Scan Leviticus chapters 1–7 and then read all of Leviticus chapters 11 and 19. Watch The Bible Project video on Leviticus.

Here is a hypothetical project: you and a group of your trusted friends are required to sit down and come up with rules and rituals that will guide and shape every aspect of your life. This is what Moses and the array of judges came up with over time: 613 rules and rituals. Instead of calling them rules (blech!), they enchanted them a bit and called them "the pathway." Walk on the pathway, and you will all be okay. This is what is called in Hebrew the *Halacha* or the pathway.

Here is the tricky part. How many of these 613 Hebrew laws that make up the pathway do you want to read and study? Then a harder question, how many of these rules and rituals are we supposed to follow today?

"All of them!" you might say. "It's the Bible."

And I would understand why one would be inclined to say such a thing. However, many of them do not translate to a different time and culture. This is where the practice of biblical interpretation comes into play. There are a wide variety of laws that covered every aspect of their life together: property, marriage, family, workers' rights, and slavery. How to treat different kinds of foreigners as well as other religions and their practices. How to take care of the poor and vulnerable, the accumulation of wealth. An explanation of different sacrifices, the behavior of priests, and various kinds of punishments for crimes.

- **Aliens.** Treat foreigners with kindness because you yourselves were once strangers in a strange land. (Contrast this with the earlier command in Exodus to not intermarry and to smash the altars of other religious cultures they might encounter.) This is another example of a tension within the scriptures that is often hard to resolve.

Add all of them up across Exodus, Leviticus, Numbers, and Deuteronomy and you get 613 rules or guiding principles. A legend says a pomegranate (kind of fruit) has exactly 613 seeds, the same number as the Halacha. That would be a fun afternoon activity, right? Buy a pomegranate and count the seeds. You can see a list of all these rules arranged by categories here: http://www.jewfaq.org/613.htm

Some of these laws are found in the book of Exodus, but most of them are found in the book of Leviticus. Leviticus is sort of notorious for being a weird and confusing book full of strange laws. Admittedly, it doesn't flow like some of the previous stories you have been reading. Instead, it lays out three basic ideas about how to be in the presence of God:

1. Rules about rituals (sacrifices and worship) to be in God's presence.
2. Rules about priests who act as mediators between God's presence and the people.
3. Rules about purity that govern how people can be near God's presence.

▸**Gleanings.** Don't harvest everything from your fields, but leave some on the ground for the poor, disabled, foreigners, and those abandoned by their providers. Don't harvest the corners of your fields at all. Leave that for the needy also. They can come in at the end of the day and "glean" (collect) from what is left over.

Think about the big picture. God's presence was one of the good things human beings enjoyed in the Garden of Eden, and it was the thing that was taken away from them when they disobeyed God. Even though God is available to people after the Garden of Eden, God has never been as *intensely* present as he was then, that is, until now with Moses. But we have seen that even that relationship is tenuous. These three areas of the Halacha helped them find a way to be in God's presence again.

Animal sacrifices were the primary way the people were to relate to God and there were three basic kinds:

1. Sacrifices that acted as apologies for wrongdoing. The blood of the animal served as a kind of payment for the sins the people had committed.

2. Sacrifices to say thank-you to God.
3. Sacrifices that celebrate with fellow Israelites (these were the offerings that people would offer to God and then turn around and eat them, like that holy barbeque).

Many of these laws have become part of our everyday language, as highlighted in the BVCs (Bible Vocabulary Concepts) within this chapter.

▸**Scapegoat.** The priest symbolically places all the sins of the people onto a goat and then it is driven into the wilderness to die. The term is now used to describe someone who has been blamed for someone else's mistakes.

Questions for Reflection or Discussion

1. Discuss some of the rules in your home that help shape your ability to live together and guide you into being healthy people. How do those rules help you achieve those things?
2. Can you name any rules, either at school or at work, that seem outdated and don't really help form and shape healthy living?
3. God gives the Hebrews a guideline for how to care for people who are helpless or who struggle. How does your family care for people in need?

28
More of the Halacha and the People Complain

Read Numbers chapters 11–13 and Leviticus chapter 23. Watch The Bible Project video on Numbers.

We will now be doing two things at once. We will be looking at a few of the laws from the Halacha and then jumping ahead to keep up with Moses and the Israelites as they continue to live in the wilderness. They wandered in the wilderness for forty years before they finally headed back into Canaan, the land promised them through Abraham.

More Big Ideas from the Law

Every seventh year the people were to let the land rest, called the *sabbath year*. Today, farmers rotate crops on different parts of their land each year to accomplish this, but the command to do so every seven years also lightened the workload for the farmer and gave the soil a chance to replenish. They still had plenty to do, but farming was not one of their tasks.

> ▸**Sabbath year.** Every seven years let the land stand fallow to recoup its nutrients.

This guideline grows out of the notion of the sabbath day of rest. Some academic institutions and churches give teachers and ministers "sabbaticals," or a period of time when they take a break from their normal duties and do something different to give them a mental and spiritual break. In theory, these sabbaticals are given every seven years, but they are not offered as often as they once were. This is where you would hear the phrase, "I need to take a sabbatical."

Take seven sets of seven years, forty-nine years, and on the fiftieth year proclaim it as a year of economic forgiveness and reset. This was called the *Year of Jubilee.* All those who were sold into indentured slavery were allowed to go free. Property that was sold to pay debt is returned. Historical research suggests it was applied sparingly. You can imagine it was not a good prospect for those who loaned money. However, the idea was meant to keep things from becoming too imbalanced and unfair in society. Every fifty years try to balance things economically. This was an idea that was radical for that time and region.

- **Year of Jubilee.** Every seven sets of sabbath years, on the fiftieth year, you must do an economic reset: forgive debt, return property taken as interest, and set your slaves free.

The term *Jubilee* is now used to suggest large-scale actions that involve forgiveness of various kinds. In the 1990s, there was an effort to convince first world wealthy nations to forgive the debt of poorer countries. Bono, from the rock band U2, is a practicing Christian and helped initiate this effort. He enlisted Bill Gates, the computer billionaire, to help. The head of the Roman Catholic Church, Pope John Paul II, also encouraged this act of Jubilee.

Unusual Laws

Some laws in the Halacha are very peculiar to modern readers. One is not to mix two different kinds of cloth, most likely wool and cotton. It made for a cloth that would draw up unevenly and would be useless. You were also not supposed to plant two different crops side-by-side, but keep them separate.

There is a law about a woman who comes to the assistance of her husband by punching the other guy in his private parts (Deut. 25:11–12). The law commands that her hand be chopped off. One explanation for such a strange law is that having children was so central to survival of the community, that to harm that area of a man was to deny him the ability to perpetuate his family. Perhaps this is why it was such a serious offense. Most laws or rules have a story behind them. Something happens and a rule is born from the incident. Perhaps that is what happened here.

There is a test for a husband who suspects his wife is cheating on him (Num. 5:11–28). Stir dirt from the floor of the tabernacle into a glass of water and make her drink it. If she gets sick and/or she miscarries, she is guilty. If not, then she is innocent. There is no corresponding test for a woman who suspects her husband to be cheating. The culture then was very male dominated, what I would call one of the dark underbellies of that culture.

Leviticus 11 is a detailed description of various laws about food being clean or unclean. Some of these laws have a rationale to them: you don't eat pigs because they will eat anything (and I mean anything), and this was seen as unclean. The same reasoning could be applied to bottom-dwelling fish: catfish, shrimp, and lobster. Again, the same principle was applied to scavenging animals. It seemed unsanitary and could make them sick. But some of the laws are more esoteric, like not eating meat and dairy together. Simply stated, Kosher food laws served two purposes: (1) to keep one away from getting sick and (2) fostering a tribal identity.

These laws and guidelines had a greater purpose: to form and shape the culture of a people committed to God and make them holy, preparing them to be a kingdom of priests who would advocate for all the nations of the earth.

Leadership and Giants

If you have ever been in a position of leadership, you know how hard it can be. Even the most organized, thoughtful, even-tempered people are second-guessed by those they are trying to lead. The reason is that living in community is *always* an emotional algebraic equation, with multiple variables on all sides. There is some beautiful imagery in these stories, giving others a portion of your spirit so they can also be leaders. There is also a lot of complaining by the people. When are we going to get there? We don't want to follow these rules!

And then there is the description from God about the various ways he speaks to people. Face-to-face? Or in dreams, visions, and riddles? We will look at this encounter more closely in chapter 31.

Remember that as we read the Bible we are doing two things: we are (1) looking at portions of the Halacha and (2) staying up with the advancement of Moses and the people in the wilderness to the land of Canaan. Moses continues to wrestle with the people and deal with their complaining and doubts, including his brother and sister, Aaron and Miriam.

In Numbers chapter 13, Moses sends spies into Canaan to see what challenges lie before them as they finally make their move into that land. The spies see that the produce of the land is abundant but that the people they will need to fight are huge! Notice verse 33? These large people are associated with the Nephilim we read about in Genesis 6:1–4 (see page 18). There was a belief that anyone who was unusually large must be a descendant of these hybrid human-angel beings.

Questions for Reflection or Discussion

1. Think about the Ten Commandments as the foundation for the 613 laws of "the pathway" and thoughtfully answer: what would be the "ten" foundational rules that shape the pathway you walk every day?
2. What do you think about the idea of giving everybody a chance to start over? It's not fair to the people lending the money or buying the property, but it would help keep society in balance. What do you think?
3. What do you think about the idea of every seven years giving workers a little bit of a rest?

29
The Shema, Blessings, and Curses

Read Numbers chapters 16–17 and Deuteronomy chapters 6 and 11.

There are a couple of things within Numbers and Deuteronomy that are of special importance, especially for understanding much of what you will read moving forward. Pay close attention. What follows is found *everywhere* in the Bible, both explicitly and implicitly.

Blessings and Curses

If you reread chapter 11, look for patterns. One you will see is "if, then. . . ." If you will obey all of these commands, then I will bless you. It is in chapter 11 explicitly using the if-then language but also found implicitly in other places. It is also called the *Deuteronomy Formula.*

I sometimes refer to this as ancient *Hebrew karma*. If you stay on the pathway, then things will go well for you. If you get off the pathway, then things will start to fall apart. This was applied to every aspect of life: health, wealth, fertility (both the land and conceiving children), and in times of war. It is also referred to as "blessings and curses." If you obey, you will be blessed; if you disobey, you will be cursed.

It is different from the eastern concept of karma, which is tied more closely to ethical and moral behavior. Issues of right and wrong are a part of the Deuteronomy Formula in the sense that many of the laws of the Halacha are ethnically based, but they aren't exactly driving how things will work. Rather, it is specifically faithfulness to God and God's laws that cause blessing or curses, not good acts for good and bad acts for bad.

If you are inclined to take issue with the idea, you would not be alone. Even voices within the Hebrew Scriptures take issue with God about its validity. Keep that in mind as we move forward.

And let me say again, this notion of *blessings and curses* is going to be present in nearly every encounter we read from here on out. It is "in the air" so-to-speak, and one cannot accurately understand the intention of the writers of the Hebrew Scriptures from this point forward without having blessings and curses in the mix.

Another important passage in this reading is found in Deuteronomy 6:4–9. It is called the *Shema,* pronounced *she-maw.* It is the Hebrew word "hear" or "listen" and is the first word of this foundational statement of faith for the Hebrew people, established here by Moses. An observant Jew recites it twice a day:

> Hear, O Israel: The Lord our God, the Lord is one.
>
> *She-maw Israel, ado-nai ela-haynu, ado-nai a-hawd.*

A different translation, though not as literal, would be: Hear O Israel, the Lord is God, God alone. It is followed by a central summation of Hebrew piety: Love the Lord your God with all your heart and with all your soul and with all your strength.

What follows is an admonition to take the laws and teachings of the pathway, the 613 laws of the Halacha, and to teach them to your children, bind them on your arms and forehead, and to the posts of your door. This was most likely intended as figurative language, that Halacha ought to shape every aspect of life. But as we often do in religious culture, a literal ritual was created to emphasize a figurative or spiritual idea. *Tefillin* and *phylacteries* are those leather straps and small boxes that contain a representative sample of the Halacha that are then bound to the head and arms of one who is praying. A *mezuzah* is a small box that contains teachings that are posted to the doorframe of one's house. It is fashioned at an angle, but the exact reason why has been lost. Some say it is to signify that the teaching of Torah should be "pouring into the home."

Lastly, if you read Deuteronomy 6–11, you'll notice that Moses is getting them ready to move back into the land of Canaan. The blessings and curses formula will determine how they will fare against those tribes they encounter as they move back. If they are faithful, they will easily win the land; if they are unfaithful, they will have extreme difficulty. At the same time, you read how God wants them to treat foreigners fairly. Both attitudes exist. This prepares us for our next reading, which moves them out of the wilderness and back into the land of Canaan.

Questions for Reflection or Discussion

1. Blessings and curses. What if the world worked this way all the time? If something bad happens to you, then it must mean you have disobeyed one of God's guidelines? What do you think of this? Do you think it still applies today?
2. God told them to write the Law on their arms, heads, and household doorways. Do you think God meant this literally? If not, what does it symbolize?
3. Do an image search for tefillin, phylacteries, and mezuzah. Do you think following such instructions would help you put guidelines into practice?

30

A Bronze Snake and Balaam's Ass

Read Numbers chapters 20–22.

The people grumble *again* about no water. Moses is fed up, goes to God, and asks for help. God tells him this time to "speak to the rock." However, in a fit of frustration with the people, Moses strikes the rock like before. God is angered by this disobedience and forbids Moses to enter the Promised Land. Were you taken aback by the severity of the punishment? Moses has been through a great deal with these people and with God. He has been far from perfect, but overall he has stayed faithful. God leaves him in the wilderness to die. He can see Canaan from Mount Nebo, but is not allowed to enter. It is a puzzling turn of events.

Leadership asks a lot of a person, and in some ways it can do damage to us. These stories are flush with this kind of symbolism. You can be in charge of an important long-term project, do most of the hard work, and then because it is such a difficult endeavor, be made the *scapegoat* (Bible Vocabulary Word) by taking the blame for the wrongdoings of others when the project is finally finished. You have, symbolically, been left on Mount Nebo to watch from a distance.

Note: Martin Luther King Jr. references this story in a speech delivered in April of 1968 in Memphis, Tennessee, when he tells other civil rights activists that "he may not get there with you."

The appearance of poisonous serpents in the desert (Num. 21) repeats the above themes, but becomes important in the New Testament because Jesus compares himself to the bronze snake on the pole. And it's a pretty cool story . . . well . . . because of the snakes.

Lastly, the story of Balaam's "ass" in Numbers 22. This is important because it is a transitional story that plays with the tribal tensions between the Hebrews and the surrounding tribes as the descendants of Abraham move out of the wilderness back into the land of Canaan. Balak is the king of the Moabites, a land the Hebrews must pass through to get to Canaan. He is none too pleased that this huge tribe of people will be passing through his land. He pays one of his witches (warlocks), Balaam, to curse them. Balaam tries, but God intervenes and asks him not to do it. In fact, Balaam ends up blessing them instead.

There is significance in God is using a different religious cleric, from a forbidden tradition (witchcraft), to bless the Hebrew people. The way that God ultimately gets Balaam's attention is by sending an angel to speak to him, but he refuses to see the angel. His donkey, however, sees the angel and freaks out. Balaam keeps punishing the donkey until the animal is finally given speech by God and yells at his master, "Stop hitting me!"

At that point Balaam sees the angel, and then he gives a series of four blessings to the people passing through his land. You might wonder if this means Balaam converted. Perhaps he considered it, but later in the book of Joshua, as the Hebrews move into Canaan, this same Balaam is condemned by God: "In addition to those others slain, the Israelites killed the fortune-teller Balaam, Beor's son, with the sword" (Josh. 13:22).

If you have time, watch *The Bible Project* video on Numbers once more. This ends our readings in the "Torah" or Pentateuch, the first five books of the Bible, also known as the Books of Moses.

Questions for Reflection or Discussion

1. God used a Moabite witch to bless the Israelites. Would you say that God possessed the witch?
2. Here was a donkey that God allowed to speak to Balaam, the Moabite witch. Name some other stories where animals spoke wisdom to someone who needed to hear it.

31
The "Voice of God"

Read Numbers 12:1–22.

Christians read portions of the Bible in gathered worship, and many of them when they finish say, "The Word of the Lord." What exactly do they mean by this? It depends on the tradition.

These readings come from a variety of genres, across 2,500 years of biblical history (circa 2500 BCE—100 CE). The Bible read by the majority Christians worldwide is comprised of about eighty-two books (the Orthodox and the Roman Catholic Churches have a slight disagreement on what to include). Protestant denominations who separated from the Catholic Church in the sixteenth century consider sixty-six books to encompass the Bible. (They see the value of the other books, but don't feel they should be included in the collection for a variety of reasons.) Regardless, both collections have about forty different authors. In other words, the Bible didn't just drop out of the sky. It took hundreds of years to determine which books ought to be included (and why) from numerous scholars, discussions, and church leaders.

This gives you some perspective on the complexity of the book(s). When people say things like "This is the Word of God," it is often a complicated thing to say.

In worship settings when some Christians end the reading by saying "The Word of the Lord," they are implying that God is speaking in the stories. In religious studies this is called *revelation* because God is revealing something. There are a wide variety of revelations, but the main ones are typically spoken or written. The Bible is a written record of various revelations people had from God. Some of them are very direct and others are more indirect.

When someone says the Bible is "God's Word," what does this really mean? Let's begin by looking at an encounter that is the set of readings we are currently grappling with. Read again Numbers 12:1–8:

> When they were in Hazeroth, Miriam and Aaron criticized Moses on account of the Cushite woman whom he had married—for he had married a Cushite woman. They said, "Has the Lord spoken only through Moses? Hasn't he also spoken through us?" The Lord heard it. Now the man Moses was humble, more so than anyone on earth.
>
> Immediately, the Lord said to Moses, Aaron, and Miriam, "You three go out to the meeting tent." So the three of them went out. Then the Lord descended in a column of cloud, stood at the entrance of the tent, and called to Aaron and Miriam. The two of them came forward. He said, "Listen to my words: If there is a prophet of the Lord among you, I make myself known to him in visions. I speak to him in dreams. But not with my servant Moses. He has proved to be reliable with all my household. I speak with him face-to-face, visibly, not in riddles. He sees the Lord's form. So why aren't you afraid to criticize my servant Moses?"

God is making a distinction between two different kinds of revelation. One for the general population—everyday folks. In the first form God speaks in dreams, visions, and riddles. This is called *indirect revelation.* For Moses, it was more direct. God spoke to him "face-to-face."

It can be assumed that in the direct form, Moses is hearing an audible voice. In the other instances, it requires you to solve a kind of puzzle. I gather that most people (I include myself), when they say God has spoken to them, it is very much this indirect version. It is a sense of something: logic, advice of trusted friend, something seen in a movie or read in a book, a reaction to a reading or a story.

Most modern readers would be less sure of someone saying they heard a voice. I'm not saying God didn't do it then, or that it is outside the realm of possibility today, but I am saying that indirect revelation is how most of us "hear" from God.

The Bible is a collection of those experiences people had in the past. We read these stories looking first for how they spoke to the original audiences they were written for; secondarily we read as to how they might speak to us today. Sometimes the meaning is clear, but often it takes a little collective rigor. This is what is called *interpretation*. The more academic word for it is *hermeneutics*.

Questions for Reflection or Discussion

1. Do you ever feel like God has spoken to you? If yes, how did God use to speak? Was it an indirect way and how so?
2. If God conveys messages using indirect revelation most of the time, is there a more accurate way to describe that process instead of saying, "God spoke to me?" Is that the best way to express it? How would you share such a revelation?

Unit Two

Joshua and the Conquest of Canaan, the Dark Period of the Judges, and the Call of Samuel

Joshua, Judges, and 1 Samuel

32

Canaan as a Symbolic Abstraction

Read Joshua chapters 1–3.

The twelve tribes of Israel had been organizing during their years wandering in the wilderness. This is a good time to remember their origins. Ten of the tribes were descended from the sons of Jacob (who was renamed "Israel" after wrestling with God), but the other two were the sons of Joseph, Manasseh and Ephraim, Jacob's grandsons who were born in Egypt. Levi was also a son of Jacob, but the role of the Levites (as organized by Moses) was to be priests for all the other tribes. They were not allotted tribal land, but would disperse, living in every tribal land. Aaron and Moses were essentially the first high priests, both of whom are from the tribe of Levi.

The land of Canaan is referred to by two other names: (1) "the Promised Land," because it was the land that was originally promised to Abraham and Sarah some 500 years earlier and to which they were now returning, and (2) a "Land Flowing with Milk and Honey" because of portions of the land that were fertile. It was also centrally located for regional trade, which made it profitable. It should be noted that the tribes who inhabited it while the Hebrews were slaves in Egypt for those 400 years would not be easily removed.

The first place we heard the name "Canaan" was in the Noah story. Canaan was Noah's grandson who did something sketchy in his grandfather's tent after Noah got drunk. It was likely an attempt at tribal usurpation, overthrowing his grandfather. Noah curses Canaan as well as all his future descendants. They settle in this region and become the "Seven Tribes of Canaan." The stories in Exodus, Leviticus, Numbers, Deuteronomy, Joshua, and Judges depict them as cultures that were corrupt. The religion they practiced included fertility rites that involved all kinds of inappropriate sex, and there is repeated reference to the practice of child sacrifice. So when the Halacha tells the Hebrews not to intermarry or practice Canaanite religion, that helps explain why their laws were so strict. But it also doesn't mean all the people in the Canaanite tribes were evil. This was a brutal time, but like any place where people live together, the cultures were varied and complex.

Taking back the land of Canaan was difficult for many reasons. As you read, try to have some sympathy for those displaced tribes. Can you imagine if a group of people showed up in your town demanding you give them all of the houses in town because their ancestors lived there 500 years before? Even during the time their ancestors once lived there, they likely only numbered a few hundred people. Now they are over 300,000!

Despite this history and reality, God tells Moses and Joshua that this land was prepared for them and they should get ready to take it by force. It makes me wonder, if Jacob and his sons had not stayed so long in Egypt and returned to Canaan after the famine was over, could this bloodshed have been avoided? We'll touch on this more in the next chapter.

Earlier as we read Genesis 24, we noted that Abraham insisted on paying the inhabitants of the land for the burial plot where he buried Sarah. This is a short and obscure reference, but significant. There was a way of living respectfully together in that land, but it seems that those variant cultures had progressed too far down that road. Diverse cultures living together takes hard work, and perhaps it is impossible if one of the cultures has been corrupted beyond help.

Land of Canaan as an Abstract Idea

The "land of Canaan" is one of those concepts in the scriptures that people use in a variety of ways. Martin Luther King Jr., in his efforts to bring civil rights to America, compared that process to a journey toward a *promised land*. He even went as far to compare himself to Moses, saying he would "not get there with you," but that his calling, like Moses's, was to lead them through the initial phases of that struggle, the *wilderness* of the civil rights movement.

When I went to college in the 1990s there was a band called the Indigo Girls who had a song called "Land of Canaan":[1]

I'm not your promised land
I'm not your promised one
I'm not your Land of Canaan, sweetheart,
Waiting for you under the sun.

The person in the song is lonely, wants to be with the other person, but she insists that despite the loneliness, the other person is not her *land of Canaan*.

Obviously, the narrator is not talking about a strip of land in the Middle East. Instead, *Canaan* serves as an abstract idea. It represents a place, a person, or a situation that was safe and permanent. It represented home. If your goal in life is to find a true love and get married, then remaining single might feel like a type of "wilderness" in your life. When you finally meet the person who shares your values, you make it permanent. They become your "land of Canaan."

Now this may seem obvious, but it is important in understanding how the scriptures are used by various readers. I call this the *practice of abstraction*. You take a story, an image, or idea and abstract it, or pull it away, from the scriptures. That idea is first associated with its original context, but then you remove that idea from that original context and treat it as an abstract idea that can be applied to other contexts. This is often done with ideas, images, and stories in the scriptures. The "land of Canaan" is an idea that has been commonly used as a symbol or abstraction for other settings.

The African-American spiritual "Off to Canaan Land" is sung in anticipation of being in a place where there will be civil rights and equal opportunity for all people. There is an orphanage in Uganda called "Canaan Land Children's Home." What about you? What is your "land of Canaan"?

1. *https://youtu.be/lUmEfp_mq_U*.

Questions for Reflection or Discussion

1. How would you feel if someone came up to your front door and told you they wanted to live in your house because their ancestors once lived in that area 500 years earlier?
2. Do you have a symbolic "land of Canaan" in your life now? Is there a place where you feel most at home, loved, and safe?

33
Joshua and the Conquest of Canaan

Read Joshua chapters 4–7 and 10:6–16. Then scan the remaining chapters of the book.

The name "Joshua" means "savior." In Hebrew it is *Ye-o-shua,* the Aramaic pronunciation is *Ye-shua*, and over time it was westernized and eventually pronounced *Jesus.* Jesus, the first-century Jewish rabbi who instigated the Christian faith we will study later in this text, was named after this folk hero who lived 1,500 years prior.

In the opening chapters, he repeats the covenant that God made with the people: if you will follow in God's statutes, then reentry into the land of Canaan will be easy. This is the Deuteronomy Formula mentioned earlier (see pages 87 and 126). Did you recognize it when you were reading? Then Joshua repeats what has become his mantra, "Be strong and courageous." Be confident in your chances for success but only if you are being true to the covenant God made with you.

At this point it is important to mention "point-of-view" in religious histories. The book of Joshua is an ancient Jewish history about a group of people returning to a land that was occupied by their ancestors some 450 years earlier, alongside a variety of other tribes. As mentioned in the last chapter, during the time the Hebrews (Israelites) were living in Egypt, the land of Canaan remained occupied by other tribes and cultures. As the descendants of Abraham returned to Canaan, they would be displacing those people. How would they do that? Pay for land? Military conflict? Negotiation? Merging tribes? The reality is that all of these approaches were used in some form, but military conquest was the primary method. This is often called the "Period of the Conquest." It lasts for about 500 years, and is a very long time of transition.

If you keep up with current events, then you might see a correlation between these stories and the conflict between modern Israel and Palestine. It would be naive to suggest these ancient stories do not play some role in modern attitudes about the conflict over that land, but it is not the same set of circumstances. The ethos of the scriptures still shape current understandings of land conflict, on both sides of the issue. Interfaith and intercultural coexistence has always been hard, in the past as it is today.

One of the characters mentioned who is from a competing tribe is the prostitute Rahab. A prostitute is a person who exchanges sex for money, in most cases in the Bible it is a woman. This practice is downgrading to women and is forbidden in the Halacha; it is illegal in most modern cultures.

That means that one of the heroes of the *Conquest of Canaan* is a prostitute from a Canaanite tribe. God is using a sketchy person to accomplish a greater good. Rahab lives in Jericho, and she has heard about Moses, Pharaoh, and the Red Sea. She agrees to help a group of Hebrew spies in exchange for her family's life. She helps them hide and escape. The signal not to harm her family is a *red cord* tied to her door. After the battle, she converts to the Hebrew faith and is part of the lineage of Jesus.

> ▸**Rahab and the red cord.** This was the signal to the Israelite army not to harm Rahab and her family in return for helping the Israelite spies. This is a typology of the blood over the doorposts in the Passover (Josh. 2:1–22).

The Israelites set up camp at Shittim, on the east side of Jordan, and they use the Ark of the Covenant to miraculously bind up the waters of the Jordan, mimicking the crossing of the Red Sea. This repetition in religious texts is called a "typology," when a type of thing, image, or idea repeats itself. The repetition calls up an association of the previous event or idea and all of the emotional and spiritual significance associated with it. Once they cross the river, God gives Joshua specific instructions about how to take the city of Jericho. In fact, the red chord that Rahab is told to put over her door is a typology of the blood of the lamb put on the doorposts at Passover during the exodus from Egypt. The initial story is called the "type," and the one that mimics it is called the "antitype," or the type that comes afterward. We will see more of these as we continue to read the Bible.

> ▸**typology.** When stories, ideas, or images repeat across time periods to recall important stories of the past and show a connection across time. The first story is the type, the repeating story is the antitype.

God gives Joshua instructions on how to take the city of Jericho: (1) Circle the city once each day in silence, blowing the shofar (ram's horn), following the Ark of the Covenant. Do this once, for six days. (2) On the seventh day, circle the city seven times, and on the seventh time, blow the shofars and shout.

The walls came tumbling down and they took the city, sparing the family of Rahab. God puts a curse on Jericho, saying anyone who attempts to rebuild it will be cursed. There is an attempt by the rebellious King Ahab 400 years later to rebuild Jericho, and it doesn't go well for him (1 Kings 16). There are some warnings about not taking the religious artifacts of Jericho for fear they will tempt the Israelites to adapt the Canaanite faith and culture. One Israelite soldier, Achan, tries to sneak some, and it creates all kinds of problems.

There are a couple of items in this reading worth noting. Did you notice that when Joshua asked the "man" (angel) who God was supporting, the response was, "Neither" (Josh. 5:13–15). Isn't that interesting? It suggests that what God is looking for is a people willing to be faithful and it doesn't matter who it is. Rahab? It was a way of God telling the people to "check themselves."

Also, what about that awkward description of the adult men needing to be circumcised (Josh. 5:2–7)? This was the ancient mark for Hebrew men that distinguished them as members of Abraham's (God's) tribe. They cannot enter into this endeavor without being certain they are in the right relationship with God. Remember that bizarre exchange Moses had with God about his son Gershom (Exod. 4:24–26)?

In chapter 10, there is a significant story for modern readers, especially those skeptical of biblical miracles. Joshua has a victory over the

Amorites, but needs more time to complete the battle. He prays to God and is given another full day of sunlight. The story is set as Hebrew poetry and says that God "made the sun stand still." This raises certain questions about the mechanism of this miracle. If you need twelve hours more of daylight, what exactly would need to happen for that to occur? It isn't the sun standing still (from science class you know that the sun does actually rotate on its axis every twenty-five days and orbits around the center of the Milky Way galaxy). Rather, if more hours of daylight were needed, the earth would stop rotating on its axis. The earth would need to stand still.

Those who want to discount the science in the scriptures often point to this story. The idea of the earth being a sphere was still unknown to the most of the pre-Enlightenment world (the ancient Greeks had some notion about a spherical planet), so a Hebrew writer would not perceive this correctly. When reading ancient religious stories, it is best to first accept them on their own terms; that will help you grasp the author's intended meaning. Questions about the science are important, but secondary to the intended meaning: God intervened to help Joshua win a military encounter.

The remaining chapters of Joshua detail the distribution of the land. Remember, even from their own account, this process takes over 500 convoluted years. Keep this in mind for what you will be reading next, the book of Judges.

Questions for Reflection or Discussion

1. What if a group of Native American tribes collectively announced that they wanted their lands back after 400 years of European-American occupation? Can you see how that would be similar to what the Israelites were attempting in Canaan?
2. The angel says he is neutral while one of the heroes of the story is a Canaanite woman. Do you think our prejudices can make us fail to see the value of others? Can you name some of the people you might have prejudices against?

34
The Period of the Judges

Read Judges chapters 1–4.

The book of Judges is the worst book in the Bible.

This is a strange thing to say, but there is scholarly, theological merit to it. Judges is a book that records some horrific behavior and overall it is set up like a long winding downward spiral, getting worse as it moves toward its ending. As mentioned before, there are passages in the book of Judges that are very hard to read, and if given a movie rating, it would be called a "hard R."

The key verse in Judges that captures the atmosphere of most of the book is found in Judges 17:6: "In those days there was no king in Israel; each person did what they thought to be right." Not every story in the book is so dark, but many of them are. Think about an undulating spiritual life, one that is like a roller coaster. You see this upward and downward spiritual life described in chapter 2:16–19. If the people had a faithful leader, they flourished. But when that leadership died, they began to tank. Most of us have seen this in some form in our families and businesses. Leaders who are competent and have integrity matter for the health of community.

There are some infamous stories early on. The story of the judge Ehud killing King Eglon of Moab is one example (Judg. 3:12–26). He goes under the guise of paying his taxes but ends up thrusting a sword into the king's fat belly, so fat that it consumes the sword and spills his guts on the ground. Ehud leaves, locking the door behind him. The king's attendants think the door is locked because the king is going to the bathroom and the smell coming from his quarters confirms this. Eventually they realize that he is not well and break in to find him dead—dark humor in an ancient form.

A similarly dark story is described in the exploits of the one female judge in the period. Deborah is a strong and faithful leader, and she inspires a Kenite woman named Jael to kill an opposing general named Sisera by driving a stake into his head while he is sleeping in her tent (Judg. 4:17–22). Chapter 5:1–31 concludes the early sections of Judges with a song praising Deborah for her leadership and faithfulness to God.

Questions for Reflection or Discussion

1. In many ways, the book of Judges is about the effects of leadership. Can you name some leaders in your life who help you (or organizations you are a part of) thrive? Conversely, do you know of any leaders who are not very good and have created some negative outcomes for groups?
2. Deborah is the only female military and tribal leader in the Bible. What women in your life are strong, intelligent, and faithful leaders?

35
Canaanite Religion and Biblical Interpretation

As we have reviewed numerous times, the biblical origins of the name "Canaan" come from the Noah story in Genesis 9–10. Canaan, the son of Ham, fell out with his grandfather in some unknown power struggle and was cursed as a subjugated tribe. After the flood, Ham's descendants settled in Egypt in what is now called the Levant, the area most think of today as the Middle East. In the stories that follow in Genesis, Canaanites are looked down upon as people of questionable culture, and members of Abraham's family are encouraged not to intermarry with them.

Eventually, seven main tribes from a grouping of those living in that area are named as the Tribes of Canaan. They typically are Amorites, Hittites, Perizzites, Canaanites, Girgashites, Hivites, and Jebusites. These are the primary cultures that Moses, Joshua, and now the judges, are trying to displace, merge with, negotiate with, or convert to the Hebrew religion and culture. They will need to be very careful as they attempt all of these approaches.

The Torah (first five books) and the Nev'iim (the prophets or histories) describe these tribes as characterized by two unacceptable practices: (1) They practiced child sacrifice as a way of appeasing their god's wrath (Exod. 22:29–30; Lev. 18:21; Lev. 20; Deut. 12:30–31, 18:10); and (2) their worship was rooted in fertility rites; the idea that if women priests were fertile (able to get pregnant), then the land would be fertile (produce crops). As a result, their religious rites and practices involved many different kinds of inappropriate sex. This is in great part why the laws in the Halacha about sex are so strict. God wanted the Israelites to be different, a holy people, set apart to be a kingdom of priests for the entire world.

Think of it this way: most parents want their kids to be kind and respectful to every person they encounter. That doesn't mean they want them to be friends with every person they meet. Rather, parents want their kids to be friends with others who share their values and will help their kids grow into the kind of people they want them to become. Marriage is the same way. You should show respect and decency to every person you meet, but you wouldn't marry someone who was harmful to themselves or to others. Apply this on a cultural level and it helps you to understand how the Israelites tried to strike a balance between respecting neighboring tribes while at the same time rejecting any of their practices they believed were wrong.

This is a loose version of biblical interpretation, which in its most simple form has three steps:

1. Try to understand what is happening in the story on its own terms. Who is writing? To whom are they writing these things? Do they have an agenda?
2. What is a general principle you can pull away from the story (abstract it) that stands on its own?
3. What is a smart and thoughtful way to apply that principle to a different context, like your life or some other situation?

Let's apply this concept to the book of Judges:

1. Israel must keep themselves separate from the Canaanite tribes who practice polytheistic child sacrifice and inappropriate fertility rituals.
2. God wants us to be holy for the purpose of being able to be a priestly advocate for other people.
3. We follow healthy principles, a modern-day Halacha, that will keep us on track to grow into the kind of people God wants us to be, including who we choose to be close friends with, all the while showing respect and kindness to all people.

We applied this same principle to the study of the Halacha when we thought about guidelines and principles that shape your life (see page 98). It isn't that the laws of Torah don't apply to your life. Some of them most certainly do, but not all of them, not because they are wrong, but because they were laws given for another time and place. Interpretation is the skill of figuring out which ones still apply, and when they don't, how to apply abstract principles from the scriptures to a different situation. The good news is, you need not do that by yourself. Interpretation happens best together with other people you trust, under the guidance of the Spirit of God.

Questions for Reflection or Discussion

1. Name some people God wants you to be kind to and respect but maybe doesn't want you to be close friends with because they might lead you toward behaviors that aren't the best for you.
2. Who in your life would you trust to help you interpret scriptures to apply them or their principles to your life?

36
Gideon, Jephthah, and Shibboleth

Read Judges chapters 6–7 and 11–12.

Gideon

The middle section of Judges has a series of stories about Gideon. For the most part, Gideon is presented as one of the faithful, "good" judges. He is best known for "laying out a fleece," a sign he asked God to give him to assure him of God's presence. A fleece was an animal fur throw (like a sheepskin) used to keep warm, and it's where we get the name for our fuzzy jackets. Drawing inspiration from this story, over time the phrase "lay out the fleece" has been used as an attempt to discern God's will. In the story, Gideon sets the fleece outside his tent and asks God to keep the fleece dry from the morning dew as a sign. God does so. But Gideon very presumptuously asked him to do it a second time for assurance, but to switch it around: make the fleece wet and keep the ground dry.

Does this remind you of any previous stories we have read?

Remember Moses pestering God with the same questions about God's presence? He wanted multiple reassurances that God would be with them in the wilderness. And his second-guessing changed that relationship with God, from face-to-face to "only seeing his backside." Gideon's doubt is a typology of Moses doubting.

In your reading you may have made this connection, and might even remember the concept of "typology," a concept or theme that repeats over time across different stories. It was introduced in the story of Joshua crossing the Jordan River (a type of Red Sea). Gideon's fleece story is a typology of the earlier Moses account, but the consequences are harder to see.

▸**Laying out a fleece.** The sign Gideon asked from God to ensure that God would be with him in a battle against the Moabites. Used now to refer to someone looking for a sign.

The reason he is so scared is because the Midianites have 135,000 soldiers. God says he is going to be with Gideon, but God sets Gideon back on his heels by asking him not to send his full strength of 32,000 troops into battle. Rather, he tells him to send home those who are scared, which is 22,000, leaving him with 10,000 soldiers against the 135,000. To make it worse, God tells Gideon to reduce his numbers even more with an unusual test: send the men to the river and have them take a drink of water. Almost 10,000 of them shove their face into the water and "lap it like a dog." Three hundred of them scoop up the water in their hands to drink.

Which method shows the better soldier? The men who scoop it up; they can drink and still stay aware of their surroundings. If you shove your face into the water, someone can sneak up on you and attack you. God tells him to take the 300 who drink it in their hands. So you want to question God? He may just make you go into battle the hard way, so that you will need to depend on him.

The 300 then surround the Midianite camp with lamps inside clay jars. On signal, they smash the jars, blow the shofars (ram's horn), and start screaming. The Midianites panic and end up fighting each other.

Jephthah

Next we jump to a dark story. I often question whether this story should be read (trust me, there are ones worse in Judges), but we need to see the undulating spiritual life in Judges that was described earlier in the book. This is the story of Jephthah the Gileadite in chapter 11. The tribal leaders of the Israelites ask Jephthah, a member of a neighboring tribe that was partially allied with Israel, to lead a pro-Israel attack against one of their old rivals, the Ammonites. This sounds good enough, but Jephthah makes an unnecessary vow to God that if given a victory, he will sacrifice the first person he sees coming out of his house upon his return, as a tribute to God. He wins, and who comes out of his house as he strolls up the driveway? His daughter.

He wails and moans but keeps his commitment, confessing to his daughter his deep regret, but insistent to her that he keep his vow. She agrees, but asks him to allow her and her closest friends to go on a two-month retreat in the mountains to grieve the loss of her future. Upon her return, he puts her to death.

You might wonder about the decisions of these people. Why not just go back on your promise to God? People do it all the time in these stories, right? We might also be puzzled as to why the daughter came back from her mountain retreat. It begs the question, "Is this okay with God?" The answer is *no*. Human sacrifice is forbidden by the Halacha. The implicit point to this story is Jephthah and his daughter are so deeply influenced by the Canaanite culture that they are unable to see what God wants. In an indirect way, this story conveys the convoluted, up and down, extremely poor spiritual instincts of the people during this period of their history.

Shibboleth

The last bit in this reading that is of note might be called "Bible Nerd Knowledge." Have you ever heard of a *shibboleth*? It is a term that means insider language or a kind of cultural code word. Most cultures have some version of this, as well as fraternities, clubs, and most organizations. For example, Episcopalians have insider, fancy words for a lot of things. Janitors are called sextons. The lobby to a church is called a narthex. So fancy.

> ▸**Shibboleth.** This was the word that the Gileadites used to determine who were Ephraimite traitors because they could not pronounce the "sh" sound. It is now used to refer to insider, code language.

The idea of a shibboleth comes from Judges 12. The Ephraimites attacked the Gileadites and lost. The defeated Ephraimites tried to sneak back home, but the Gileadites set up a checkpoint to capture them. At the checkpoint they asked people to say the word "shibboleth." As it turns out, Ephraimites cannot pronounce the "sh" sound and can only say "sibboleth." If they couldn't pronounce the word correctly, then the Gileadites killed them as traitors. Over time the word "shibboleth" has come to mean insider language that distinguishes you as being part of a certain group of people or a word regarded by others as empty of real meaning. Admittedly, the vocabulary word is just as obscure as this story from Judges.

Looking Ahead

Our last reading from the Judges is the story of Samson, in its entirety, chapters 13–16. As a teaser, know that this story has typically been cleaned up for children's church school. This is the unedited version and Samson is the prototype hero for the period of the Judges. You will see what I mean as you read.

Questions for Reflection or Discussion

1. Like Moses and now Gideon, have you ever found yourself doubting God's presence or care for you?
2. What are some practical steps you can take to make sure you understand God in the best possible way?
3. Are you part of any groups that have shibboleths? Insider language or inside jokes that only people in the group know?

37
Samson the Antihero

Read Judges chapters 13–16 and then watch The Bible Project video on Judges.

Samson is a hot mess. It's tempting to see him as a superhero of the Hebrew Bible; in the New Testament he is listed by the writer of the Letter to the Hebrews as a man of great faith. But there is something more complex going on, particularly because it is located in the larger dark narrative of the Judges.

Samson's mother, the wife of Manoah, has a hard time getting pregnant and makes a plea to God (a typology of Sarah, Rebekah, and Rachel). When she is blessed with a son, they dedicate him as a Nazarite to God, who will lead his people in defeating the greatest enemy of that period, the Philistines. The Nazarite vow was prescribed in the Halacha (Num. 6) for those that wanted to live an especially devout life. Nazarites were required, among other things to:

- Follow the Halacha closely
- Abstain from wine or any sort of grapes or raisins
- Never cut their hair

People generally understand the prohibition against wine. But grapes and raisins? The answer is nebulous. Some sources say it was because grapes were associated symbolically with blood, and a Nazarite was not to handle blood. Or it could be that grapes and raisins were associated with sacrifices made by fertility religions. This applies also to raisin cakes.

Grown to full stature, Samson demands his father allow him to marry a Philistine woman. Samson has an attraction to Philistine women. These are ancient stories, so they aren't always going to spell things out for you, but this one should seem obvious. The last thing a Nazarite would do is unite himself to a woman who practices a different religion. But did you see what the parenthetical said?

> His father and mother didn't know that the LORD was behind this. He was looking for an opening with the Philistines, because they were ruling over Israel at that time. (Judg. 14:4)

Wait! What? It was from God? This raises all sorts of questions. Is God using hypocritical behavior as a means of positioning Samson to fight Philistines? Is Samson's lackadaisical commitment to his Nazarite vow a guise? A ruse? A secret identity? Is this ancient counterintelligence, a kind of Hebrew spy? Or is he just a lousy Nazarite?

What is set into motion are a series of what could be called "seedy" stories about Samson. He:

- touches a dead animal, forbidden by Jewish law, and eats honey out of the carcass;
- feeds this impure honey to his parents without their knowledge;
- loses an impossible bet with his Philistine bridegrooms because his Philistine fiancé manipulates him.
- pays the bet by killing thirty men;
- when his Philistine father-in-law gives away his bride, Samson burns down the village with 300 helter-skelter, flaming foxes;
- and when arrested for burning down the village, Samson kills a thousand Philistines with the jawbone of an ass.

Here is a literary pattern: a reckless man throwing himself boorishly into various situations, inevitably leading him to kill Philistines, which was the purpose of his birth. Which leads to the most well-known story: Samson and Delilah. See again the introduction to this story at the outset of chapter 16: "One day Samson traveled to Gaza. While there, he saw a prostitute and had sex with her" (Judg. 16:1).

Visiting a prostitute is not something the Halacha allows. But it reinforces the sketchy nature of our hero. He later meets Delilah, a Philistine woman, who then tries repeatedly to kill him by asking for the source of his super strength. Each time he lies to her, killing the men that she unleashes on him. Remember that parenthetical?

> His father and mother didn't know that the LORD was behind this. He was looking for an opening with the Philistines, because they were ruling over Israel at that time. (Judg. 14:4)

Then, for no apparent reason whatsoever, he tells her the truth, this after three attempts at killing him. If you cut off a Nazarite's hair, he will lose his strength. The men fall upon him, gouge out his eyes, and send him to prison. Eventually, his hair begins to regrow and he performs one last feat, collapsing the temple pillars with 3,000 Philistines on the roof. It is there that Samson dies in blaze of glory.

A hot mess.

Literary terminology calls this an "antihero." An *antihero* or *antiheroine* is a protagonist who lacks conventional heroic qualities, such as idealism, courage, and morality. They often possess dark personality traits such as disagreeableness, dishonesty, and aggressiveness. In other words, the exact opposite of the typical hero.

> ▸**Antihero.** A protagonist that is ethically challenged but accomplishes good outcomes in spite of, and sometimes because of, their moral ineptitude.

Though the writers of Judges may not have been explicitly aware of the device, an antihero is what they were writing about, and it fits into the larger atmosphere of the book of Judges. They were a people struggling to live into their identity with their God while following the ethical edicts presented in Halacha. The complexity of this story is in that pesky parenthetical. Is this what God wanted? Does God use flawed and sketchy people to accomplish his purposes? What about the archetypal hero? What about the life well lived, what about the hero? Those are also found in the book of Judges, the undulating up-and-down spiral downward that characterizes the book. Just as when we came to the story of Noah, it applies to this one also, "Samson is not a children's story."

Questions for Reflection or Discussion

1. Do you think Samson's sketchy behavior was an intentional "disguise" to get him close to his enemy, or did he lack integrity?
2. Do you think it is okay to lie and be dishonest if it helps achieve a larger purpose?

38

Ruth and the Stages of Israel's Life

Read the entire book of Ruth (it's short). You might also watch The Bible Project video on Ruth.

It may be helpful to use a mnemonic device to help you remember the larger story of the Bible at this point. I call this one the "Stages of Israel's Life." The idea of "Israel" works on a variety of levels:

1. Israel was a person, the grandson of Abraham. His name was Jacob but was changed to Israel after a night wrestling with God. The name means "he who wrestles with God."
2. Israel became a cultural tribe of people.
3. Israel eventually becomes a geographical location, a place (the land of Canaan).
4. Israel is a religious faith. You can convert to Judaism if you were not born a Jew or lived in Israel.

What follows is a metaphor of the birth and development of the multi-faceted idea of Israel, the cultural religious group that descended from the grandson of Abraham. And just like a person has stages of life as they grow up, I found that the stages of life symbolically match up, in some fashion, to the events and stages of Israel's life.

Conception. In the creation stories, the Garden, the Fall, Cain and Abel, and the Flood, there was no formal Judaism. But after the fall, God "conceived" of a culture that would eventually "be born" and usher in blessing for all the families of the earth. Judaism (Israel) had not been born yet, but it had been conceived.

Infancy and Childhood. The fall was the problem; the answer to the problem was to create a culture through which humanity could be repaired. When God called Abraham and Sarah to start a culture that would bless all the people of the earth, a religion was "born." They were small, like an infant, but hopefully will one day grow up and "be a blessing" to all the people on earth (Gen. 12:3–4).

Abraham's family grew when he had Ishmael and Isaac. It grew further in size and self-identity through his grandsons Jacob and Esau and expanded even more through Jacob's twelve sons and one daughter. And just like an infant grows into a child in size and self-identity, their culture expanded and grew from a family to a tribe.

Teenage Years. Eventually Israel (formerly Jacob) moves to Egypt during a famine. They remain in Egypt initially as guests but eventually are enslaved and remain there 400 years. During this phase, they become full-grown in size as a culture, hundreds of thousands of people. But as they leave Egypt and move into the wilderness, they, like a teenager, find themselves living *in-between* who they are and who they eventually will become. Like a teenager, they have some attributes of adulthood, but they are not quite fully there. They are a little rebellious (golden calf, constantly challenging Moses), and they need rules (the 613 laws of Halacha) to keep them on the path.

Young Adult Phase. Many young adults, though certainly not all, go through a period of duplicity. They are acting like adults, but they are also living carefree and somewhat selfishly. They are trying to figure out what kind of an adult they want to be, and they are inclined to float around and not commit to much of anything. This fits accordingly with the period of the Conquest and the book of Judges: selfish, acquiring land, an undulating spiritual life, and a shaky commitment to God. This part of the Mnemonic metaphor can be called the "Justin Bieber" phase of Israel's history. Justin Bieber is basically a good guy who most of the time wants to do the right thing, but in his early twenties he tended to get distracted and did some dumb and selfish things. That is the period of the Judges.

The Book of Ruth

The book of Ruth begins by saying, "During the days when the judges ruled. . . ." The most recognizable passage from Ruth is one you may have heard at weddings:

> But Ruth replied, "Don't urge me to abandon you, to turn back from following after you. Wherever you go, I will go; and wherever you stay, I will stay. Your people will be my people, and your God will be my God. Wherever you die, I will die, and there I will be buried. May the LORD do this to me and more so if even death separates me from you." (Ruth 1:16–17)

You can hear the poignancy for a wedding, but when you read the book you realize these are words spoken between a mother-in-law and her widowed daughter-in-law. However, in the sense that a marriage between any two people is a convergence of two cultures, the words fit perfectly.

The significance of the book of Ruth is two-fold. It's about the confluence of two cultures and it lays some genealogical groundwork for what will become the most celebrated king in Israel's history—David. Both of these things are important to larger themes within the Hebrew Scriptures.

Before we focus on Ruth's story, weave back to previous stories you have read in order to highlight one of the more important themes in the Bible: tribal identity and interaction. Remember God's initial covenant with Abraham and Sarah?

> "I will make of you a great nation and will bless you. I will make your name respected, and you will be a blessing. I will bless those who bless you, those who curse you I will curse; all the families of the earth will be blessed because of you." (Gen. 12:2–3)

Part of what is being worked out over their history (bird's-eye view of the Bible) is how to be a chosen people, unique and set aside by God, a kingdom of priests, whose ultimate mission is to bless all the tribes of the earth and not see your culture as superior or of higher value than others. The idiom "threading a needle" is useful here, because this is something hard for all of us. We are tribal creatures. The Israelites were building a culture with a lofty purpose.

Blessed by God

To be a blessing

Accomplishing this without it inflating your cultural ego, so to speak, would be a tricky thing to do. You see this needle thread in the marriages of Isaac and Jacob: go marry someone from your own tribe, and whatever you do, don't marry a Canaanite (Gen. 24:1–4 and 28:1). You see this needle thread in the development of the Halacha in the Wilderness: "Don't mistreat or oppress an immigrant, because you were once immigrants in the land of Egypt" (Exod. 22:21), and "this is what you must do with these nations: rip down their altars, smash their sacred stones, cut down their sacred poles, and burn their idols" (Deut. 7:5). You see it thread when God uses a Canaanite prostitute to win a battle or a Moabite witch named Balaam to bless Israel.

The books of Joshua and Judges are much harder to "thread." There are no simple interpretations of those accounts. A displaced people, fleeing slavery, needed to settle somewhere, with their ancient home from 400 years earlier in Canaan being the place to which they hoped to return. Could they have negotiated for that land? Our idealism would hope so. As mentioned earlier, there are accounts of Abraham paying for land he acquired when he moved into Canaan. We have all observed how difficult cultural diffusion is in modern contexts. How much harder it must have been in ancient settings.

The book of Ruth is a bright moment in the midst of all this brutality. As it begins, a Hebrew woman named Naomi has married her sons to Moabite women. Moab was one of those regions the Hebrews had to pass through on the way back to Canaan. Naturally there was some cultural mixing. Her sons die unexpectedly, and Naomi tells her Moabite daughters-in-law to go back to Moab. Orpah returns to Moab, but Ruth stays. And Ruth makes a vow to her mother-in-law to join her tribe and religion permanently. Ruth eventually becomes the great grandmother of King David. The fact that she is a Moabite convert is important to that larger theme of God's universal blessing of all tribes.

But it's messy, and it will get messier. Hang in there: it is a long and winding road. A couple of things to note from Ruth: Oprah Winfrey was named after Orpah, but the hospital misspelled it on the birth certificate as Oprah. When Ruth "uncovered Boaz's feet" (Ruth 3:4), that was a euphemism for a physical romantic relationship. Strange, eh?

Questions for Reflection or Discussion

1. Are you friends with anyone who comes from an entirely different culture or race?
2. What about other cultures do you like?
3. Is it possible to separate religious beliefs from ethnicity and culture?

39
Job, the Man from Uz

Read Job chapters 1–3.

We now are going to leave the History books (the Nev'iim) and take a closer look at one of the books from the "Writings" (Ketuv'iim)—the book of Job (pronounced *jobe*). We are doing this because one of the bigger themes in Job relates specifically to an important theme we have studied in the Torah. When we are finished with Job, we will return to our reading of the History.

Job is often referred to as a *theodicy*. The technical definition of a theodicy is "justifying God" or God's goodness and providence in view of the existence of evil, such as why people suffer. As you take a close look at the book of Job, you will see that is not really what the book is doing. The more traditional understanding of a theodicy is usually put forth this way: "Why does an all-powerful, all-knowing, all-loving God permit evil, and by extension, suffering in general? Why do bad things happen to good people?" Again, that isn't what the book of Job is doing either. Job isn't really a theodicy; it does have a purpose, but answering those questions is far down on the book's agenda.

▸ **Theodicy.** Generally the study of why bad things happen to good people. Its root meaning is God justifying his ways to human beings.

How you react to these first two chapters depends greatly on your religious background. Most likely, if you didn't grow up reading and discussing Bible stories, or the idea of God in general, this premise could be a turn-off. God is making bets? With Satan? Bets about what would happen if God allowed Satan to wreck the life of one of his most faithful followers? The wager is that if God allows Satan to destroy Job's business and kill his children, then Job will abandon his faith in God. In spite of the pain of these events, Job remains faithful.

So Satan ups the ante. "Harm his body," he says, "and Job will curse you to your face." In that second wager, Job remains faithful, while his wife taps out. "Curse God and die!" she says. And Job's response?

He said: "Naked I came from my mother's womb; naked I will return there. The Lord *has given; the* Lord has taken; bless the Lord's name" (Job 1:21).

This opening stirs up so many questions that will never be fully answered in the book.

Questions for Reflection or Discussion

1. What do you think of the opening premise, God making wagers with Satan?
2. Medical science also attempts to answer the questions of why bad things happen to people. Can you name a disease that has a medical, scientific explanation?
3. Job's children were killed in a whirlwind. What is the scientific explanation for a tornado?

40

Job's Three (Four) Friends

Your reading assignment will be Job chapters 22, 23, and 24, but read the first part of this chapter and you will get a prompt when to start reading the scripture.

As a traditional theodicy, the book of Job isn't very comforting nor is it very profound. The reason for Job's suffering is that he is the pawn in a wager about what motivates people to be devoted to God. It doesn't fit the picture of God that most of us have. Because of that, we are not going to tiptoe around one of the larger questions raised: Is the book of Job a real story, or is it a Hebrew short story? Is this history or is it fiction?

There is a great deal in the book itself that suggests it is a short story, or what you might call a *thought experiment* about suffering and faith:

- In the Jewish tradition, the book is included in the genre of Hebrew books known as "the wisdom writings" and not in the history genre collection.
- The majority of the book is written in poetic form.
- The sketchy premise.
- The "land of Uz" is mentioned a few times in scripture but has never been definitively associated with any region. In fact, one interpretation of Uz is that it means something close to "Timbuktu" or "a land far, far away."
- There is a long, detailed description of what can only be a "fire breathing dragon" in a list of the things God created. We will discuss this in the next chapter.

Having said that, I would venture that the story of Job is based on a true story. A good man who was faithful to God experienced the loss of his business, the death of his children, and a debilitating disease. The major themes of this book would remain the same whether this was a historical story or a short story based on true events. Seeing a good man go through such suffering would move someone to write a "wisdom" book that explores the reasons why.

That is what the book of Job sets out to do, but in a roundabout way. It is a long book, mostly written in dense Hebrew poetry that is very hard to read. Most of the book is a drawn-out argument between Job and his three (and later a fourth) friends, arguing with each other about why these terrible things have happened to Job. In the end, God enters the discussion and then rewards Job for his faithfulness, restoring Job's wealth two-fold and giving him a new set of children.

▸**The patience of Job** is a common saying today that refers to Job enduring his suffering without knowing exactly why it was happening to him.

What are the main themes? The argument between these friends gives us the clue to the main theme of the book. I want you to trudge through one portion of the discussion between Job and Eliphaz.

Job's three friends—Eliphaz, Bildad, and Zophar—believe with all their hearts that the reason Job is suffering is because he has secretly been living a wicked life. Remember, the beginning of the story describes Job as the most faithful man in the whole land. But his friends cannot imagine any other reason for his suffering other than he is being punished for wrongdoing.

We came across this worldview when we were reading the book of Deuteronomy and in the introduction of Joshua. Do you remember? It is called blessings and curses or the Deuteronomy Formula. If you follow Halacha (613 laws of Torah, which include faithfulness in worship to God), then you will be blessed (wealthy, healthy, lots of kids). If you do not follow it, you will be cursed (what has happened to Job).

Now read Job chapters 22, 23, and 24, a sample of this argument between Job and his three friends.

Did you see the list of things Eliphaz speculates Job must be doing in secret?

Does he rebuke you for your piety,
bring you in for judgment?
Isn't your wickedness massive,
your iniquity endless?
You have taken payments from your family for no reason;
stripped the naked, leaving no clothes;
denied water to the thirsty,
withheld bread from the starving.
(The powerful own land;
the favored live in it.)
You have sent widows away empty;
crushed orphans' resources.
For this reason, snares surround you;
sudden dread brings panic to you
or a darkness that you can't see;
rushing water will cover you. (Job 22:4–11)

Job's response to his friends is that they are insane, insisting that he has been faithful:

My feet have stayed right in his tracks.
I have kept his way and not left it,
kept the commandments from his lips and not departed,
valued the words from his mouth more than my food. (Job 23:11–12)

Job eventually turns his frustration toward God, demanding to know why these things are happening and why it seems like the wicked in this life get off scot-free. Eventually, a fourth friend, Elihu, steps into the argument and suggests that maybe there are some deeper things going on besides just the justice of God. Maybe it is through suffering that we gain wisdom or depth of soul.

Questions for Reflection or Discussion

1. Job's friends believe the Deuteronomy Formula or blessings and curses is the way the world works. If this was how every detail of life worked, would you like that or not? If things started to go wrong, you would know it was because you had done something wrong and you just needed to fix it for things to get back on track. Would you like this or not?
2. Who are the friends or family in your life that would come and just sit with you for seven days while you were hurting? Which of your friends or family would be the most likely to speak honestly to you if they thought you were suffering because of something you did wrong?
3. Which kind of friend would you tend to be? Would you sit quietly with them or challenge them if you thought they were wrong? Or would you be like Elihua and search for deeper meanings in the suffering?

41

God Answers Job

Read Job chapters 38–42. Watch The Bible Project video on Job.

Job and his friends argue back and forth for thirty-six chapters and then in chapter 38, God finally breaks into the conversation. God's answer? "I made the heavens and the earth, in all their complexity. Who are you to question how or why things work the way they do?" God's response is not comforting. The theological word for this is *sovereignty*, which means since God is all encompassing and made the rules that govern creation, God has the prerogative to follow them or not, even to change them, if God feels it necessary.

God gives Job a list of everything that was done in the work of creation in all its fathomless mystery, basically saying to Job, "How dare you ask for an explanation." Well, um, okay. Awkward.

This might lead you to think one of the messages of the book is that we are not supposed to question God. Based on the text you could make that argument. But the very fact that this book so deeply lines out Job's questions and protest communicates the opposite. Hebrew wisdom tradition always asks questions of God. It doesn't always have God providing answers, but the conversation is there. When we are hurt and suffering, we want answers as to why, and we go to God and ask these questions.

Main Themes of Job

These are the three main themes of Job:

1. Don't follow God only for blessings.
2. The Deuteronomy Formula (blessings and curses) is not always true: bad things do happen to good people and vice versa.
3. Though we can question God, God's mystery and sovereignty is absolute, and we are not entitled to answers.

There is one more thing happening in the book of Job that isn't easy to see. In the midst of God's long list of creation, did you see what is described in chapter 41? It is a fire-breathing dragon. The Hebrew word is *Leviathan*, and it is paired with another fierce beast called *Behemoth*. Both of these are described as horrific, unpredictable, and destructive. One theory as to why they are among God's list of things created is that they represent that part of nature that is destructive and unpredictable, a natural part of the ebb and flow of life. This same word, Leviathan, is used in the first creation story among the order of created beings:

> God created the great sea animals (leviathan) and all the tiny living things that swarm in the waters, each according to its kind, and all the winged birds each according to its kind. God saw how good it was. (Gen. 1:21)

In other words, unpredictable suffering may just be a part of the natural cycle of life. It does not lessen our pain when we are experiencing it, but the authors of the book of Job are admitting it is a reality.

Curiously, in Job 28, there is a literary break from the argument that Job is having with his friends that asks some strange questions. The passage asks: Where can someone go to get wisdom? Can they buy it in the marketplace? Can they trade for it, can they mine it from the ground?

What this may imply is that to truly acquire wisdom, one needs to go through all of life's experiences, even some suffering. The appearance of the Leviathan and Behemoth as part of God's complex order may be pointing to that truth. The message of Job's fourth friend, Elihu, conveys these ideas.

The notion of theodicy, or why bad things happen to people, is one of the questions science attempts to answer, but in a different manner than theology. When a family member gets cancer, the medical/scientific culture essentially asks why? What comprised the cells? What weakened the immune system? Every painful episode in our lives has a rabbit warren of questions as to the source of that hurt and pain. Some of those pursuits lead us to answers, some do not. There is a rich tradition within every major religious faith that explores the value of pain and suffering.

The purpose of Job is multifaceted. The main message of Job is that we shouldn't assume that suffering is always God's punishment for wickedness. Bad things do happen to good people. As the book of Job says in a convoluted way, it just isn't that simple.

Questions for Reflection or Discussion

1. Do you know a really good person who has experienced suffering? Explain.
2. Do you know a mean or terrible person who seems to have a great life? Explain.
3. What is the hardest thing you have ever been through? What did you learn after the hardest part of it was over? Did it make you wiser?

42
The Call of Samuel

Read 1 Samuel chapters 1–3.

The period of the Judges ends as the prophet Samuel is born.

His mother's story is what we have been identifying as a "type" of story. She is having trouble conceiving (similar to Sarah, Rebekah, Rachel, and Samson's mother), and even her husband thinks she is drunk when he sees her sobbing from despair. God helps her conceive, and in gratitude Hannah dedicates her unborn child to God. Samuel is born and after she has weaned him (finished nursing the child from breastmilk), she sends him to the house of Eli to be reared as a priest. Though it does not say so in the story, it is very likely that Hannah accompanied her son and worked in the house of Eli to help raise her son.

Eli is a good priest, but he has raised wicked sons, Hophni and Phinehas. Remember, the period of the Judges is characterized by inconsistent leadership. Eli's sons disregard the strict dietary laws of the priesthood, and they sleep around with the young women who work at the tabernacle (see chapter 26, page 76 to remind yourself what the tabernacle was).

An important aside: look at the language used to describe the young boy Samuel. He served in the home of a priest, was being trained to become a priest, but he "did not yet know the Lord." What does that mean?

If you were raised in a Protestant tradition such as Baptist, Nazarene, Life Church, etc., this makes perfect sense to you. Those Christian traditions want individuals to wait until they are of an age where they can decide for themselves if they want to embrace God, or in the case of Christianity, embrace Jesus and be baptized of their own free will. This ideally comes in the wake of an experience that the person has where God becomes real to them. Sometimes this is called *head knowledge vs heart knowledge*. We might also call it "experiential knowledge." Samuel may have known quite a bit about God, but he hadn't yet had an experience that made it real to him. The same thing exists in traditions that baptize infants. The baptism is considered a sign of God's love and grace for the child, but the tradition still hopes the person will grow into maturity and have experiences that will make that truth their own. Those traditions (Roman Catholic, Episcopal, Lutheran, etc.) call that experience "confirmation" because it confirms/reaffirms what they have been taught growing up with heart knowledge.

God comes to the boy Samuel in the middle of the night and calls his name.

"Samuel!"

This happens three times, and each time he thinks it is his teacher, Eli, calling for him. Finally, on the third time, Eli understands what is happening. He tells Samuel to go back and when God speaks again, to be ready to listen.

The message that God gives to Samuel will "make the ears of all who hear it tingle!" (1 Sam. 3:11). He sends him back to Eli with a message. "I told him that I would punish his family forever because of the wrongdoing he knew about—how his sons were cursing God, but he wouldn't stop them" (1 Sam. 3:13). Can you imagine having to confront your teacher with their wickedness? It's scary to speak truth to people who have authority over you. Some people have no problem doing that. What do we call that? Holy sass?

From this point on, Samuel grew in his relationship with God, and "none of his words fall to the ground" (1 Sam. 3:19, NRSV).

Questions for Reflection or Discussion

1. Do you think it is possible to know about God but not really know God? What would be an example of this?
2. Have you ever been to a church retreat or summer camp where you felt particularly close to God? Did it seem like God was speaking to you?
3. Have you ever had to confront someone who had authority over you about something they did wrong? How did you do it?

43
The Philistines

Read 1 Samuel chapters 4–7.

From this point on Samuel grew in his relationship with God, and grew to full stature. Here is a simplified timeline of where we have been thus far:

Creation Stories	5500 BCE
Abraham	2000 BCE
Migration to Egypt	1900 BCE
Exodus from Egypt	1450 BCE
Entry to Canaan	1400 BCE
Judges and Conquest	1400–1000 BCE

Since the beginning of Exodus, we have covered a period of around 500 years. Developmentally as a culture, that is a long time. To keep it in perspective, the United States has only been a republic for around 240 years. Always keep that in mind as you think about the cultural, political, and spiritual development of the Israelites. These events happened over long periods of time.

Here are a couple of stories for you to look at as you finish up the period of the Judges:

1 Samuel 4, 5, 6. The Philistines capture the Ark in battle, but end up sending it back because it wreaks some playful havoc while being stored in their temple. Notice how Eli dies: he falls over backwards in his chair and breaks his neck (4:18). How many times have you been told not to lean back your chair? Bad idea, right? See? It's in the Bible!

1 Samuel 7. Samuel oversees a military victory over the Philistines. As an emblem to God, he sets up a victory monument called the "Ebenezer

Stone" which means "help." This is the source for the name "Ebenezer" of Charles Dickens fame. This section is also the source for the name "Ichabod," meaning "no glory."

Our next unit begins at 1 Samuel 8 around the year 1,000 BCE, with the prophet Samuel.

SECTION THREE

The United Monarchy, Divided Monarchy, and the Prophets

Unit One

The Rise and Fall of Saul and the Rise and Fall of David

1 Samuel and 2 Samuel
with Some Ezekiel and Exodus

44

Israel Demands a King

Read 1 Samuel chapters 8–12.

Be careful what you wish for. That is what the prophet Samuel told the people when they asked for a king. "We want to be like the other tribes around us." The form of government in place was a smattering of tribal judges influenced by priests and prophets. Remember, this was a long meandering period of about 500 years since the time of Moses, so the role of a "judge" evolved from a district advisor to something similar to a regional military commander and governor. Even so, these leaders were still heavily influenced by priests and prophets. This request for a monarchy was a rejection of their religiously shaped culture and would mean a shift in the power structure.

Note: This "rejection" will become important later when we look at the significance of Jesus and the emergence of Christianity. Also notice the practice of anointing. That too will continue to have significance moving forward in our study.

God told Samuel, "They haven't rejected you. No, they've rejected me as king over them" (1 Sam. 8:7–9).

God chooses a king: Saul of Benjamin, a tall handsome man from the smallest of the twelve tribes. During an effort to locate a herd of stray donkeys, Saul meets the prophet Samuel, who conveys to him that God has chosen him to be the leader of his people. Samuel anoints him with olive oil and tells him there will be three "signs" to confirm that this comes from God. Saul will:

1. find his lost donkeys;
2. encounter a stranger who will give him two loaves of bread; and

3. meet some dancing prophets and preach with them and he will be overcome with the Spirit of God.

The prophets did appear, and Saul danced with them. The language used to describe what happens to Saul is fascinating, "God changed his heart." Have you ever had a "mountaintop experience"? This can often happen at summer camp: cloistered with good friends, out in nature, singing around campfires, praying to God with friends about your life, the experience can be very overwhelming. I remember coming home from camp when I was a kid wondering why the rest of the world couldn't be as authentic and accepting as camp seemed to be. My heart had been changed. That same thing still happens in a different way when I go away on retreats as an adult.

There is also something in religion called "ecstatic prayer languages." You might have heard of this as "speaking in tongues." Essentially, someone is so overwhelmed by the presence of God that they start to speak in a language that only that person and God understand. There are different forms of it in various eastern religions and some pagan faiths. That is not what is happening to Saul, but it is similar. He has an emotional, transforming experience.

Samuel gives authority over to the new king, repeating his earlier warning. Be careful about giving power to kings. They will overtax you. They will conscript your sons for warfare. They will put your daughters into service. Recall that one of the reasons the people ask for a king is that Samuel's sons were corrupt and greedy (1 Sam. 8:1–6). Remember that when Samuel was called by God as a young boy, God's first message to him was to condemn his Eli for his inability to properly raise his sons (Hophni and Phinehas) with integrity (1 Sam. 1–3). Seems the apple didn't fall far from the tree. Samuel was better than Eli, but still failed in raising decent heirs.

In the past, including with Eli and Samuel, what is important to note is that there seems to be an ever-present possibility of a crisis of leadership. Samuel is depicted as a godly man, but his sons (Joel and Abijah), who were destined to succeed him, were corrupt. In spite of that, Samuel warns the people that giving absolute power to a king will go poorly.

Even so, God agrees and gives them Saul, son of Kish, of the tribe of Benjamin. God chooses him, anoints him, and changes his heart. But it won't take long for it all to fall completely apart.

Questions for Reflection or Discussion

1. How do we ensure that our leaders will be good, fair, and do the right thing? Samuel is described as a good leader, but his sons who would replace him were corrupt jerks. A king isn't necessarily the solution because power can corrupt them also. What do you think can be done to ensure leaders stay "good"?
2. Have you ever had a "mountaintop" experience at a summer camp, retreat, or somewhere else where you felt changed by God?

45
Things Fall Apart

Read 1 Samuel chapters 13–15.

Saul starts off well. He organizes troops and engages the Philistines in battle. But then it somehow all goes sour, for reasons that we as modern readers might not easily understand. Not long after Saul is anointed king, he falls out of favor with the prophet Samuel. You can almost hear Samuel saying, "I told you so." The scriptures later tell us that Saul reigned a total of forty years, and we are not sure how much time passed in these early years before things went sour. It seems quick, but it could have been years or even decades. During this time period, there are three actions that lead God to reject King Saul:

1. Samuel tells Saul to wait for him to make a sacrifice to God. Saul, fearful of their chances against the Philistines in battle and anxious about a pending military engagement, jumps the gun and offers the sacrifice himself. Samuel is none too happy and chastises the new king, telling him that God has chosen another to replace him, one who is "a man after God's own heart." Saul's reign seems to be a failure before it even gets fully established.
2. Saul, again anxious about his chances in battle, orders his soldiers to fast, believing this will win God's favor. It weakens troop morale. Even Prince Jonathan, Saul's son and military commander, calls it stupid, and eats some honey in front of the troops. When he does, his "eyes brighten."
3. Saul refuses to obey an order given by God through Samuel about their military engagement with the Amalekites. He orders Saul to "utterly destroy them." Soldiers, men, women, children, infants, and most their livestock die. Saul takes the king of the Amalekites captive and saves some of the livestock for his troops.

Genocide.

Here we must stop to ask some very hard questions of the biblical narrative. It is counterproductive to sugarcoat the story. We first ought to read it on its own terms and call this what it is: God ordered genocide. I wish it were not the case. It would make reading and understanding the scriptures easier. But it exists and we ought to make a thoughtful effort at understanding why.

There are many interpretative approaches or "readings" for handling stories like this, from very traditional and conservative to more liberal and even secular readings. In that vein, here are four interpretations of this violence:

> **Literal.** This is a more conservative reading with not much nuance. If the story says that God wanted that culture eliminated, then that is what it means. The Amalekites were a marauding band of pillaging thieves that the Hebrews had encountered as they fled Egypt (remember Moses holding his staff over his head in order to win the battle at the end of Exodus 17?). One could make a case for destroying the soldiers of a destructive tribe, but it becomes mystifying when the order is to kill children and infants. Also, these ancient stories were often exaggerated. We know this, in part, because the story suggests that he only spared the king and the animals and every other Amalekite was killed. But Amalekites show up later in Samuel and Chronicles.
>
> **Allegorical.** The story is symbolic for some other struggle. Early Christian theologians, some eleven centuries later, tended to read these Hebrew stories this way because they were shocked by the examples of brutality. These harsh accounts were used as allegories for some other difficult struggle, an inward spiritual battle, or some other difficult situation to be "utterly destroyed." So the story is read as primarily symbolic of the struggle of good versus evil. This created a dispute in the early Christian Church that the God of the Old Testament must have been a different God than the one depicted in the New Testament. Traditional Christian belief rejects this division of God, but it isn't always easy to reconcile these descriptions of God.

Moral Evolution of Human Civilizations. I seem to hear this one referred to the most. Earlier in human development we were more brutal and combative, so that was the manner in which God interacted with human beings. As we matured and evolved as a species, God changed the way God interacted with us. Again, you see this demonstrated in the early Christian Church a thousand years later, as the scriptures were embraced and then interpreted by Greek and Hellenistic Christians. This holds true in the history of Judaism also as it developed more progressive understandings of these stories.

Projection onto God. The last view is a nonreligious view from an anthropological understanding. It was not God who was asking for the annihilation of the Amalekites but rather Samuel and the people. In other words, to justify their actions, they said God asked them to do it, when it was actually their own idea.

Which one do I think is accurate? Honestly, I float between the last two. It simply is too difficult for me to imagine God ordering the killing of innocents. And my questions and struggles have been shared by readers of the Bible across the centuries. St. Augustine in the fourth century BCE developed a theology of *just war*, coming up with a spectrum of scenarios in which war might be allowable in light of Christ's teaching about loving your enemies. *Just war theory* is taught in our military academies to officers who are required to make nuanced, complicated decisions about war. There is another term in war theory called *collateral damage*, which refers to the level of harm that is done to innocent people when trying to kill or apprehend a guilty person. If a criminal or enemy sets up their headquarters in a children's school, is it okay to bomb that school? You may get the "bad guy," but you will also be killing a large number of innocent people.

Is this what was occurring with the Amalekites? Why couldn't the Israelites go after the warriors and leave the women and children? Could they adopt the children of the Amalekites after the war? War and violence is always a tragedy; a society saturated with violence was the specific reason given for the rebooting of human civilization in the flood account in Genesis 6. God abhorred violence because it did damage to the *imago Dei* (Gen. 9).

A modern equivalence, though not as saturated with religious questions, was President Harry Truman's decision to drop atomic bombs on Nagasaki and Hiroshima in 1945. Both bombs completely annihilated populations, including innocent adults and children. Truman, a devout Christian, tormented by his decision, ultimately felt those hard decisions would save more lives than were lost. War is so profoundly ugly, regardless of our best efforts to keep it "fair."

Samuel chastises Saul for his disobedience and insists that God prefers obedience over animal sacrifices. Samuel then takes a sword and kills the king of the Amalekites. Saul, in desperation, reaches out for Samuel and grabs him by his tunic, begging forgiveness, ripping the cloth. The prophet sees the tear in his robe and declares that God will: "search for a man following the Lord's own heart, and the Lord will commission him as leader over God's people, because you didn't keep the Lord's command" (1 Sam. 13:14).

Questions for Reflection or Discussion

1. Which of the four theories interpreting violence in the scriptures do you think is the best one? Why?
2. Leaders of countries do not need to make hard decisions in war all alone. They can ask for advice from wise people as to the best thing to do in a difficult situation. Who would you ask to be your advisor if you were a leader needing to make difficult decisions in war?

46
God Anoints David

Read 1 Samuel chapters 16–20.

God rejects Saul for disobedience, and in the wake of this rejection says he will anoint another to be king. Earlier, when Saul made an unsanctioned sacrifice (1 Sam. 13) and angered the prophet, Samuel predicted he would one day anoint another as king to replace Saul, *a man after God's own heart*. That day has come.

Samuel travels to the little town of Bethlehem, home to the tribe of Judah, where God says he will anoint a son of Jesse to be the new king. Jesse has eight sons, seven of them are strong, strapping soldiers. But God does not reveal any of these as the next king. Samuel says something beautiful regarding this, "Humans see only what is visible to the eyes, but the Lord sees into the heart" (1 Sam. 16:7). Remember that Saul was handsome and tall, popular with the people, and that had failed. He asks if Jesse has any other sons. David, his youngest son, is out in the fields with the sheep. Samuel anoints David with oil, the next king of Israel.

The story describes David as handsome and "ruddy." This could mean he had a glowing, rosy complexion, or possibly that he had red hair. Either way, it is ironic that though "God looks at the heart," it just so happens that David is a looker.

David is drafted to work in Saul's court. He will play the lyre for Saul to soothe him when he is depressed. Did you notice the source of Saul's torment? God sent an evil spirit to torment Saul. So begins a long period when there are two anointed kings, Saul and the young David. David

Note: In about 400 years after David, the prophet Isaiah, when predicting the coming of a future super king, says that there will be nothing about his appearance that will draw people to him, but rather a spirit of wisdom. (Isa. 53:1–2)

soon gains notoriety from his showdown with the Philistine giant Goliath, and the public falls in love with him. Women sing songs written in David's honor: "Saul has killed his thousands, but David has killed his tens of thousands" (1 Sam. 18:7).

Saul becomes insanely jealous and twice tries to kill young David while he is playing the lyre for him. It gets even more complicated. Michal, King Saul's daughter, falls in love with David. Saul sees this as a chance to arrange David's death. He tells David that if he will kill 100 Philistines, and bring him their foreskins, then he can marry Michal. David ends up killing 200. Was it God's blessing? David's passive-aggressive sass? A little bit of both? Regardless, it is an ever-growing complicated relationship.

How much time passes while David works in the court of Saul as a soldier and lyre player? It is hard to determine, but it was an extended period of time and a tense situation for David. The scriptures tell us later that David was thirty years old when he eventually assumes the throne, so it appears to be a period of about fifteen to twenty years.

David is anointed king. Saul is rejected as king. Why doesn't David just overthrow Saul and set up the new reign?

David's fame and notoriety has made Saul jealous. The story never tells us whether Saul knows David has been secretly anointed. Regardless, you sense the tension between the two. David works for the king, both as a soldier and as a musician. Twice Saul has tried to kill David by throwing his spear at his head while he played music for him. So you might ask, "Why doesn't David just leave?" A question emerges: "When will David rise?"

It's a very soap operatic situation. It would make a great "Housewives of Gilboa" TV show (in fact, ABC tried to make a version of this story with a rustic "Game of Thrones" feel called "Of Kings and Prophets," but it was canceled after two episodes because it was too racy and offended Christians. Um, have they read the Bible?). David is married to Michal, Saul's daughter, and is best friends with the king's son Jonathan. Even Jonathan has recognized that David will one day be king instead of him. So again, why doesn't David just flee, raise up an army, and overthrow Saul?

As you read, David eventually does flee after conferring with Jonathan.

Questions for Reflection or Discussion

1. What do you think it means for someone to have a heart after God's own heart?
2. Can you think of a leader who isn't traditionally good-looking but in that leadership position because they are intelligent and good?
3. David was hired to play music for the depressed king. When you are sad and discouraged, what music do you choose to listen to? Most people, as they grow older, listen to less music than they once did when they were young. What was, or what is now, the music of your soul?

47
Saul Chases after David

Read 1 Samuel chapters 21–26. It's six chapters, but you can do it.

What ensues in these chapters is a game of cat and mouse. Both David and Saul are fighting Philistines, but at the same time Saul is also trying to find and kill David. David enlists the help of the priest Ahimelech, asking for food and weapons. The priest gives David forbidden bread, the bread of the presence of God that was kept in the tabernacle, bread that is reserved symbolically only for God. David takes the bread and feeds his men. He also asks for any weapons the priest might have, and the only one he has is the sword of Goliath, which he gives to David. Saul finds out the priest helped David and has the entire cohort of priests slaughtered.

Note: The priest giving David bread that was set aside for God (the bread of the presence) will have a future significance as Christianity emerges about 1,000 years down the road. Jesus will be a descendent of David (in some sense he will be the future "perfect" version of David), and since Christians believe that Jesus was God in human form, there is symbolic foreshadowing in David being allowed to eat the bread of God. To be sure, David is not God, but his descendent Jesus will be. Jesus is a typology of David (Matt. 12:1–8). This is a kind of typology, with the bread of God's presence being the type, David eating the bread being the "antitype," and Jesus, the very presence of God, being a further "antitype."

You also might enjoy the way David convinces a Philistine king not to kill him. See 1 Samuel 21:10–15. What do we call this, the slobbering idiot defense?

David finally has a chance to kill Saul. While David is hiding in a cave in the desert of En gedi, who enters into the cave "to relieve himself" but King Saul? Saul seems to take a while to do his business, as Joab and David have quite a conversation in the back of the cave. Joab, David's military advisor, is ecstatic! "God has delivered your enemy into your hands! Go sneak up on him and cut his throat!" he whispers to David. David responds in the negative:

> "The LORD forbid," he told his men, "that I should do something like that to my master, the LORD's anointed, or lift my hand against him, because he's the Lord's anointed!" (1 Sam. 24:6)

He refuses to kill Saul for what seems like spiritual reasons: he is God's anointed king, let God end Saul's reign.

Who is to say in this context and culture that God was indeed trying to do that very thing. The story already says that God not only abandoned Saul but was sending demons to torment him. So Joab was essentially making the case to David, "God *is* ending Saul's reign. God has delivered him into your hands!"

Instead, David sneaks up on Saul and cuts off the corner of his robe. Later that same day, from a distance, he shows the piece of cloth to Saul and begs him to stop pursuing him, insisting they are not enemies.

"When will David rise?"

The Case of David's Wives

David leaves and gets embroiled with a wealthy sheep herder named Nabal, asking for food and supplies. Nabal refuses to help David because he considers David a political traitor, and it would not be good business to upset the king (maybe he heard what happened to the priest Ahimelech). David plans to invade Nabal's home and steal food for his men. Nabal's wife Abigail helps David behind her husband's back. When she tells Nabal, he has a heart attack and dies. David finds out and asks her to be his wife. David has now also been married to multiple wives: Michal, Ahinoam, and now Abigail. Although the story tells us that Michal, Saul's daughter, was given to another man when David fled.

And just to complicate things even more, there is a good chance that Ahinoam might actually be King Saul's wife, who left with David when he fled. The theory is that Saul's wife Ahinoam in 1 Samuel 14:50 is the same woman David married in 1 Samuel 25:43. Recall right before David fled, Saul yelled at his son Jonathan, calling him a "son of a stubborn, rebellious woman" (1 Sam. 20:30). Could it be because Saul's wife and Jonathan's mother (Ahinoam) ran off with David? Did David steal the mother of his best friend Jonathan? Later, after David is made king, the prophet Nathan tells David that God "gave your master's house to you, and gave his wives into your embrace" (2 Sam. 12:8). If this is the case, that means David was married to Michal and maybe Michal's mother. Maybe. Saul likely had multiple wives, so perhaps Michal was daughter to Saul by a different wife or a different Ahinoam. We can't know for sure, but what we do know is that their situation was a mess.

Real housewives of Gilboa? Welcome to the Bible.

More Intrigue

David has a second opportunity to kill Saul as David stumbles upon the king's camp while Saul is sleeping with no one on guard. Again, Joab pleads with David to take the opportunity God has given him, and again David refuses to "harm God's anointed." Instead, he sneaks up on Saul, thrusts Saul's spear into the ground next to his head, and takes his water jar. The next morning, he shows Saul the water jar from a distance and begs him to stop his pursuit. Saul "apologizes" and asks David to return home. David does not.

Is David's cautiousness a spiritual act of trusting in God's timing? Or is it a sign of weakness? When will David rise to the throne?

A couple of other things to notice before this reading ends. A story that is rarely told about David is found in chapter 27. David, at this point, tired of waiting to be king and tired of Saul's attempts to kill him, crosses enemy lines to fight as a mercenary alongside the Philistines. Strange. He does some tricky maneuvering to ensure that he isn't fighting and killing Israelites, but it is still a peculiar choice.

Sometimes things have to get worse before they can get better.

Question for Reflection or Discussion

1. David refuses to kill Saul because he is God's anointed, but he knows Saul is mentally imbalanced. Do you agree with David's patience or with his military commander Joab's encouragement to strike?
2. How do stories like these sound like reality TV?

48
David Rises to the Throne

Read 1 Samuel chapters 27–31 and then 2 Samuel chapters 1–2.

When will David rise? Soon, very soon. David gets nervous about working as a mercenary for the Philistines and decides to head back into the wilderness of Israel. You can't be king if you are working for the enemy of your people. Saul, on the other hand, goes completely "round the bend," and does something expressly forbidden by the Halacha. He seeks out a witch to conjure the ghost of Samuel (See Exod. 22:18, Lev. 20:27, and Deut, 18:9–13).

The Witch of Endor (the same name used by George Lucas for the moon-planet inhabited by the Ewoks in *Return of the Jedi*) does as Saul requests, though she fears for her life because she knows the Hebrew law. Samuel, groggy from his sleep in *Sheol* (the grave), chastises Saul for his insolence and repeats his earlier curse. God departed from Saul decades ago and he will now be delivered into the hands of his enemies. That is what happens during a battle against the Philistines.

As Saul is about to be captured in battle, he orders his attendant to kill him, a practice not uncommon for a king to prevent capture by an enemy, drawing out his death and using it to humiliate his people. The attendant refuses to kill the king, so Saul falls on his own sword.

Did you see the discrepancy in 2 Samuel 1:1–6? An Amalekite comes bearing the news of Saul's death to David, bringing Saul's crown to give to the king-in-waiting. He tells David that he killed King Saul on the battlefield as an act of mercy. Which is it? Did Saul fall on his own sword or did the Amalekite servant kill the king to protect him from humiliation at the hands of the Philistines?

It could be that the rivalry between David and Saul at this point was well known and the Amalekite servant saw this as an opportunity to rise in the new court of David. However, consistent with David's character thus far, the servant misreads David completely. David executes him for raising his hand against King Saul: "You *do not* harm God's anointed!"

Then David does something else consistent with this thread. He writes a sad song, called a lament, for King Saul and for Jonathan, who also died in the battle. He issues a decree in Judah that the lament be learned by everyone, in part:

Note: The description of the friendship between David and Jonathan in the song says that their love was "more amazing . . . than the love of women" (2 Sam. 1:26). There are some who want to see this as a description of a homosexual relationship between the two. There is no other supporting evidence that this was the case (in fact, quite the opposite) and more likely this suggests David and Jonathan were soul mates, and they trusted each other more than one would trust a spouse.

> Saul and Jonathan! So well loved, so dearly cherished!
> In their lives and in their deaths they were never separated.
> They were faster than eagles,
> stronger than lions! (2 Sam. 1:23)

What is going on? Is David being honest?

Two things: First, David is a spiritual person who trusts God. At this point, he could have turned to Joab and said, "See, I told you so. God took care of it." Second, there is more going on behind his actions; the clue is found in chapter 2 when you read about a seven-year period when there are essentially two kings, David in Judah and Ishbosheth (Saul's son) in Israel. David is from Judah, in the south. Saul is from Israel, in the north.

North and South. Israel and Judah

This can be confusing. If you recall, "Israel" is a general term that refers to all twelve of the tribal groups that were descended from Jacob and were settling into the land of Canaan after 400 years of slavery and forty years in the wilderness. But it also refers specifically to the collection of ten of those tribes, the ten northern tribes.

One way to think of this is the word "democrat." As Americans, we are all democratic, but only some Americans are part of the Democratic Party—Democrats. You could also say the same thing with the term "republic," as we are all part of the republic (the United States), but we are not all part of the Republican Party. This was true of the Hebrew tribal organization. All twelve tribes were descendants of Israel, but ten of those tribes, the northern ones, were specifically part of Israel. Israel is in the northern region where there were ten tribes. Judah is the southern region where there were two tribes.

David does not want to be only the king of Judah. He wants to be the king of the twelve tribes united together, Israel and Judah. Even though it is not said explicitly in the text, this desire explains his earlier hesitancy in killing Saul.

If you want to be king of Judah (south, where you are from) *and* king of Israel (north, where you are not from), you do not want to alienate the northern people whom you eventually want to rule. Saul may be crazy, but if you are from the north, he was *your* "crazy." David is wise enough to know this, which is why he writes a song honoring the northern king and requires his people in the south to learn it. David is being spiritual by trusting God's timing, but he is also being politically savvy. Is it possible to be both?

You also do not want to set a precedent that it is permissible to assassinate a king, under any circumstances, even if that king is a terrible ruler. When David rises to power, he does not want anyone to think they are allowed, by David's precedence, to "harm God's anointed." So he takes the slow, deliberate route rising to the throne. He is patient, wise, and trusting. David knew how to play the long game, like a third order Jedi playing chess on a two-level board.

David takes the reigns as the king of Judah only for about seven years. Eventually he will converge with the northern tribes of Israel into one united kingdom, strong enough to finally defeat the Philistines and drive out all of the Canaanite tribes.

Questions for Reflection or Discussion

1. Is David patient and trusting in God's timing or he is politically savvy and does not want to sabotage his ability to be king for all the tribes? Which do you think is truest? Can both be true?
2. Have you ever been in a situation, either on a sports team or maybe at work, where someone in charge was not the best person for that position and you were tempted to try and sabotage them to get someone better in that position? What did you do?
3. Would you consider yourself like David, trusting the long game and waiting on God to make things happen? Or are you more like Joab, wanting to take matters into your own hands and seeing those opportunities as given by God?

49
David Builds Unity

Read 2 Samuel chapters 5–7 (8–10 are optional). Watch The Bible Project video on Samuel, part I.

In reality, there are two versions of David, as there are typically with all leaders: the symbolic version and the actual person. This is true with a lot people who have multiple roles in life and take on unique traits for each. As we move forward in 2 Samuel, you will get a glimpse of "the other David," while continuing to show you the good, strong, and spiritual David. Both people exist. All of us are complicated, with a variety of aspects to our lives. David is the shepherd-king who would watch over his people, protect and care for them as a shepherd would, but he is far from perfect.

What is David's challenge? In 2 Samuel it is to develop strength among the united tribes. To do this, he wants to cultivate *one* cultural identity of the twelve tribes of Israel (ten in Israel and two in Judah). This will enable them to defeat their long-term enemy, the Philistines, and finally establish a homeland in Canaan.

At this point, I sense that perhaps Israel's original cultural purpose has been lost. Do you remember Abraham and Sarah's original Vision Quest? Genesis 12 called Abraham and Sarah and their offspring to become a blessing to all the nations of the earth. How are they doing with that vision thus far?

Anyone who has led a diverse group of people knows how tricky it is to build and maintain unity. Have you ever been in a situation in your group of friends, family, business, or church when the group was trying to make a change? It's a harrowing experience. Most people, and especially groups, dislike change. The process requires a great deal of wisdom and patience. David sets about the work necessary to bring all these people together in the following ways:

Chapters 1–4. After seven years of a divided reign, Saul's son concedes his reign in the north, making David the king over all the tribes.

Chapter 5. David conquers Jerusalem and establishes it as the capital city in northern Judah and renames it Zion, after the name of the hill on which it sits. It is also referred to as the "City of David." He also defeats the Philistines.

Chapter 6. David brings the tabernacle and the Ark of the Covenant, which had been moving from house to house throughout the tribal lands, to the new capital city. He does this with a celebrative processional, dancing before the Ark in his ephod (Jewish undergarment). Michal, his somewhat ex-wife (Saul's daughter, who was given to another man after David fled), watches David with contempt. David says he will gladly embarrass himself before the Lord in praise for all God has done.

Chapter 7. Bringing the tabernacle to Jerusalem was a first step in centralizing sacrifice and worship. This didn't happen completely until David's son Solomon built the temple, but David began to encourage people to stop making sacrifices locally and travel to Jerusalem to offer sacrifices. David passes a law that sacrifices can no longer be made on altars in each of the tribal regions and villages, or the "high places," but rather must be done in Jerusalem in the tabernacle. And "high places" had a tricky association tied to it. Those certain Canaanite tribes that performed child sacrifice had done so on high places. So even though it made sense for Israelites to offer animal sacrifices to God on high places, those locations became conflated with that abhorrent practice. David wants to phase out that association, requiring people to bring their animal sacrifices only to Jerusalem.

Chapter 8. David defeats the Philistines, which begins a period of unity, peace, and economic growth.

Chapter 9. David allows Jonathan's crippled son Mephibosheth to live in his court, a sign of mercy and unity.

David is uniting his people. He is doing this by appealing to the northern tribes by honoring Saul. He writes a song in his honor and requires the southern tribes to learn it, he sets up a common capital in a city on the border of the north and south, and then he starts the process of centralizing worship in that capital city, asking all the tribes to make a common pilgrimage to make sacrifices.

A new prophet is now in the land; Nathan tells David that God will establish his household forever and will never abandon David. David wants to build a temple for God and a resting place for the Ark of the Covenant, but Nathan tells him that his son will be the one to build it and makes a strange prediction about his son being beaten publicly by his enemies.

Did they all lived happily ever after? Well, you've read a good deal of the Bible at this point. You might be able to imagine what happens next.

Note: There is a legend about the "Star of David" that is unlikely true, but it fits with the understanding of David's significance in uniting the tribes of Israel. David wanted to create a symbol that would unite his people from all the tribes. He envisioned that a right-side-up triangle would represent the north, and an upside-down triangle the south. Overlay the two triangles together, and you come up with the twelve-sided star of David. Most Jewish scholars place the development of the Star of David around the seventh century CE, some 1,700 years after the reign of David.

Note: Solomon, David's son, does build the temple, but there is no clear event connected with any public beating. Christians believe this is a prophecy or foreshadowing of the arrest and beating of Jesus, some 900 years into the future, who is a "Son of David."

Questions for Reflection or Discussion

1. Most people have at least two "lives." This is sometimes called your public identity and your private identity. How are the two different for you? How do you act different in public than you do in private? Are they so different as to be dishonest?

2. Have you ever been in a position on a team, at school, or work where you had to bring people who were different together for a common purpose? In what ways was that difficult? In what ways was it enjoyable?
3. Things that bring people together are often called "instruments of unity." Can you name the instruments of unity that schools use to bring people together? What about in your city or state? Some have described the United States as a melting pot or stew of different cultures and religions. Is this an accurate and uniting description?
4. Did you know we have a National Cathedral in Washington, DC, similar to David's vision of a temple in the capital city of Jerusalem? It was envisioned and built by the Episcopal Church to be a place of worship for all Americans, even people of different faiths. Look it up on your search engine as an activity. Is the very city of Washington, DC, our nation's capital, an instrument of unity?

50
David and Bathsheba

Read 2 Samuel chapters 11–12.

After having immense success against their enemies, David's reign brings stability to the region and unites the twelve tribes as well as the northern and southern regions. What will David do next? Screw it all up.

Walking on the roof of his palace in Jerusalem, David sees a beautiful woman across the way taking a bath. He calls her over and learns that she is married to one of his commanders, Uriah the Hittite. David and Bathsheba have a romantic dalliance, and she gets pregnant.

There is a Hebrew ritual within marriage called the *Niddah*, a time of separation between a man and woman during the woman's menstruation. During those days the husband and wife do not touch each other, because the woman is considered ceremonially unclean. This sounds misogynistic (demeaning toward women), but there were equivalent laws for men concerning their bodily fluids, all of which were part of the wide range of purity laws in the Halacha that were created around bodily functions.

When the Niddah was over, the woman would take a ritualistic, prayerful bath (mikvah) and then be reunited with her husband and um . . . ahem . . . well . . . you know. It just so happens that those days after a woman's period are also the time of a woman's ovulation, when the egg from her ovaries is dropping and she is most able to conceive a child. So the Niddah has a myriad of purposes: spiritual cleansing, prayer, intentional separation, reunion, and the possible conception of a child.

▸**Mikvah** is a word that sounds like the word "hope" in Hebrew and refers to the variety of ritual baths connected with Hebrew spirituality and being made pure before God. Priests washed before entering God's presence in the tabernacle. A man who had done work that

> might have made him impure took a mikvah upon his return home. Hebrews who had fallen away from God and needed to be made spiritually clean took a mikvah. Anyone wishing to convert from another religion to the Hebrew faith took a mikvah as their final act before becoming an Israelite. As you might imagine, mikvahs are the ritualistic precursor to Christian baptism, something we will talk about more down the road when we turn the corner toward the life of Jesus.

This story specifically mentions that Bathsheba was coming to the end of her monthly period, and so she was most definitely taking her mikvah. When David calls her over to his palace, what happened was exactly what was bound to happen. There is a good chance David knew precisely what kind of a bath she was taking, but he didn't care. He wanted what he wanted.

He tries to cover up the pregnancy by calling Bathsheba's husband Uriah back from the front lines under the guise of needing a report of the battle. He then encourages Uriah to sleep with Bathsheba so the baby will be assumed to be theirs. But Uriah, in an act of devotion to his men, chooses not to go to Bathsheba, because his men are not able to be with their wives. David even gets him drunk hoping that will do the trick, but still Uriah refuses.

So David has him killed. He sends him back to the battle with a note that he is to be put on the front lines. He dies. David marries Bathsheba.

When the prophet Nathan learns what happens, he confronts David, but he does not do it directly. Part of the king's duties, you may remember, is to serve as the head judge over the tribes, ruling on the direst issues. Nathan asks if he may share a pressing matter with the king and begins to tell him the predicament: A rich man had boorishly stolen a poor man's lamb for a party he was throwing. David is furious and demands that the man pay back the poor man four times over and then be put to death. David demands to know the name of the man.

"You are that man!" Nathan told David (2 Sam. 12:7).

It is difficult confronting powerful people, sometimes called *speaking truth to power.* Let's say some students caught a teacher in some shady behavior, what would they do? Most students say they would tell some other adult and ask them to confront the teacher (there are always a few who insist they would have the courage to confront the person head on). But the point is the same. When you confront people who have power over you, you have to be subtle, or oblique about it. If not, then you could lose your good standing, your job, or worst-case scenario, your life. Speaking truth to power needs to be handled delicately because the person you are confronting can harm your life.

▸**Speaking truth to power.** Saying things to powerful people that they need to hear, but do not want to hear. This can be difficult because they can hurt you or kill you in retaliation.

David immediately apologizes and asks if he must die. Remember that Nathan already promised David that God will establish his "house forever" (2 Sam. 7). He will not be removed from power and will not be put to death. However, there is a new promise to accompany the first promise: calamity (violence) will never depart from the House of David. And the child conceived by David and Bathsheba will die. The story is framing these promises: David's House is established forever. (David commits a sin of adultery, deception, and murder.) David's House will forever be cursed with violence.

David later writes Psalm 51, which is about this sin:

Create a clean heart for me, God;
  put a new, faithful spirit deep inside me!
Please don't throw me out of your presence;
  please don't take your holy spirit away from me.
Return the joy of your salvation to me
  and sustain me with a willing spirit. (Ps. 51:10–12)

Prepare yourselves. What happens next is a fulfillment of the curse that Nathan has proclaimed on the House of David and one of the worst stories in the Bible.

Questions for Reflection or Discussion

1. Speaking truth to power: If you caught one of your teachers or one of your bosses in corrupt or inappropriate behavior, what would you do? Would you tell someone? Would you confront them directly? Or would you not take the risk and just let it alone?
2. It has been said that power and money corrupt a person and that absolute power corrupts absolutely. What are some things a leader can do to help make sure this doesn't happen?

51
David's House Falls Apart

Read 2 Samuel chapters 13–15 and 18 (16, 17, and 19 are optional) and then watch The Bible Project video, Samuel, part II.

David commits adultery and murder. In the wake of this sin the prophet Nathan makes a declaration: "The sword will never leave your own house" (2 Sam. 12:10).

Immediately, in this biblical narrative, the prophecy comes to pass. The next part of the story is one of the most horrific we read in our survey of the Bible. To fully understand what the larger arc of the Hebrew-Christian Bible is saying about people and about God, we must walk through the worst parts of the story. You can't fully appreciate the good news of redemption unless you have some understanding of what needs redeeming.

The Rape of Tamar

David's son Amnon rapes his half-sister Tamar.

Rape is an act of violence that is mixed with sex; rape is attacking someone with unwanted sex. Sex was created by God to be a mutual loving experience between two consenting adults, to bring them closer together. Rape is a horrific corruption of that purpose. Even worse, this story is about a brother attacking his half-sister, something forbidden by the Halacha and against the law in nearly every culture in human history. This awful practice is called **incest.**

It is truly an awful story, one that should be treated with the utmost seriousness when read in a class. Amnon is hateful, selfish, and depraved. He attacks his half-sister physically and emotionally abuses her, which also shames himself, his family, and the kingdom. To make it even worse, he blames her! It is a disgusting display. She flees to Absalom (her full brother) and they report the crime to their father, King David.

David. Does. Nothing.

Rape and incest were a crime punishable by death in the Hebrew Halacha. The story says that David was angry at Amnon's actions, but it just ends there. Look at the transition from chapter 13, verse 21 to 23. It says, "Two years later . . ." This inaction on the part of King David festers, like an infected wound, and it poisons his family. Absalom, disgusted with his father's moral weakness, takes matters into his own hands and kills his half-brother Amnon.

"The sword will never leave your own house."

Absalom flees for fear of his father's punishment. Why? If David wasn't going to put Amnon to death for the shameful raping of Tamar, then why would Absalom think his father had the moral temerity to punish him for doing what David lacked the character to do? Still, Absalom flees. Eventually, he is allowed to return to court but is denied access to his father. In Absalom's eyes, his father has lost all moral authority. He camps out at the gate of the palace and spends the next four years undermining his father's administration, telling people his father is a weak leader, unwise and unjust. He is planting the seeds for a rebellion.

The Death of Absalom

This leads to Absalom raising an army and attempting to overthrow his father David. As David sends his men to engage the traitor, he begs them, if it is at all possible, not to harm Absalom. During the pursuit, Absalom gets caught in an oak tree by his thick luxurious hair. There, hanging by his locks, he is speared to death by David's long faithful military commander, Joab.

When the news reaches David he is inconsolable. "Oh, my son Absalom! Oh, my son! My son Absalom! If only I had died instead of you! Oh, Absalom, my son! My son!" (2 Sam. 18:33).

Joab chastises the king for mourning the loss of his traitor-son rather than thanking his men for their devotion.

> Joab came to the king inside and said, "Today you have humiliated all your servants who have saved your life today, not to mention the lives

> of your sons, your daughters, your wives, and your secondary wives, by loving those who hate you and hating those who love you! Today you have announced that the commanders and their soldiers are nothing to you, because I know that if Absalom were alive today and the rest of us dead, that would be perfectly fine with you! Now get up! Go out and encourage your followers! I swear to the LORD that if you don't go out there, not one man will stick with you tonight—and that will be more trouble for you than all the trouble that you've faced from your youth until now." (2 Sam. 19:5–7)

There is a song by Pierce Pettis that I would encourage you to listen to. It is called "Absalom, Absalom" on his album *Making Light of It* (released in 1996).[1]

The next reading is a bit off course, but you will see why.

Questions for Reflection or Discussion

1. This is a difficult story, but an important one. How did David's sin with Bathsheba and his attempt to cover it up poison his family?
2. If you were David, would you have had the courage to punish Amnon the way he was supposed to be punished?
3. Why do you think David does nothing?
4. What do you think of Absalom's actions? Did he do the right thing in overthrowing his father?

---

1. *https://youtu.be/l1nBRCpS4GI.*

52
The Parents Eat Sour Grapes: Three-Fold Interpretation

In chapter 35 (page 107), when we were reading about the Canaanite tribes, we introduced a very basic three-step method of interpreting and applying religious stories to life. Some form of this basic three-step approach is done across religious traditions, whether it be the Hebrew Bible, Christian Scriptures, the Koran, Bhagavad Gita, or Buddhist texts (*Tripitaka*, *Mahayana Sutras*, and the *Tibetan Book of the Dead*). It looks something like this:

> **Story.** What the writers of a particular account intended to say to the people to whom they were originally writing. Sometimes this is clear and sometimes it requires work deciphering the historical background and cultural understanding of the time.
>
> **Abstraction.** Is there an abstract idea or concept that can be lifted from the story?
>
> **Application.** Can the abstract idea or "lesson" drawn from the story be applied (responsibly and carefully) to a different situation or context? This is the work of basic of biblical interpretation.

Here is how it might apply to what we have been reading in 2 Samuel:

Modern readers might not relate to being shepherds or warriors in a tenth-century tribal society, but they do understand the struggles for power within their own subgroups at school or work. We understand the difficulty of building unity among different groups of people, and how frustrating it is to be subject to a bully (such as King Saul) who has influence and uses it in a mean and hurtful way. David was learning to be patient, to trust the process of his rise to power, to manage the complicated relationships all around him, to maneuvering through difficult situations, and trust in the invisible hand of God. Reading these stories frames those abstract ideas and invites us to apply them to other situations.

I believe that one of the primary tasks of a healthy religious community is to frame the important issues of life and find the best ways to maneuver them. Recall the ancient Hebrew culture called this Halacha (pathway) or law (Torah). We are still doing the work of finding the best paths and best principles to shape our lives. Review the three layers we've read in 2 Samuel:

1. What is going on in the tenth-century BCE political-religious culture?
2. What are the abstract principles from those stories?
3. How can those principles be applied to the life of a thirteen-year-old or a forty-five-year-old or whomever is reading it?

We must be extremely careful because the applications can be dark. For instance, how we "apply" or interpret the story of God telling the prophet Samuel to instruct King Saul to kill Amalekite men, women, children, and infants certainly takes spiritual intelligence.

And so it goes with the overall story of the rise and fall of Saul and the rise and fall of David. David committed a horrible act with Bathsheba and the murder of Uriah. The prophet said that God would not abandon him but that it would poison the culture of his household.

Read Ezekiel chapter 18 and Exodus 20:4–6.

With this in mind, read the opening portions of Ezekiel's teaching in chapter 18 and revisit a portion of the Ten Commandments. Over the centuries, the leaders in Hebrew culture noticed that children tended to repeat the behavior of their parents. If the parents set a good example, the kids tended to do well. If the parents were wicked, the kids tended to be wicked. Of course, this isn't always the case. There are exceptions where people "break the cycle." But modern psychology has observed that it often takes intentional strategies to form new patterns of behavior different than your parents.

And that, in a sixth-century prescientific manner, is what the prophet Ezekiel is saying. Even if your parents set a bad example, even if your grandparents or great grandparents set into motion a family culture of self-destruction and harm, even if your "house is plagued with calamity," God says (through the prophet) that, even so, you are now responsible to correct your own life's course. You cannot control the behavior of your parents (i.e., Saul, David), but you do have control over your own formation.

It isn't always easy, but with the guidance of the Holy Spirit, the best of our collective thinking, and the help of healthy relationships, it is possible. In the New Testament, Paul said it this way:

> Don't be conformed to the patterns of this world, but be transformed by the renewing of your minds so that you can figure out what God's will is—what is good and pleasing and mature. (Rom. 12:2)

Reading these stories is one way, among others, to frame abstract ideas that we can apply to other situations.

So it is with David. He had the opportunity to model a love for God, to walk in the Halacha, and show the Hebrew people what it means to make mistakes and then repair the damage. Instead, he seems to have retreated to a position of fear and pride. Somewhere along the way he poisoned his children. Was the mercy shown to Amnon a sign of forgiveness, or was it a sign of moral weakness? Had David lost the respect of his children? Was he afraid to punish them because he thought he had lost the right to rule justly? Had David lost his moral authority? These are hard questions.

Forgiveness is made available by God, but it is sometimes hard to put into practice. Doing the right thing is almost always the difficult thing. Even when we make mistakes, God is ready to enter into our lives and repair what was damaged and give us a new start. Having the courage to act on that new start is sometimes difficult.

Questions for Reflection or Discussion

1. It is often said that children will almost automatically grow to parent their children in the same manner they were raised. This is a deep

conversation, but talk about how you were raised and the things you wanted to imitate from your parents, as well as the things you did not want to repeat.

2. This may also give you the opportunity to talk about your life as a parent now. Are you being the kind of parent you had hoped you would be?

53
Biblical Inspiration

Earlier, in chapter 31 (page 92), we started a conversation about how God speaks to people. The story from the scriptures that framed this topic for us was a tense exchange between Moses and his siblings Aaron and Miriam in Numbers 11. They resented that Moses claimed to have a special relationship with God. "God speaks to us also!" they insisted. God intervenes in the argument and says, yes, he speaks to most people in "dreams, visions and riddles." But to Moses, he speaks directly, face-to-face.

This process is called revelation because God is revealing something. There are two categories for the different kinds of revelation: general and special. General revelation (or revealing something) is akin to the wisdom we get from observing the way the world works and what are reasonable, best practices. Special revelation is more like the dreams, riddles, visions, and audible voices mentioned in Numbers 11.

The Bible contains both types of revelation. We dig into these stories for ideas, messages, and impressions that we then say are from God. In this way, God also speaks through the Bible to us today. Sometimes it is more direct and other times it is like solving a puzzle. As you have read through the stories and worked through my commentary on the scriptures, we have been doing some of this work.

Another way people talk about the Bible is as an "inspired" revelation. Inspired means "to be filled with spirit," meaning the spirit of God enters into the stories of scripture and our task is to extract God's message from them. But there are some formal descriptions for how this actually works. Like most things, the views tend to fall along a spectrum, from a traditional conservative approach to a more liberal one, even nonreligious understanding, and everything in-between. The five traditional theories of revelation are:

Dictation Theory. God dictated the books of the Bible word-by-word and the biblical authors were recording the message. What is on the page is a perfect rendition of that message.

Verbal Plenary Inspiration. The writer's personal traits and background played a significant role in shaping the story, but God's Spirit shaped the integrity of the words and ideas to maintain their integrity in all aspects. This is typically still considered a perfect revelation, if interpreted correctly.

Dynamic Inspiration. The thoughts and ideas contained in the Bible were inspired by God but were profoundly shaped by the individual writer's background and knowledge, to a greater degree than in a verbal plenary conception. This theory tends to allow for mistakes that result from the message being passed through the perception of the writer's imperfect life. The message of God is contained in the writing, but it requires interpretation.

Form Criticism. The scriptures, in all their different genres (religious history, law, poetry, proverb, short-story, fable, apocalyptic visions), have discernible roots in history, mythology, or ancient cultural/cultic practices. The stories are divinely inspired, but with mixed elements, so the themes can sometimes be inconsistent. Readers look for overarching messages across all the various stories rather than for particular and perfect unity. Because of this, form critics attempt to separate the kernel of inspired truth from the husk that contains it, through various interpretative methods.

Historical Criticism. This is similar to Form Criticism but not concerned whether the stories or ideas are inspired by God or hold truth. This form tends to look at religion using a scientific, phenomenological (observing evidence) approach. This view sees the writings as imperfect and descriptive of the writer's experience and agenda only.

As a middleweight theologian and teacher, I tend to move back and forth between dynamic and form criticism theories of inspiration, but I have students who come from families that understand inspiration from a dictation and plenary point of view as well as historical. It can be tricky terrain to navigate and never dull when there are a variety of biblical interpretations represented in a Bible study. As we have read together, you may have at times found my interpretations not matching up with your own. While unavoidable, having different perspectives helps us think more deeply.

Questions for Reflection or Discussion

1. Which one of these descriptions do you think best captures the way the Bible contains an inspired message from God?
2. Can you identify a story from the scriptures that you felt God has "in-spired" or put a message in there for you?

Unit Two

The Reign of Solomon, the Temple, the Divided Kingdom, and the Prophets

1 Kings, 2 Kings, Proverbs, Ecclesiastes, Song of Songs, Isaiah, Hosea, Amos, Jeremiah, Ezekiel, Daniel, Ezra, Nehemiah, Esther, 1 Chronicles, and 2 Chronicles

54
Abisha the Shunammite

Read 1 Kings chapters1–4, scan 5–7, then read chapter 8.

Abishag had a peculiar job. Old man King David was cold and no manner of blankets could keep him warm, so they called one of his concubines to come and snuggle with him. (The story underscores that this was snuggling only.) Abishag is a fairly unknown character in the Bible, but she has come to represent a larger issue that is important to touch on when reading the scriptures—the value and treatment of women in biblical cultures.

A *concubine* refers to women who served in the king's court or served in the household of a wealthy and powerful man. The word *concubine* sanitizes the situation, as these women were essentially slaves. Though they worked as servants in households, one of the potential duties of a concubine was sexual. It isn't a pleasant thing to discuss and it can be an embarrassment for those who value the Bible because slavery is not strongly condemned, at least to the degree and manner one thinks it ought to be. The exploitation of Abishag the Shunammite, and those like her, is often dismissed as "part of the times."

In the Garden Story, when Adam and Eve disobey God and access the knowledge of good and evil before it was allowed, one of the consequences conveyed was a broken relationship between men and women. As I stressed in the Genesis story (see chapter 4, page 12), this subjugation was not God's intention for the relationship between men and women. You see the vestiges of this in many of biblical stories, and Abishag is among them.

As you have read, Abishag becomes a pawn in the struggle for succession after David's death. Solomon and Adonijah compete for the throne, and Solomon's mother (Bathsheba) uses subversive power to make sure her son is crowned. Adonijah concedes, but he makes one seemingly simple request, to be allowed to marry Abishag the Shunammite. Seems a fair enough compromise, but it infuriates Solomon and he has Adonijah put to death. Why?

In that culture, to be given one of the king's concubine was to imply that the man was an equal to the king and a possible heir to the throne. Adonijah made a passive-aggressive move and Solomon called him on it. You can see how women are valued and used in this culture: exploitation, misogyny. It's part of the Bible that should not be ignored.

▸**Misogyny** is the belief and practice that men have a higher intrinsic value than women, which leads to the mistreatment of women.

Solomon is made king and has a dream in which God grants him one wish. As he is young, he is afraid he will not be able to rule effectively, so he asks for a discerning heart. He knows he needs wisdom. God is so pleased that he asked for wisdom, God grants him wealth and power also. The story at the end of chapter 3, about Solomon "cutting the baby in two," has come to represent his wisdom in dealing with people.

▸**Cut the baby in two** is a reference to the story that demonstrates Solomon's wisdom and is used to describe a difficult situation that requires unconventional and wise solutions.

Building the Temple

I would encourage you to scan chapters 5 through 7. As you'll recall, King David wanted to build the temple but was told it would be the task of his successor (who is now Solomon). Practically speaking, David's major accomplishment was to unite the tribes—the northern and the southern regions—and conclude the regional conflicts that beleaguered Israel during the conquest of Canaan. Solomon has no wars to fight, so that gives him money and human resources to build the temple and deepen and enrich the intellectual culture of Israel. You can read a description of this in chapter 4.

> Solomon's wisdom was greater than all the famous Easterners, greater even than all the wisdom of Egypt. He was wiser than anyone, more wise

than Ethan the Ezrahite or Mahol's sons: Heman, Calcol, and Darda. His reputation was known throughout the region. Solomon spoke three thousand proverbs and one thousand five songs. He described the botany of trees, whether the cedar in Lebanon or the hyssop that grows out of the wall. He also described cattle, birds, anything that crawls on the ground, and fish. People came from everywhere to listen to Solomon's wisdom; even the earth's kings who had heard about his wisdom came! (1 Kings 4:30–34)

▸**Wisdom of Solomon.** Solomon was known for asking God for wisdom. Many of the wisdom sayings in the scriptures are attributed to him, so this phrase is often used to describe a person who is wise.

Read 1 Kings chapter 8.

This is a repeat of the covenant that both Saul and David made with God. It is the blessings and curses, the Deuteronomy Formula applied to kingship. If you will be faithful, then you will be successful, but if you fall away, then you will experience curses.

Questions for Reflection or Discussion

1. When reading the Bible it can seem like women were often treated unfairly and as unequal to men. Back then, if a woman was going to wield power, they had to be sneaky about it. Do you think girls or women are still treated unfairly? In what situations?
2. What steps can you or others you know take to ensure that women are treated the same as men?

55
Wisdom

Read Proverbs chapters 7–8, then Ecclesiastes chapters 1–3, 7, and 11–12, and then go back and read Proverbs chapter 31 and Song of Songs chapter 1. Watch The Bible Project video on Proverbs and Ecclesiastes.

As noted in chapter 24, the Bible is a collection of books written in an array of genres. There is ancient history, law, short story, political-religious history, poetry, allegory, parables, proverbs, letters, and poetic prophecy. A quick review: the Hebrew tradition divides what Christians call the Old Testament into three larger categories: Law (Torah), History (Nev'iim), and Writings (Ketuv'iim). The acrostic of these three Hebrew words is TNK. So the Hebrew tradition refers to this collection as "The TaNaKh."

What you are reading in this chapter is a selection from the Ketuv'iim, or the Writings. The writings are a mixture of poetry, proverbs, short story, and histories (with high amounts of figurative language). The Ketuv'iim is typically made up of the following books:

Psalms
Proverbs
Job
Song of Songs
Ruth
Lamentations
Ecclesiastes
Esther
Daniel
Ezra
Chronicles

Most of these writings are attributed to Solomon, though some of the writers would have been advisors in his court, or teachers in various institutions he had created.

You started by reading Proverbs 7 and 8. They are two sides of a metaphorical coin. In chapter 7 you have the writer encouraging young men to avoid the *adulterous woman* who wants to lead them astray. In chapter 8 it is the *woman of virtue and wisdom*, calling them toward a healthy and productive life. Both wisdom and folly are personified poetically as women. Which woman will you choose, young man?

The introduction to Ecclesiastes is pretty dark and cynical. Meaningless! Everything is meaningless! Another translation of that Hebrew word is *mist* or *smoke*. Everything is transitory. Ecclesiastes almost didn't make it into the Hebrew *canon* (a canon is a collection of endorsed books) because it was so cynical. There are some beautiful passages in the book (the intro to chapter 3 on the rhythms of a balanced life among them) but peppered throughout are some pretty jaded views of life. Chapter 7 is a collection of proverbs about the search for wisdom and contains one of my favorite passages:

> I have seen everything in my pointless lifetime: the righteous person may die in spite of their righteousness; then again, the wicked may live long in spite of their wickedness. Don't be too righteous or too wise, or you may be dumbfounded. Don't be too wicked and don't be a fool, or you may die before your time. It's good that you take hold of one of these without letting go of the other because the one who fears God will go forth with both. (Eccles. 7:15–18)

But then toward the end is a peculiar passage:

> See, this is what I found, says the Teacher, examining one matter after another to account for things. But there's something that I constantly searched for but couldn't find: I found one man among a thousand, but I couldn't find a woman among any of these. See, this alone I found: God made human beings straightforward, but they search for many complications. (Eccles. 7:27–29)

Solomon, to whom these writing are attributed, had difficulty in his relationships with women, something we will take a closer look at in the next chapter. But notice his struggle within the context of the other wisdom writings in a book that almost did not make it into the Bible because of all of its wanton cynicism.

Also, read his admonition to young people:

> Rejoice, young person, while you are young! Your heart should make you happy in your prime. Follow your heart's inclinations and whatever your eyes see, but know this: God will call you to account for all of these things. Remove anxiety from your heart, banish pain from your body, because youth and the dawn of life are pointless too. Remember your creator in your prime, before the days of trouble arrive, and those years, about which you'll say, "I take no pleasure in these." (Eccles. 11:9–12:1)

There, coming from a man who has had too much money, too much power, and has been worn down by the worries of life. There is a saying for this that comes from the hip-hop culture, "Mo' money, mo' problems."

To balance and juxtapose Solomon's cynical view of women and marriage, read Proverbs 31, a writing of King Lemuel, who describes a strong, smart, independent, spiritual woman, and holds her up as an example for all people.

Then glance at a sampling of the romantic love poetry in Solomon's Song of Songs. This book also was nearly excluded from the collection of scripture because it was so risqué for its time. In fact, the romance described between the man and the woman was later interpreted as being an allegory for the love between God and Israel. We will look at that further when we read the prophets.

Finally, I commend to you portions from the wisdom writings that are found in the apocryphal books The Wisdom of Solomon and the Book of Sirach. The *Apocrypha* is a collection of books that were generally written in the interbiblical period, the timeframe between the Old and New Testaments. Not every Bible contains these books. Both Jews and Christians see these books as important, but various Christian traditions disagree about whether they should be included in the Bible. Catholic and Orthodox denominations (such as Roman Catholic, Episcopal, and Greek Orthodox) include them. Protestant denominations (those who were formed during the Reformation in the fifteenth and sixteenth centuries, such as the Lutheran and Methodist Church) value their place in religious history but do not see them as official scripture. Having said all of that, the wisdom books in the Apocrypha are worth exploring.

There are thirty-one chapters in the book of Proverbs. Some people make it a daily discipline to read one chapter of Proverbs each day, something you might try.

Questions for Reflection or Discussion

1. The call of a woman to a young man is used metaphorically in both positive and negative ways to describe life choices. Why do you suppose the writers of Proverbs did that instead of using men as a metaphor?
2. Can you name a woman in your life who fits the description of the one described in Proverbs 31?
3. Who is the wisest person you know? What makes them wise?
4. If God granted you one wish, what would you ask for?

56
The Downfall of Solomon

Read 1 Kings chapters 8–12. Watch The Bible Project video on Kings.

A few years ago our school chapel theme for the year was "wisdom." A guest speaker started his chapel talk by asking our students, "Who was the wisest person in the Bible?" There was the normal amount of hesitation but within a few seconds someone said, "Solomon." "Correct!" the preacher said, and he proceeded to speak on something in the wisdom literature (the Ketuv'iim).

Sitting from my perch in the chapel, having walked numerous seventh graders through 1 Kings and the saga of Solomon, I couldn't help but wish that at least part of their hesitation in answering the question was that some knew the *whole* story of Solomon. This king started out asking for wisdom and no doubt cultivated much of it along the way, but eventually he turned from it and wrecked the kingdom.

Solomon had a problem, a big problem. You read about it in 1 Kings chapter 11. He *collected* 700 wives and 300 concubines. Corrupt beyond comprehension, in no way does it capture the spirit of the Halacha. Solomon allowed money and power to corrupt him. Besides his mistreatment of women, 1 Kings 9 describes how Solomon levied high taxes to pay for the building of the temple and implemented slavery to provide cheap labor. Scholars who study his reign characterize it as a restitution of the slavery Israel fled in Egypt some 500 years earlier. Solomon undid what Moses did and became a reincarnation of Pharaoh.

A close reading of Solomon's problem with women identifies the larger sin, not as infidelity and a narcissistic collection of women (as awful as that is), but rather the women he married were of foreign cultures who practiced distant religions. For each of his wives Solomon built shrines and temples in the high places. Remember, one of the unifying policies David instituted was regulating worship. No longer were people allowed to make sacrifices on the high places in their villages and regions but rather had to make a pilgrimage to Jerusalem to the temple. This pilgrimage would unite the tribes and cultures around the worship of one God in one special place.

Solomon dismantled what David, his father, created.

This tragedy may not seem important to us. As Americans, we value the religious freedom our secular society provides. The separation of church and state ensures a plurality of religious practice in our nation. But at that time in Israelite history, unity was considered a necessary strength. The cults (religions) Solomon allowed to resume were also a return to the fertility cults they had worked so hard to avoid, including the practice of child sacrifice.

Chapter 11 describes a slow fragmentation of the nation. The kingdom would split (undoing what King David had done) again into two regions. Ten tribes would form in the north and the tribe of Judah in the south (the inclusion of Simeon was assumed, making it twelve). Ahijah the prophet uses a dramatic illustration, tearing his new fancy one-piece robe into eleven pieces, giving ten of them to a northern king and one piece to a southern king. It's all downhill from here on out. This sets up the rest of the Old Testament history, from c. 900 to 300 BCE. There will again be two factions in Israel, a divided nation; Jerusalem will be the capital in the southern kingdom, and Samaria will be the capital in the northern kingdom.

Solomon destroyed what Moses and David worked to create.

Questions for Reflection or Discussion

1. Have you heard the phrase, "Power and money corrupt. Absolute power and money corrupt absolutely?" Do you think this is true?
2. Was it the power and money that led Solomon to forget God? Or could it have been something else?

57
Fertility Religions and the Prophet Elijah

Read 1 Kings chapter 16:21–34 and then chapters 17–19.

The tribes divided, ten in the north, two in the south sets the tone for the remainder of the Hebrew Bible. The book of 2 Kings tracks both lines of kings, north and south, back and forth, assessing them for whether or not they promote unity and faithfulness to God, following in "the pathway" or whether they promoted the worship of other gods. All the kings in the north were corrupt, and only eight out of twenty in the south were considered faithful.

The reading this time focuses on one northern king in particular, Ahab. It names three things that he did that were detestable to God. One, he married Jezebel, a queen who promoted fertility cults. Two, he set up temples and fertility poles for the worship of Baal and Ashtoreth. And three, he sacrificed two of his sons to get the blessings of the fertility gods (refer to Deut. 12:29–32, 16:21–22, and 17:9–14).

> ▸**Jezebel.** Since Queen Jezebel rebelled against God by promoting fertility worship, the name is often associated with a woman who has loose morals or has indiscriminate sex with lots of people.

Fertility worship is a tricky thing for modern readers, but it is important in understanding the context for the religious conflict of that time. Baal and Ashtoreth were fertility cults, built on the idea that if a priestess became pregnant, that would be a sign of the coming fertility of the land. So ritualistic sex was part of their worship. The more you "worshipped," the higher chance the gods would respond.

The prophet Elijah emerges. God causes a drought, something fertility cults would see as a bad omen. Elijah lives in the desert and is cared for by ravens. He visits the widow of Zarephath, a non-Israelite and her son, both of whom are starving to death; he asks her for their last bit of food. She gives the prophet her last meal and miraculously the flour and oil are perpetually replenished. (There is a tradition during the Jewish Passover to set an extra place at the table just in case Elijah shows up asking for food.) However, after this miracle the widow's son dies, but Elijah raises him from the dead by laying on top of him three times. Pretty strange.

Note: The people had essentially been practicing a form of *syncretism*, which is when you take elements of two or more religions and you mix them. If a Buddhist and a Muslim get married and each maintain their own religion, that is not syncretism. But if they get married and each takes elements of each faith and combine them into a new hybrid religion, that is a form of syncretism. The Israelites had been mixing their Judaism with fertility cult practices.

This sets the stage for an epic showdown between the God of the Hebrews and the fertility gods Baal and Ashtoreth. Elijah challenges the prophets of these gods to prepare a sacrifice on Mount Carmel, as will he to the God of the Hebrews. Each will call on their deity to set their sacrifice on fire and whichever does so first is the true God. The prophets of Baal get so frustrated at their gods' lack of response that they begin to cut themselves to provoke their gods. Elijah taunts them, asking if their gods are sleeping or have gone on vacation. He even soaks his offering with twelve jars of water. God then sends fire from the sky and licks up the water and sets the offering ablaze, as well as the offerings made by the fertility cults' prophets.

▸**Syncretism** is when you mix two or more religions into one, changing and corrupting the practice of both. It is not practicing different religions separately, but rather a mixture of the two.

But God's fire from heaven inspires those who see it and they change their minds on the spot. They rise up and kill the 950 prophets of Baal and Ashtoreth.

When the challenge is all over, Elijah receives a message from Queen Jezebel that she is going to enact revenge and kill Elijah. His response is peculiar. He flees to a cave on Mount Horeb and hides for fear of his life. Why? Didn't God just reign down fire on a sacrifice?

Modern interpretations of his actions superimpose a psychological diagnosis. Is this a kind of ancient manic-depression? Did Elijah get up for the showdown and then emotionally collapse after his victory? Surely God can save him from Jezebel if he can rain down fire from the sky? Why the collapse?

Regardless, Elijah experiences three dramatic occurrences: an earthquake, fire from the sky, and a fierce wind. Each time the story says that God is not present in the dramatic phenomena (earthquake, wind, fire). Instead, God is found in the *sheer silence*. Sometimes this is translated from the Hebrew as the *still small voice*. God instructs Elijah to return to Damascus, where he will have him choose a new king. It is also where God will have Elijah choose his own successor as a prophet.

An interesting aside. Jezebel, the queen who promoted fertility worship, meets a strange and gruesome death later in the book of 2 Kings (2 Kings 9). The nefarious King Jehu throws her from a balcony, where she is trampled by horses, and then eaten by dogs (all but her hands and feet).

Questions for Reflection or Discussion

1. Elijah tested the dying woman and her son by asking them to give him their last bits of food. He was testing their faith in God's ability to help them. What would you have done if you were the widow?
2. We don't have anything like fertility worship in our culture, but we do have people who treat sex like it is a recreation and not a sacred expression between two people committed to each other for life. Why is it important to treat sex with respect and holiness?
3. The Hebrew people were trying to play both sides of the situation, practicing syncretism. Do you think it is ever okay to mix elements of different religions?

58

Elisha the Miracle Worker

Read 1 Kings chapter 19:19–21:29 and then 2 Kings chapters 1 and 2. Then read 2 Kings chapters 3–6 as an option.

When it is time for the Prophet Elijah to end his work, he chooses a successor. As if the Bible isn't confusing enough, he chooses a man named Elisha. That's right. Elijah is replaced by Elisha.

Elijah places his cloak, or *mantle*, on Elisha's shoulders, signifying he has passed his authority on to him. Elijah then asks his protégé Elisha if there is anything he can do for him. Elisha requests, "Give me a double portion of your Spirit." There is a poignancy and beauty to this exchange. If you ever had a teacher, coach, or mentor that you admired so much that you tried to pattern yourself after them, then you understand this request. "Give me twice as much of you." There was a practice at that time of giving your oldest child twice as much, or a double portion of the inheritance of any of the other children. Elisha is Elijah's spiritual son.

▸**Passing the mantel.** Elijah places his cloak onto Elisha's shoulders as a way of passing his role onto him. The phrase is now used when a position is passed from one person to another.

Note: It has been identified that if you count the number of Elijah's miracles (seven) you will notice that Elisha did twice as many (fourteen), or a double portion.

I had a mentor named John when I was in college, a minister in Louisiana that I very much wanted to emulate. Years later when I happened to be watching myself on video, I couldn't help but see his mannerisms and his "spirit." He and I are different people and I eventually developed my own approach to ministry, but no doubt his imprint is still on me. Give me a double portion of your spirit.

A fiery chariot descends from heaven and separates Elijah and Elisha, and Elijah is taken up to the heavens in whirlwind. He is one of only two individuals in the Hebrew Bible who "did not die" but were taken by God.

▸**Chariots of fire.** How Elijah "died" (and also a movie with a well-known theme song, based on an Olympic runner who was a committed Christian.)

The other is Enoch from Genesis 5. This is significant because there really is not a well-developed concept of the afterlife, heaven or hell, in the Hebrew Bible. The predominant understanding was that when a faithful Hebrew person died, they laid dormant in Sheol (ground), sometimes referred to as sleeping in the ground. It is only around the beginning of the fourth century BCE when Hebrew culture began to converge with Hellenistic culture of an afterlife in their thinking.

Note: By the time of Jesus, the Jewish culture had split into two camps, those of "the resurrection" and the traditionalists. Jesus was part of the side believing in resurrection, as he tells the thief on the cross, "today you will be with me in paradise." But this was an idea that was revealed or unfolded over time.

What you read from this point on are a series of miracles that are performed by Elisha, many of them typologies (repeating stories and images) from earlier Hebrew accounts. Some of them (from our Christian perspective) foreshadow the work of Jesus.

- Dividing the Jordan River with his mantle (2 Kings 2:6–8) and the Hebrews crossing of the Red Sea (Exodus 14:21–22)
- Healing of the water (2 Kings 2:19–22) and Moses making the bitter water clean (Exodus 15:22–27)
- Elisha sics bears on insolent youth (2 Kings 2:23–25) is an interesting and humorous incident; Elisha did twice the number of miracles as Elijah (or a double portion)

- Restoring the Shunammite's son to life (2 Kings 4:8–37) and Jesus restoring the life of the widow's son in Nain (Luke 7:11–15)
- Making the bitter stew clean (2 Kings 4:38–41)
- Reproducing bread for a hundred men (2 Kings 4:42–44) and Jesus multiplying the fish and loaves (Luke 9:10–17)
- Healing Naaman from leprosy (2 Kings 5:1–14) and Jesus healing the lepers (Luke 17:11–19)
- Making the axe head float (2 Kings 6:1–7)

Taking all of these things into account, one of the overarching messages of these miracles is that despite the unfaithfulness of the Israelite people, God is with them. The miracles are a sign of God's presence, even in the midst of their demise.

Kings and Prophets

What happens next are a series of foreign occupations over a period of about 800 years. Assyria invaded from the northwest in the eighth century BCE and occupies Israel. Babylon invades from the east in the seventh century. Persia conquers Babylon and occupies Israel and Judah in the sixth century.

The prophets you see listed as books the Bible are each preaching during one of these foreign occupations. Their messages vary, but a central theme runs throughout each of them; the Israelites are punished or disciplined by God because they are not faithful, a rebellion that started in great part with Solomon. It is more complicated, but this gives you a simplified framework to approach the remaining books of the TaNaKh:

Assyria: Hosea, Amos, Micah, Isaiah

Babylon: Jeremiah, Ezekiel, Daniel, Nahum, Zephaniah, Habakkuk, Obadiah

Persia: Haggai, Zechariah, Malachi, Joel, Ezra, Nehemiah

Our next readings are from the prophet Hosea, chapters 1–2, and then Isaiah chapters 1, 6, 9, 11, and 53. Then a chapter from the prophet Amos. Hosea, Isaiah, and Amos were all preaching during the Assyrian invasion.

Questions for Reflection or Discussion

1. Has anyone ever "handed you the mantle"? Have you taken over something important from someone else?
2. Is there any teacher, coach, employer, or supervisor in your life in whom you wish you had a "double portion" of their spirit?

59

Assyria Attacks from the North: Isaiah, Hosea, Amos

As we study the Prophets, we begin with Hosea and Isaiah because they lived during the invasion of Assyria, which happened first. Remember that we are in a period of history where there are three successive foreign occupations over a period of around 400 years: Assyria, Babylon, and Persia.

It might be helpful to remember this with ABP, *Always Be Positive*. The *positive* reminds you that Persia was the occupier who let them return home and rebuild Jerusalem and the temple that Babylon destroyed. All of these prophets listed in the Bible are preaching to the various kings (of either Israel or Judah) during one of these ABP occupations. Hosea is preaching during the first invasion from Assyria and so are Isaiah and Amos. To review, in dated chronological order by conqueror:

Assyria (A): Hosea, Amos, Micah, Isaiah

Babylon (B): Jeremiah, Ezekiel, Daniel, Nahum, Zephaniah, Habakkuk, Obadiah

Persia (P): Haggai, Zechariah, Malachi, Joel, Ezra, Nehemiah

Isaiah is considered one of the three major prophets, along with Jeremiah and Ezekiel. They are called major not because they are more important but simply because their writings are longer. The rest of the prophets are referred to as minor prophets (shorter writings). Daniel is considered by some to be one of the major prophets, but that book fits into a different category (apocryphal) because of its dating and genre.

The Book of Isaiah

Read Isaiah chapters 1, 6, 9, 11, and 53 and watch The Bible Project video on Isaiah, part I.

Isaiah is an incredibly important and pivotal book in the Hebrew Bible. It is long and most scholars agree that it is made up of three books, written over a period of around 200 years. Sections two and three of Isaiah actually concern events that happened long after Isaiah died.

The first section is about the invasion of Assyria during Isaiah's life; the second and third are about the invasion and occupation by Babylon, which took place around 100 years later. One theory is that God gave Isaiah a vision of the future, but the more accepted view is that the later parts of the book were written by some of Isaiah's disciples who followed in his teaching, not an uncommon practice of the time.

In the first chapter of Isaiah, he is preaching against Israel's syncretism, which has led to wickedness and disregard for the poor. Then in chapter six, God asks who will speak for him. Isaiah does not feel worthy, so an angelic being cauterizes his mouth with a hot coal, purifying him to speak. Whether this is a vision, dream, or literal occurrence is unclear. But Isaiah then says, "I'm here; send me" (Isa. 6:8). He is sent out to speak God's message.

In chapters 7, 9, and 11, he speaks of a coming anointed king (messiah) who will repair the broken kingdom. The term "messiah" means the same as it did with previous kings, but in Isaiah's poetry it seems to take on added weight. This will be a "Super David" of sorts, not a reincarnation of David, but a future, perfect version of an anointed king from the line of David. The poetry in chapters 9 and 11 paint a picture of the kind of king he will be and the kind of world he will bring. He will be wise and strong, and a just government will rest on his shoulders; wolves will live with lambs, lions will lie down with calves, infants will play with snakes. The destructive world as they knew it will be turned upside down into a place of healing, justice, and love.

Jumping ahead to chapter 53, which was written generations later during the captivity of Babylon, "second" Isaiah makes a prediction that the future king will suffer and die for his people, atoning for their sins. This future king will be the hope and expectation of the people of Judah and Israel for the next 800 years. With each ensuing foreign occupation there is hope that this king will finally come and bring unity and strength to Israel and Judah. But something new is introduced in these promises—not only will this king rescue Israel and Judah, he will also bring peace and justice to all the nations. It is a tall order, this messianic expectation.

It was a long and arduous process for the Hebrew people and culture: first Assyria, then Babylon, and then Persia. After that, the Macedonians or Seleucids (Alexander the Great) took a turn and eventually the Romans. It was 800 years of hoping and waiting for a king to come rescue them and give them their nation back.

Note: Do you remember what the Vision Quest of Abraham and Sarah was? At the time we first read it, I said this could very well be the thesis of the entire Bible. *I will bless you so that through you and your descendants all the families (nations) on earth will be blessed.* Christians believe that Jesus is the eventual fulfillment of this Messianic expectation. I will be making that connection as we move forward.

One last important note that fits one of our emerging themes. Read the very short chapter 20 in Isaiah. God asks Isaiah, like Hosea, to do a peculiar thing to help get his message across to the people. He tells him to preach naked for three years. Why? When the people ask him why he is embarrassing and shaming himself by "baring his buttocks," Isaiah is to tell them that it is *they* who are embarrassing and shaming themselves by making alliances with Egypt against Assyria. They are depending on others and not God, and it is to their "shame." The prophet as performance artist. This will not be the last of it. Prepare yourself, it gets even weirder.

I wish we had more time to take a closer look at some of these passages. That is truer with Isaiah than most of the other books. Isaiah is truly a work of literary art, and I recommend you take a deeper look and a longer read. Especially chapters 40 and 59–62. With all these books, do an internet search for the videos on Isaiah from *The Bible Project* on YouTube. They are of tremendous help for beginning readers of the scriptures.

The Prophet Hosea

Read Hosea chapters 1-2 and watch The Bible Project video on Hosea.

God tells Hosea to marry a whore named Gomer.

Shocking, but that is the story's intention. A prophet of God marries one of the local prostitutes—not a former prostitute who has changed her ways, but one still practicing prostitution. When people ask Hosea why, he tells them it is because they have "cheated on God." To make it worse, Hosea and Gomer conceive and have children, naming them:

- Conflict (*Jezreel* was a valley known for conflict and war)
- Not Loved (*Lo-Ruhamah*)
- Not My Child (*Lo-Ammi*)

Can you imagine the therapy these kids needed?

Why would God ask a man of God to do this? It's a real-life morality play, with Hosea playing God as the faithful husband and Gomer playing the unfaithful people of Israel and Judah. The children represent a religious culture that has embraced other religions, ignored God's morals and ethics, become greedy, stopped caring for the poor and vulnerable, and weakened the spiritual fabric of their culture. Amos is a prophet acting as a performance artist; his dysfunctional family are the actors and the script. The people of Judah and Israel have been cheating on God, and yet God stays with them in spite of their waywardness.

The story does end with a sign of hope. God tells Hosea and Gomer to rename *Not Loved*, to *Loved* (Ruahmah) (Hosea 2:21–23).

I will point out again the misogyny in this piece of performance art. Typically, men tend to be the ones to wander and cheat. Certainly both sexes have the potential to be unfaithful, but could God have cast the characters in the play differently? God could be the "wife of noble character" like we read about in Proverbs 31 and the wandering-eye, cheating husband would represent Israel and Judah. Perhaps she is playing the role of Israel for the symbolism of their children. How can Hosea be sure they are his kids if she was a prostitute?

Regardless, it is a strange story.

The Prophet Amos

Read Amos chapter 5 and then watch The Bible Project video on Amos.

It's important to read a little bit of Amos because one of the problems he points out with the people's unfaithfulness was the mistreatment of the poor by the wealthy. The Halacha was very explicit about caring for the poor and vulnerable, stressing that you not underpay and abuse your workers. Amos tells them that part of returning to God is being fair and establishing justice in the land. Martin Luther King Jr. included passages from Amos in his "I Have a Dream" speech in 1963:

> But let justice roll down like waters,
> and righteousness like an ever-flowing stream. (Amos 5:24)

Questions for Reflection or Discussion

1. Isaiah 11 is poem that describes animals that are typically enemies living together in harmony. It is a poetic picture of a changed world. Can you think of other poetic images that could be a picture of a world completely changed?
2. Hosea's family is set up to be a symbol for Israel's unfaithfulness to God. Could there be a better way to get this message across? If so, how?
3. Amos condemns not paying workers fairly. What do you think is a fair wage for one hour of work?

60

The Babylonian Conquest: Jeremiah the Weeping Prophet

Read Jeremiah chapters 1, 25, 27, and 29. Watch The Bible Project video on Jeremiah.

ABP: Always. Be. Positive. Assyria, Babylon, Persia. These are the successive foreign occupations during the period of the prophets. The "positive" one works well for the Persian occupation because it was King Darius who allowed the Hebrew exiles to return home and rebuild Jerusalem and their temple.

We now begin an overview of the prophets who preached during the invasion of Babylon, in the sixth century BCE: Jeremiah, Ezekiel, and Daniel. The minor prophets (shorter books) are Zephaniah, Obadiah, Nahum. We will only glance at the biggies: Jeremiah, Ezekiel, Daniel.

Jeremiah is called the weeping prophet. He weeps over the destruction of Jerusalem. King Nebuchadnezzar invades and pillages the treasures from the temple. He also takes the smartest and brightest young people as slaves back to Babylon. This makes practical sense; if you acculturate young talented slaves, they can enrich your culture by becoming doctors, engineers, and even religious scribes. Nebuchadnezzar sought to reeducate them with Babylonian culture.

The entire book of Lamentations was written by Jeremiah. It consists of stark, depressing poems about this invasion and exile.

There is a troubling dark theology within Jeremiah's prophecies, stemming from the reason why the invasion and exile is happening. It is God's discipline and judgment, for Israel and Judah's falling away and unfaithfulness.

Think about the implications. God uses military invasion and slavery to punish the people. Horrific, but a consistent premise of the prophets.

Read Jeremiah chapter 25 again. Jeremiah tells the kings in Israel to stop resisting their captivity and not make any military alliances with Egypt against Babylon. "Give up," he says. "This is God's doing." The Israelite king threw Jeremiah in a cistern and left him there to die for saying such things. Jeremiah did not offer popular advice.

There are specific ways this idea gets worked out. Jeremiah 29:11 is one of the most loved passages from all scripture:

> I know the plans I have in mind for you, declares the Lord; they are plans for peace, not disaster, to give you a future filled with hope.

This is printed on greeting cards, posters, knitted into pillows. It is often shared at graduations because it looks forward to what God has in store for people in the future. The verse that come before complicates the passage:

> The Lord proclaims: When Babylon's seventy years are up, I will come and fulfill my gracious promise to bring you back to this place.

Wait! How long? Seventy years? Stay put in Babylon for seventy years, and *then* I will give you a future and a hope? Consider the context: God has allowed a foreign entity to invade their nation, destroy their infrastructure, pillage their wealth, burn their temple to the ground, and then take captive the brightest of their children. And what is God's message? God has allowed this to serve as discipline and punishment for their unfaithfulness. Stay in Babylon for seventy years, and I will allow you to return and then I will give you a future. Putting it in context is important.

Reading chapter 29 from the beginning allows you to see the expanded message from God through the prophet Jeremiah. Not only will you be a captive in Babylon, God wants you to invest in their land. Get married, have kids, purchase property. It even says they should have grandkids, invest in the people of Babylon. Then, only after living in exile for seventy years, will you be allowed to return home. The message of *a hope and future* may not be for those held in captivity now, but for their grandchildren or great-grandchildren.

Once again review the three-tiered method for biblical interpretation. This example demonstrates how tricky interpretation can be:

> **Story.** What did the writers of a particular account intend to say to the people to whom they were originally writing? Sometimes this is clear, and sometimes it requires work deciphering the historical background and cultural understanding of the time.
>
> **Abstraction.** Recall reading about "The land of Canaan" (page 97) and looking at David as a father (pages 170–71). Is there an abstract idea or concept that can be lifted from the story?
>
> **Application.** Can the abstract idea or "lesson" drawn from the story be applied (responsibly and carefully) to a different situation or context? This is the work of basic of biblical interpretation.

For Jeremiah 29 it looks something like this:

> **Story.** God's people are "allowed" to be taken captive and live in oppression as a means of discipline and punishment; they are to endure this period until a future time when God will bring them into a new future.
>
> **Abstraction.** Hope for a future while living under oppression. Another abstract idea is being a slave to something.
>
> **Application.** In what difficult situations do people find themselves where they have little choice to leave? And what does hope look like for them? Most of us have some situation like this in various degrees: a job you feel like you cannot quit or a relationship you cannot leave. For situations like these, the words of the prophet take on an added weight. God is with us in these difficult situations and asks us to endure them until a later time when he will fulfill a greater purpose and give us a future and a hope.

We need to be thoughtful and intelligent in the way we apply these abstractions. Being stuck in a difficult job that you don't like is very different than being held as a slave in a foreign land for a period of seventy years. We should never use stories like these to justify oppression, slavery, and injustice. Someone could flippantly tell another who is stuck in an abusive relationship that God is using that situation to discipline them or punish them, and that they need only endure it for a period of time until they come into God's future and hope. Do you see how this gets tricky?

Yes, God often allows us to endure difficulty and hardship for a period of time, but each situation is different and has different outcomes. We must be wise and open to determine how God is present in each situation. Jeremiah and Israel's situation is not our situation. They may be similar in some ways but are dramatically different in others. God forbid our situation be the same. Recognize there are people in the world today that do live under those kinds of conditions. Are they being punished by God? Disciplined? Most of us would say no.

This is the art of biblical interpretation, and it takes sensitivity and spiritual discernment. In the Christian tradition, we also speak of being led by the Spirit of God in interpreting these stories.

A couple of additional things to note about Jeremiah that are important. God asked him to do something strange in the same vein as Hosea and Isaiah. Because God did not want Israel to establish a military alliance with Egypt, he told Jeremiah to walk around preaching tied to an ox yoke. This was an object lesson to "yoke" themselves to Babylon; his message to the people and the kings of Israel was "accept your punishment, yoke yourself to your captors." They didn't care much for this message and threw him in a pit. Again, here we have a prophet as a performance artist.

The next reading is a little longer. Read the first three chapters of Ezekiel and the first three chapters of Daniel. Both of these prophets were during the Babylonian invasion and were taken as captives in Babylon.

Questions for Reflection or Discussion

1. The opening of Jeremiah says God called him to be prophet even before he was born, in his mother's womb. Do you think God had a plan for you before you were born?

2. What do you think of Jeremiah's message that God is using a foreign invasion to punish or discipline his people? What if you had been one of those kids taken and you heard there was a prophet saying this? What would you think of that message?
3. Jeremiah stated it would take seventy years for God to put a "deliverance" plan into motion. What do you think about the idea that God's plan might not be for you, but for your children or even your grandchildren?

61
Ezekiel the Street Artist and Daniel the Slave

Read Ezekiel chapters 1–3 and Daniel chapters 1–3.

Have you seen or read *The Hunger Games* by Suzanne Collins? Many have read the books, others have seen the movies. This can be a helpful tool in understanding the context of these prophetic writings.

Using the book's language, these foreign invaders are The Capitol and the regions they have conquered are The Districts. The prophets are like rebels speaking out in the midst of their dystopian existence. The future anointed leader that Isaiah promised? The Messiah figure? Katniss Everdeen.

> **Note: APB**: Assyria (seventh century), Babylon (sixth century), Persia (fifth century).

The comparison has limitations, but it gives readers a handle on understanding life under oppression, exile, and judgment. The books of Ezekiel and Daniel are stories about prophets who have been captured and taken into exile in Babylon.

Ezekiel

Ezekiel is a long, strange book full of vivid imagery. Some of it is near impossible to understand, even for scholars who closely study them. The first chapter of Ezekiel contains apocalyptic imagery. He has a vision of four-headed creatures, hybrids of humans and animals with wings. These are Hebrew cherubim, a term that describes one manifestation of angels in Hebrew mythology. (Another form are seraphim, illuminated snake-like creatures with wings. Most angels that appear in scripture have a human form with some unnamed quality that distinguishes them as messengers of God.)

Then Ezekiel sees a structure of interchangeable spinning wheels, covered in eyeballs. Listen to "Wheels in the Sky" by Journey.[1] The song is not a direct take on Ezekiel's vision, but the atmosphere of the song is sad and has a dystopian feel. Sitting on top of these creatures is a throne with a figure sitting on it who looks like "a Son of Man," a figure sometimes used to depict God, since we were created in the image of God. An *imago Dei* is sitting on this throne.

So what does it mean? The eyes festooning the wheels might indicate a "watchfulness" on God's part. The prophet Jeremiah (who was left back in Jerusalem) has a vision of an almond tree, and God says, "You are right, for I am watching over my word until it is fulfilled" (Jer. 1:12). The Hebrew word for almond is a pun of the word "watch." So the eyes may be a different play on that theme. Nebuchadnezzar destroyed the temple in Jerusalem and it likely is an image of God's presence being portable, on wheels, traveling to be with them in Babylon.

A modern-day reading of the wheels is that Ezekiel is possibly seeing a UFO. Some skeptical readers suppose he might be hallucinating from a psychedelic drug. The skepticism comes from the fact that the books of Ezekiel and Daniel are the first strange visions like these to appear in Hebrew literature. At this point in their history, there has never been anything like this in the scriptures.

▸ **"Wheels in the Sky."** Imagery in the song by the band Journey of a sad dystopian landscape.

Apocalyptic visions are a kind of code language, sending messages back and forth from Babylon and Judah that cannot be understood by their captors. This same basic understanding can be applied to the visions in Daniel chapters 7–12 and the Revelation to John in the New Testament (the political power being eluded to is Rome). In fact, the books of Daniel, Zechariah, and Revelation swap and share similar imagery.

1. *https://genius.com/Journey-wheel-in-the-sky-lyrics.*

The Jewish Talmudic tradition, which is a series of interpretations and expansions on the Tanakh, held that Ezekiel was only to be read and studied by Hebrew men over the age of thirty. This was, in part, because these apocalyptic visions could easily be misinterpreted and used to manipulate vulnerable people. The book of Ezekiel also has some imagery similar to the metaphor of Hosea and Gomer, or "Israel cheating on God." Those images in Ezekiel are pretty explicit.

Chapters 2 and 3 are some of my most favorite in scriptures. Ezekiel is called to be a spokesperson for God, a prophet. He has a vision of God extending a scroll to him, God's message, asking him to "eat the scroll." It tastes sweet, like honey. But God warns Ezekiel that the people are rebellious and will not listen, so gives him a forehead of stone.

The final image in these chapters is "the watchman on the watchtower." A common duty in ancient Mesopotamia was to stand guard on a tower that scanned the horizon for coming enemy attacks. If you saw dust kicking up in the distance, you had time to warn your leaders and prepare for a defense. But if the watchman fell asleep, then the people would perish. God tells Ezekiel he is a watchman, and if he fails to warn the people about their impending spiritual destruction, then their blood will be on his hands.

The image of the watchtower was immortalized in contemporary culture when Bob Dylan wrote "All Along the Watchtower,"[2] a song that has been covered by Jimi Hendrix, U2, and Dave Matthews, among others. You might want to listen to that song also.

> ▸ **"All along the Watchtower"** is a song written by Bob Dylan that was inspired by the imagery in Ezekiel, to speak the message of people's self-destructive behavior to them even if they do not want to hear it.

What happens next is a peculiar string of messages Ezekiel gives to the people in exile in Babylon, but accentuated with weird performance art:

- God asks him to lay on his side in the dirt in the town square and play with a toy model of Jerusalem, acting out its judgment and

2. *http://www.bobdylan.com/songs/all-along-watchtower/.*

destruction. He is to do this for 360 days. When that period is over, he is to run over on the other side and do it again. Imagine a crazy man lying on the ground near the center of your town or city, playing with a toy model of your town, warning of God's destruction of the city.

- God tells him to shave the hair off his body and place it into three piles. He is told to chop up the first pile with a small sword; this represents the invasion of Judah. The second pile he is to set on fire—the destruction of the temple. The third he is to throw to the wind, representing the people being scattered. Then he is to take a small pinch of hair and put it in his pocket. This is the small remnant of faithful people that remain.
- God asks him to cook his food using his own dried excrement as fuel (it had always been a common practice to use animal dung infused with grass as fuel when no firewood was available). But your own excrement? This was unclean according to Halacha and would represent the uncleanliness of their spiritual condition. Ezekiel begs God not to make him do this, and God concedes.
- God tells Ezekiel to pack up his bags and give the appearance that he is "leaving town," and then to turn around and do it over and over again. When people ask him what he is doing, he says this is a reenactment of the exile.
- God tells Ezekiel to take two sticks, on one write the name *Israel*, on the other, *Judah*. These two "sticks" had been divided for generations. God tells him to take the two sticks and to tie them together, a glimpse of the unity that God will one day bring to them once again.

Ezekiel—the ultimate performance artist.

These prophets are exhibiting what has often been called "the prophetic voice." The prophet is tasked with telling people things they do not want to hear, so the source of the message may need to be packaged in peculiar and strange ways in order to get the attention of the audience. Artists are often portrayed as being "prophetic." The most common art form being music and movies. You might occasionally come across a performance artist and they want you to wonder, "What message are they trying to convey?"

▸ **Prophetic voice.** Speaking to people about things they would rather not hear, but need to hear.

We don't have much time to cover the story of Daniel, but you now having a larger context by which to understand what you are reading. Many of Daniel's stories are familiar, like the Fiery Furnace and Daniel in the Lions' Den. I encourage you to read those first three chapters.

Questions for Reflection or Discussion

1. Ezekiel and Daniel were teenagers who were taken as slaves to Babylon because they were intelligent and talented. How scary would it be to be removed from your home and taken to a strange land to live?
2. Daniel and his three friends resisted adopting the diet, culture, and religion of their new home. How do you think you would handle this challenge? What three friends would you want with you in a strange land?
3. If you saw a street preacher in your city, laying on his or her side, acting out God's judgement on a toy model of the city, would you stop and listen or would you walk on by? Why this choice?

62

The Valley of Dry Bones and Daniel, Part 2

Read Ezekiel chapters 37 and 47, then read Daniel chapters 4–6, then scan Daniel chapters 7–12.

Remember that the purpose of these commentaries is to introduce you to the general framework of the Hebrew and Christian Bible, so as we finish up the Hebrew Scriptures, you will be better equipped to read other books that we have not covered.

Ezekiel is going to be one of the last prophets we read together. Remember that the prophetic books are all messages given primarily to the kings (and their people) of Judah and Israel while they were under foreign occupations. ABP helps you remember: Assyria, Babylon, Persia.

Ezekiel's messages are given under duress. God is angry at the Israelites for walking away from their spiritual devotion to God and now the nation is dissolute and scattered. Ezekiel has a vision of God leaving the temple. This is a big deal. Presence is a recurring theme in the Hebrew Scriptures:

- The Garden of Eden is about God's presence.
- God cast humans out of the Garden; they are denied God's presence.
- Abraham's unique friendship with God.
- Moses with God on Mount Sinai.
- Moses speaks to God face-to-face.
- Moses is chastised and then only sees God's backside.
- The Ark of the Covenant and "the Mercy Seat" is the hot spot of God's presence.
- The chief priest is with God in the Holy of Holies in the tabernacle.
- The Ark is taken into battle so that God's presence is with them.

- David wants to build a dwelling place so God can be present.
- Solomon builds the temple where God will be present with them.

When King Nebuchadnezzar of Babylon invaded Jerusalem and burned Solomon's temple to the ground, it contradicts their idea of "Presence." God has had enough, abandoning his people, divorcing them, in a way. These visions are very dark and depressing.

But finally, a message of future hope begins to emerge. In Ezekiel 36, the prophet hears that God will one day return. This time God will give the people a new heart, not one made of stone, but of flesh. God's Spirit will be put in the people, and they will follow God's laws not because they have to, but because they want to. What follows in chapter 37:1–14 is one of the most well-known passages in Ezekiel. He sees a valley of dry human bones. God tells him to preach to the bones, to prophesy (preach) to them. Ezekiel did and slowly the dead bones began to form sinew and muscle, then skin formed on the bones, and they began to come to life. God tells him that "these bones are the people of Israel."

▸**Valley of dry bones.** Ezekiel's vision of human bones coming back to life.

Then God gives the prophet a vision of a temple that will be built in the future. This makes sense, as the temple in Jerusalem had been destroyed. Chapters 40–46 gives detailed building plans, and it is said God's presence will return to this temple.

Remember that the temple represented the presence of God. Specifically, the sanctuary or Holy of Holies, that separate building within the tabernacle that housed the Ark of the Covenant and was the location where God's presence dwelt most intensely (Mercy Seat). The decor for that inner sanctuary described by God to Moses in Exodus is replete with garden imagery, a "typology" of the Garden of Eden when human beings existed freely in the presence of God. The portable tabernacle was designed this way, as was the sanctuary in Solomon's Temple. The temple was where God dwelled.

The plans for this future temple are very specific. This temple will be thirty-six times the size of Solomon's Temple, and it will be in the shape of man. The sanctuary will represent the mind of God, the altar will represent the heart of God, and the four porticos are the arms and legs. In chapter 47 there is a description of a small trickle of water that begins from behind the altar of this future temple, the heart of God, and grows deeper as it flows into the Dead Sea, where it will freshen the stagnant water. From this will grow trees with fruit for food and leaves for healing.

The temple that Ezekiel envisions was never built. Instead, the Persian Empire allowed the Jews to return and begin to rebuild Solomon's Temple (538–515 BCE), which was eventually enlarged by Herod the Great under Roman occupation (37 BCE). But what was rebuilt was not this larger temple described so specifically in Ezekiel's vision. Rather, it was the restoration of Solomon's Temple, with those specifications. That is why it was referred to as the "second temple." That was the temple that Jesus knew.

Questions for Reflection or Discussion

1. The valley of dry bones coming back to life is a strange and beautiful image. Can you interpret this story and apply it to some other situation?
2. What is something that was "dead" in your life that was restored and brought back to life? If not in your life, in someone's you know?

63

Freedom from Persia: Ezra, Nehemiah, Esther

Watch The Bible Project videos on Ezra-Nehemiah and Esther. There are two them.

The books that are written about the Persian occupation are Esther, Ezra, Nehemiah, Haggai, Zechariah, and Malachi. It was during the Persian Empire that the Israelites were allowed to return to Judah and Israel and rebuild their city and the temple. Ezra and Nehemiah are about the start of that process.

Now read Ezra chapters 9 and 10.

As they move back to Judah to rebuild their culture, the prophets are adamant that the people need to seek a fresh start with God. This includes a fierce commitment to spiritual purity of the Hebrew tradition. Remember what occurred during their own recent history leading to their exile? Solomon's intermarriage and syncretism (the mixing of religions) started them down this road 400 years earlier. As part of an effort to return the people to spiritual purity, the prophet Ezra insists that any marriages that had been formed while in exile were to be dissolved.

It is a dark episode in the life of Israel. Remember, what was the purpose of Abraham and Sarah's Vision Quest (covenant)? God would create a blessed culture whose purpose would be to bless all the people of the earth. How do you do that with this kind of cultural and religious exclusivism?

This question begins to be answered as Christianity emerges some 500 years later, but things get worse before they get better. At this point in their history they will work hard to rebuild their culture and their faith, and part of that will be to commit to keeping Judaism separate and pure from the other religions and cultures. The prophets and leaders did not want a repeat of the discipline and punishment they experienced as a result of Solomon's syncretism. By the time of Jesus, this "separateness" will be deeply ingrained and institutionalized in the Jewish culture. In reading the Gospels, you will see how this was epitomized by the Pharisees and their efforts to follow the laws of Torah strictly. That is what the name Pharisee is associated with—someone who is very strict religiously.

Lastly, if you have time, read the book of Esther.

Chronologically, Esther takes place before Ezra but after Nehemiah. These three books are the books surrounding the Persian occupation and the return to Israel. Esther is a story about a beautiful young Jewish woman who is part of the Persian king's concubine, who eventually is made queen. She must risk her life by exposing her Judaism in order to beg the king not to commit genocide against the other Jewish people being held captive in Persia. The Jewish holiday of **Purim**, a kind of Halloween costume-like day, celebrates this story.

Questions for Reflection or Discussion

1. Ezra let his desire for the perfect lead him to exclude people. This is sometimes called *sacrificing the good for the perfect*. Do you sympathize with Ezra at all? If so, why? If not, why not?
2. Esther risked her life to save her people. Have you ever witnessed someone being bullied and knew you should say something but were afraid to do so? Or have you been bullied and needed a friend to say something and they did not?

64

The Chronicles and the Stages of Israel, Part 2

Watch The Bible Project video on The Chronicles. This will set you up for reading through the Gospels and the emergence of Christianity out of Judaism.

This would be a good time to return to our mnemonic device that helps you remember the larger story of the Bible: the "Stages of Israel's Life." The last time we discussed this, we stopped at the "Young Adult Phase" of their history. Let's review: Just like a person has stages of life as they grow up, I found that the stages of life symbolically match up, in some fashion, to the events and stages of Israel's life.

Conception. In the Creation stories, the Garden, the Fall, Cain and Abel, and the Flood, there was no formal Judaism. But after the fall, God "conceived" of a culture that would eventually "be born" and usher in blessing for all the families of the earth. Judaism (Israel) had not been born yet, but it had been conceived.

Infancy and Childhood. The Fall was the problem; the answer to the problem was to create a culture through which humanity could be repaired. When God called Abraham and Sarah to start a culture that would bless all the people of the earth, a religion was "born." They were small, like an infant, but hopefully will one day grow up and "be a blessing" to all the people on earth (Genesis 12:3–4).

Abraham's family grew when he had Ishmael and Isaac. It grew further in size and self-identity through his grandsons Jacob and Esau and expanded even more through Jacob's twelve sons and one daughter. And just like an infant grows into a child in size and self-identity, their culture expanded and grew from a family to a tribe.

Teenage Years. Eventually Israel (formerly Jacob) moves to Egypt during a famine. They remain in Egypt initially as guests but eventually are enslaved and remain there 400 years. During this phase, they become full-grown in size as a culture, hundreds of thousands of people. But as they leave Egypt and move into the wilderness, they, like a teenager, find themselves living in-between who they are and who they eventually will become. Like a teenager, they have some attributes of adulthood, but they are not quite fully there. They are a little rebellious (golden calf, constantly challenging Moses), and they need rules (the 613 laws of Halacha) to keep them on the path.

Young Adult Phase. Many young adults, though certainly not all, go through a period of duplicity. They are acting like adults, but they are also living carefree and somewhat selfishly. They are trying to figure out what kind of an adult they want to be, and they are inclined to float around and not commit to much of anything. This fits accordingly with the period of the Conquest and the book of Judges: selfish, acquiring land, an undulating spiritual life, and a shaky commitment to God. I help the kids understand this part of the mnemonic metaphor by calling this the "Justin Bieber" phase of Israel's history. Justin Bieber is basically a good guy, who most of the time wants to do the right thing, but in his early twenties, he tended to get distracted and did some dumb and selfish things. That is the period of the Judges.

Settling Down. Young adults eventually settle into a career, find a spouse to marry, have kids, choose a city to put down roots, buy a house, and start a retirement. All of this works as a reminder of what was happening developmentally for Israel as a nation. The people asked for a king and they have 120 years of relative unity, wealth, and stability in three kings: Saul, David, and Solomon. During this period the nation settles down, chooses a capital city of Jerusalem, and builds the temple as a unifying place of worship. Even though this period is far from perfect, it tends to get idealized, particularly the reign of David, as the high point of their cultural strength, identity, and unity. In fact, the retelling of their history in Chronicles does this idealized editing of that period blatantly.

Midlife Crisis. Solomon, though initially wise, divides the nation into political "taxation" regions, marries hundreds of women from foreign nations with various religions, allows fertility religions to practice, and institutes massive slavery. The nation falls apart. The prophets emerge and among other poetic imagery and metaphor, describe this falling away as marital unfaithfulness to God. Israel is cheating on God.

Wisdom Years. If Israel is cheating on God, then God stages an intervention by bringing prophets onto the scene to bring Israel back to faithfulness. Among their messages are that the invasions from Assyria, Babylon, and Persia are God's punishment and that a future Messiah (anointed leader) will come and repair what is broken and set up a good and just kingdom.

And that sets the stage for the emergence of Christianity out of Judaism.

SECTION FOUR

Christianity Emerges Out of Judaism

Unit One

Messiah, Healer, Teacher, Divinity

1 and 2 Chronicles, Isaiah, Matthew,
Mark, Luke, John, Colossians, and Philippians

65

The Chronicles

Watch The Bible Project video on The Chronicles.

The books of 1 and 2 Chronicles seem like stories you have read before. That's because they are! Namely, they are repeats of events that happened in Samuel and Kings. But they are different. These versions are stylized versions. They have been shaped in order to get you ready for what is coming next.

In fact, 2 Chronicles ends with an incomplete sentence! So in some respects they are a summary of the TaNaKh with anticipation of what is around the corner. A big aspect of the latter half of the Hebrew Bible is the promise of a coming king who will finally bring control of Israel back into the hands of the Israelites. After Solomon's reign they had been overrun by five consecutive regional powers: Assyria, Babylon, Persia, Macedonia, and then Rome. This promised king (messiah or anointed leader) would not be any normal messiah, but an elevated, super messiah, a kind of "perfect-David." That is what Chronicles presents, a cleaned-up version of David's reign. Why? Because a super king is coming, who will be in the line of David, who will reign the way a perfect David would reign.

Questions for Reflection or Discussion

1. If you were to write your life's story for a book or a movie script, are there any events in your life you would want to "tweak" to emphasize a certain aspect of your life?
2. Can you name a celebrity that you suspect presents a more "stylized" version of themselves to the public, much different than their actual life? Do you think this is dishonest? Or is it an acceptable aspect of being a public figure?

66
Messianic Expectations

Read Isaiah chapters 9, 11, and 53.

When someone runs for president of the United States, they are often accused of having a **messiah complex**. It's typically meant as an insult. But anyone who wants that job must have a little bit of a messiah complex in order to seek the office. It is the belief that you can help, fix, and rescue the nation. Anyone who goes into any helping profession needs to have a little bit of a messiah complex. In order to help people, you have to believe that you have something to offer.

> ▸ **Messiah complex.** Usually meant in a derisive way, this description implies that someone is arrogant enough to think they can help or rescue someone or a group of people.

The term **messiah**, or *messiach* as it is pronounced in Hebrew, was a general term meaning "anointed leader" and was applied to any prophet, priest, or king. But the term changed with the emergence of the prophet Isaiah. When Isaiah speaks of a coming anointed leader, you get the sense he is speaking of something much bigger. It is an exalted anointed leader who will come—a Super Messiah. What exactly will this leader do?

Most scholars agree that the book of Isaiah is made up of three different sections, each section written about a different time period (see chapter 59). We know this because the first part references an attack on Israel from the northern power of Assyria, the latter speaks of an attack from the eastern power of Babylon. But these regional invasions are separated by about 200 years. The later writings of Isaiah are considered part of the "tradition" of Isaiah.

The main thing you need to know is that in Isaiah, the idea of an anointed leader took on added meaning, a kind of "Super David," a perfect, symbolic version of David. The promise of that leader is sustained through their 800 years of foreign occupation. Here is a basic sketch of that complicated stretch of time:

1000 BCE	United Kingdom (Saul, David, Solomon)
1000 BCE	Kingdom (Nation) divides after Solomon's reign
740 BCE	Assyrians invade from the north
586 BCE	Babylonians invade from the east
537 BCE	Persians overthrow the Babylonians
	Israelites are allowed to return and begin to rebuild the temple
336 BCE	Macedonians march through Palestine[1]
285 BCE	Rome begins its rise to power
63 BCE	Rome occupies Palestine

This really underscores the cultural significance of those 120 years when the tribes of Israel and Judah were a united kingdom under Saul, David, and Solomon. It shows why it was such a cultural disaster when Solomon began to steer them toward religious and cultural diffusion. Modern Western sensibility, where we hold the separation of church and state as important for a free democracy, might see this as strange. But remember that in biblical history, religion and government were intertwined and cultural unity could translate into national strength.

When Isaiah promises that a leader is coming who will bring unity and chase out the oppressors, what the people are expecting is a return to the unity they had under David. This is why this leader will be a "shoot will grow up from the stump of Jesse" (Isa. 11:1). You will recall that David's father, Jesse, was from Bethlehem.

Isaiah 53 takes a hard turn in an entirely different direction. This promised leader will be killed by the people he came to help. They will lead him like a lamb to the slaughter, and all of their sins will be put on

1. Palestine was a term given to this region of the Levant for the first time in the fifth century BCE. It continues to be used (in place of the State of Israel today) by many Arab Christians and Muslims who live in the occupied territories of Israel (such as the West Bank, Gaza, and Golan Heights).

him, like the scapegoat we read about in the book of Leviticus. So which is it? Will he be a conquering spiritual warrior or a leader who is sacrificed for his people? That is what we will be looking at as we read ahead. Both were promised and predicted.

As we begin to read about the emergence of Christianity, keep these things in mind: messiah means anointed leader; the Greek translation is "Christ." Christians believe that Jesus is the fulfillment of that promised leader. He certainly fits many of the attributes given by Isaiah, but one thing Jesus did not do was overthrow the Romans. The anointed leader, according to Isaiah, would establish a "government on his shoulders." Jesus was never a large-scale political leader. Hold on to this question: What does it mean that Jesus was the fulfillment of that promised Super Messiah?

One last thing to keep in mind in this reading: anytime a culture of people is oppressed by an invading power, the culture reacts with a variety of coping mechanisms, along a spectrum. The Jewish culture developed four main cultural responses to the Roman occupation, or ways the Jewish people coped with being controlled by a foreign power. These are sometimes called "schools" of thought for that time period:

> **Sadducees.** This was the ruling class of the Jewish society. They could be called the "sellouts" in that they often would compromise with the Roman government while still maintaining their Jewish identity. Because of this willingness to get along, they tended to be wealthy and well connected economically.
>
> **Pharisees.** The way they coped with Roman occupation was to lean heavily into their Jewish religious practice and culture. They resisted Roman occupation by being as non-Roman as possible. So they created a complex series of rules and practices that accentuated their faith. They are often depicted as the villains of the New Testament because some of their rules were extreme. A modern example of this would be families who never let their kids watch TV, go to any movies, or listen to non-Christian music. Pharisees were not villains; they were sincerely trying to embrace their faith in hopes that it would prepare the way for the Messiah.

Essenes. I call these the "hippies" of the time. They disconnected from the Roman society altogether, set up tent cities, and lived in caves in isolated Jewish communes. The Romans generally cared very little about these groups, save for the fact that they didn't pay any taxes, but at least they weren't being a problem. They too were waiting for the Messiah.

Zealots. These were the revolutionaries who hated the Roman occupation and wanted to overthrow them. They planned insurgent attacks on the Romans. In some historical accounts Zealots would sneak up on Sadducees and cut their throats. They attempted to raise small armed forces that would be ready to fight when the Messiah arrived.

These categories were fluid. You could be sympathetic to the Essenes and visit the tent cities, but live your life as a Pharisee. Or you could be a Sadducee and have contempt for your own hypocrisy while secretly helping the Zealots. And so on. The Jewish people had been waiting for a new anointed leader for nearly 800 years. That is a very long time to wait.

The term *gospel* means literally "good news." Matthew, Mark, Luke, and John are four different versions of the story of Jesus' life, and each are good news. We will be unpacking what that "good news" actually means to Christians.

▸**Gospel** comes from the Greek word for "good news" or "good tidings." The term was commonly used for the declaration of a political victory or change in leadership. It is now most commonly used to describe these four accounts of Jesus' life, who brought good news of God. The four Gospels in the New Testament are Matthew, Mark, Luke, and John.

Each of the four Gospels tell that good news from a slightly different perspective:

- Matthew was written primarily to Jewish readers, trying to convince them that Jesus is the promised Super Messiah.
- Matthew, Mark, and Luke are all very similar in that they have mostly the same stories, and that is why they are called *synoptic* gospels. Synoptic means "seems similar."

- John's Gospel is different from the other three. He was writing mostly to a Gentile (non-Jewish) audience, more specifically a Greek (Hellenistic) reader. That means he told his story differently than the other three, emphasizing things that would be of interest to non-Jews.

In addition to the Gospels, the New Testament also contains *epistles*, which were letters written to the early Christian church and first Christians.

Questions for Reflection or Discussion

1. If you were a Jewish person living in that setting under Roman rule, which of the four groups do you think you would associate with? Which of them would you be secondarily sympathetic?
2. Have you ever felt yourself to be a person who puts a lot of hope on a leader? Are you interested in presidential elections? What about looking forward to coaches or new teachers? Employers? How much do you tend to be a person who places your hope in leaders?

67
John the Baptizer

Read Matthew chapters 1–4.

What religion was Jesus?

As we make a decisive pivot toward Christianity, this question is a good place to start. It catches some off guard. Many want to say "Christian," but Jesus was profoundly Jewish. Over time, an entirely different religion emerges from his teachings, but to truly understand Jesus and the faith that would be birthed from his life and work, you must first understand his Judaism. Part of the premise of Christianity (and our study together) is that the collection of books in the Bible really contain one unified story, one that leads to the Jesus movement.

As you read through these first four chapters of Matthew, you can see the writer's effort to connect Jesus meaningfully to Judaism and the prophecies about the Messiah. As we read through the Hebrew Bible, we talked about the importance of "typologies," or stories and images that repeat themselves or allude to previous stories. In the Hebrew imagination, time and history are not linear, they are circular. Past is present and present is past.

The genealogy that begins the Gospel (book) of Matthew is showing Jesus' connection to the salvation history (the way God was saving and rescuing the Israelites as a people—past, present, and future). It begins with Abraham, a rock star in Hebrew history and faith. The Jewish story begins with Abraham and Sarah. Luke also has a genealogy; it "starts" with Adam, who, though part of the Jewish creation story, is more fundamentally a universal figure. Abraham is considered the first "Hebrew." See the distinction?

Joseph is called "Son of David." It was crucial that the Messiah be a descendent of King David as predicted in Isaiah, because David is remembered as the pinnacle of "anointed leaders" (messiah). From our reading, we recall that David was far from perfect, but over time he became an expanding symbol for a good king. Isaiah, the prophet who spent a lot of time predicting the coming of a messiah, is quoted repeatedly in these opening chapters.

When Joseph and Mary flee Herod, they escape to Egypt, an antitype (typology) of the stories of Abraham's tribe in Genesis who repeatedly fled to Egypt when in danger. Joseph and Mary's return to Palestine is an antitype of the return to Canaan after slavery in Egypt.

Jews do not believe in reincarnation, but there was some peripheral belief that some individuals might reappear. Many at the time thought John the Baptist was a reappearance of Elijah, who did not die but was taken up in a fiery chariot. Or because much of John's preaching was quoting Isaiah, the messianic predictive prophet, they wondered if perhaps he was a reappearance of Isaiah.

John is called the "baptizer." This is derivative of the Greek word that means to "immerse in water." Baptism is primarily associated with Christianity, but you will recall it was first a Jewish practice called mikvah, a Hebrew word that sounds like the word for "hope" and referred to a variety of Jewish ritual washings. There were three main reasons Jews took these baths:

1. **Being in God's Presence.** Priests would need to be spiritually clean before entering into the Holy of Holies, the place where God dwelled in the temple.
2. **Repentance from Sin.** If a Jewish person found themselves spiritually unclean because they has fallen off the pathway (Halacha), before they could return to normal worship they would need a ritual cleansing. They went to the temple priests to ask for this. This also applied to someone who had fallen away from the life with God and needed to rededicate themselves to God.
3. **Conversion to Judaism.** Though Judaism is not a proselytizing faith, meaning they don't seek to convert people to Judaism, they also are not opposed to people converting if they want to do so. So after a time of study, the last thing a person does before they convert is to take a ritual bath, a mikvah.

Do these last two Jewish mikvahs remind you of anything? You bet. They sound similar to the reasons Christians baptize. Mikvah is the origin of Christian baptism. Christianity, in its origins, was a Jewish sect. Matthew's Gospel shows this over and over.

> ▸**Mikvah.** Ritualistic bathing done in the Jewish tradition, later adapted by the followers of Jesus as an initiation rite for converts to the Jesus movement. Early on, it served as a substitute for circumcision for Gentile converts to the Jesus movement. It is the origins of Christian baptism.

John the Baptist was doing a rebellious, nonsanctioned, in-your-face baptism. Did you hear what he said to the Pharisees and Sadducees? He was inviting them to have a mikvah, telling them not to depend on their status as descendants of Abraham; even the rocks could convert to Judaism. In other words, John was being sassy, telling them they needed to have a mikvah of *conversion*, that they weren't being authentically Jewish in their actions. How do you think they liked that?

They didn't like that one bit.

Mikvah, a spiritual bath, sounds like the word for hope. You can have hope when you're in the presence of God. You can have hope when you need to start over in your walk with God and seek healthy living. You can have hope when you convert and start your walk with your Creator.

All of this begs many questions: Why did Jesus go to John to be baptized? Which version of John's rebellious, nonsanctioned baptism did Jesus feel he needed? We will answer that question at a later time. But get a mikvah Jesus did, and afterward a voice (God's) declared that this was God's son, whom God loved and with whom God was pleased. Jesus then goes into the wilderness to fast and pray, to prepare for his work. While there, he is tempted by Satan. We will circle back around to this encounter also.

Questions for Reflection or Discussion

1. Have you been baptized? Was it as a baby or did you wait until you were older?

2. Why do you think Jesus chose to be baptized? Which of the three reasons? What other reason might there be?
3. What do you think about the idea of a "spiritual bath" or spiritual cleansing?

68

Jesus the Healer, Part 1

Read Mark chapters 1–3 and John chapter 9.

What did Jesus do for a living?

After his baptism and temptation, Jesus was ready to formally begin his work. What exactly was that work? If you ask folks what Jesus did for a living, most would answer "carpenter." His earthly father, Joseph, was a carpenter, and no doubt Jesus learned aspects of the trade, but his vocation (from the Latin, "to call") was to be a rabbi, a teacher. But he was also a healer. Right out of the gate, he is teaching and healing the sick and disabled.

As you read the first three chapters in Mark, you see this explicitly. He is moving from town to town teaching the people and healing them. He heals Peter's mother-in-law from the flu, he heals various diseases, a man with leprosy, a paralyzed man, and a shriveled hand. Across all of the Gospels the list expands: those who are blind, deaf, mute, bleeding, and even death. Jesus heals as he moves from village to village teaching.

Let's focus on the healing found in Mark 2:1–12. He says a peculiar thing to the paralyzed man just before he heals him. "Child, your sins are forgiven!" (Mark 2:5).

What do you think of this? Imagine if you were sick and your physician came to you to discuss your treatment, but she said to you, "I want to get something straight before we begin. God forgives you of all your sins."

What would be meant by this? What are the implications? Is Jesus inferring that the man's paralysis was caused by sins he had committed? And if so, in what way? Was his paralysis a consequence of his sin? Or was it more mystical? Was God punishing the man with paralysis?

As modern thinkers living in a scientific age, we might be willing to accept that some of our illnesses are consequences of our behavior. If you smoke, you leave yourself vulnerable to lung cancer. If you abuse alcohol, you damage your liver. A bigger leap is the idea that God punishes us for something we did. That seems harsh and out of step with our best understanding of God. One line of thinking is logical, the other is mystical.

Jesus did not say this every time he healed someone. In John 9, Jesus says the opposite when a man born blind from birth is brought to him to be healed. His disciples ask him, "Rabbi, who sinned so that he was born blind, this man or his parents?" His answer? "Neither he nor his parents. This happened so that God's mighty works might be displayed in him" (John 9:2–3).

Even that is hard to comprehend. Is some suffering presented as an opportunity to experience God that otherwise would be missed? Maybe one could embrace this idea in retrospect, but in the middle of suffering that would be a hard teaching to hear.

When you are sick or suffering, are you able to see any good in it?

Human beings want there to be a reason why someone gets sick. Science often gives us logical pathways to understanding the origins of illness. But in the culture of Jesus, it tended to be mystical. It was a form of Jewish karma, or in this sense, a Jewish understanding of how the universe worked. If you recall, this was formalized in early Hebrew culture during the time of Moses and then proliferated throughout their history. It was called blessings and curses, or the Deuteronomy Formula. In the Gospels you see Jesus both embracing it and questioning it.

Questions for Reflection or Discussion

1. People want to know why we get sick. We often feel like sickness is unfair even when its source makes sense. Do you think being sick is unfair?
2. There are illnesses of which we can clearly identify the cause, like lung cancer and smoking. Do you ever think there is a sickness that God is using to get someone's attention or punish them?
3. What do you think about Jesus saying that being born blind provides an opportunity for the glory of God to be shown?

69

Jesus the Healer, Part 2

Read Mark chapters 5–8. Watch The Bible Project video on Mark.

Jesus travels to the land of the Gerasenes. In that region is a man living in a cave who is possessed by demons, so damaged that he is self-mutilating. Jesus goes to help him and asks him his name. "Legion is my name, because we are many" is the man's response (Mark 5:9). Jesus orders the demons to leave the man, and they enter into a herd of pigs nearby. Consequently they run over a cliff and drown, angering the local pig herders, who chase Jesus out of town.

Are demons real? That is a question that many ask when reading about Jesus. Modern observation of a similar person as the one Jesus helped might call his ailment a mental disorder, multiple personalities, or schizophrenia, the result of a brain chemistry that has betrayed the body. Resolving the question, if one wants to hold onto the value of spirituality, requires a convergence of two ideas.

The region of the Gerasenes was on the eastern side of the Sea of Galilee, which is in the country of Jordan today. It served as a resupply station for Roman armies who were passing through, some coming from military engagements. A hint of this were the pig herders. If this was predominantly a Jewish population, then pig herding would not be lucrative.

When Jesus asks the man his name, he says, "Legion, for we are many." A legion was a designation for a group of Roman soldiers, at that time around 5,000 (later it would be reduced to 1,500). What if this man were a Roman soldier who was suffering from PTSD (post-traumatic stress disorder)? What if this were a man who had done damage to his mind because he had committed atrocities, or at minimum, witnessed them?

Modern medical science would track the chemical and physiological damage such action or sights might cause. First-century Judaism would see this as an attack of demons as punishment for the sins this man had committed or participated in, no matter how marginally. What if the main difference between these two theories is the language used to describe them? One view sees this as a cosmic battle for the spirit of the man. One view sees this as damage to his mind caused by trauma.

Most of us, even people of faith, tend to make the medical science view the primary way of our understanding this phenomena, and only secondarily are we ready to call it "demon possession." We want to follow medicine as far as it will take us, and if there is still no relief, then we are willing to ask if this is a mystery beyond our understanding.

But what if it is *both*? Simultaneously?

You hear this language from time to time; someone is wrestling with that demon alcohol or the demon of cancer. It is poetic, figurative language for sure. But what if there is a cosmic battle happening within those scientific processes? Traumatic injury that comes from violence has a spiritual quality to it, an element of good versus evil. What if the body, the mind, and the spirit were not separate spheres of the human experience, but rather overlapping?

There may be part of us that wished Jesus had shown up, called a press conference, and once he had everyone's attention, said, "Good evening. Thank you for being here. Let me tell you all about this little thing called science." But that isn't what he chose to do. Living in that time and age, Jesus reached out to this sick man and cured him. Whether it was cell and chemistry damage or casting out harmful entities, one will never know. Both ways of understanding the world seem to be instinctive to us. We see the world as a collection of the physiological mechanism that make us up, and we see it as a great cosmic battle. In Jesus, maybe there is both.

Questions for Reflection or Discussion

1. Most of us, if we are sick, want the best medical care available. But most of us likely would also like our friends and family, and maybe even our medical staff, to pray to God for our healing, even if quietly

to themselves. But what if you could only choose one or the other? Which one would you choose and why?

2. Do you think that demons exist? Do you imagine there is a cosmic battle going on behind the scenes that is played out in our lives?
3. It has been said that people tend to lean toward either being left brained (logical, rational) or right brained (imaginative, creative). Everybody has both, but we tend to lean one direction. Which way do you tend to lean?

70
The Divinity of Jesus: God and Human

Read John chapters 1:1–14 and 10:22–42 and Colossians chapter 1.

If you remember nothing else about Jesus and Christianity, the one thing you should remember is this: Jesus is God.

"Wait, what!? I thought he was the *Son of God*? I even vaguely remember him referring to himself as the *Son of Man*. So which is it? *God? Son of God? Son of Man?*"

All three. It's confusing. Anyone explaining Christianity to someone needs to be honest about the perplexity. Having admitted the strangeness of it upfront, remember that the central idea of Christianity is that Jesus was God in human form.

Let's look at this in a roundabout way by considering some fourth-century BCE Greek rhetorical philosophy. Rhetoric was at the core of the Greek educational world because they held that language was the key to accessing truth. Thus, developing good arguments with precise language was an important skill to have. Aristotle said there were three main ways we attempt to convince people of the truth.

1. **Ethos.** You put forth an idea but associate it with people who are good and have integrity. When someone associates an idea with a good person, they are using ethos to convince you of that idea.
2. **Pathos.** This is appealing to one's emotions, so any commercial that leaves you in tears is stirring your feelings to draw you to that idea.
3. **Logos.** Logos is an expansive term in the Greek language and conveys the highest ideas that govern the universe. It is sometimes translated as logic, reason, or word. But all of these fail at conveying the complexity of the word. When a Greek person heard the word "logos" it meant the best ideas in the universe.

When the Gospel of John was written, John chose the Greek concept of ***logos*** to talk about the essence of Jesus. All the best ideas that govern the universe became flesh, and lived among us. It has been generally understood that the intended audience of John's Gospel was the Greek world. So if you are trying to convince them that Jesus was special, then describing his essence as *logos* would appeal to that audience. The *logos* was with God in the beginning, and the *logos* was God, and the *logos* became human.

The trouble with this is that the word "*logos*" translates literally as "word," which meant a whole lot more things to a Greek person when they heard it than what it means to people in English. It was a word packed with a punch. So in English, reading it as "word" sort of falls flat. People want to think it means "the Word of God" as in the scriptures. Though that is a nice idea, that is not remotely what was meant in the Greek language. It meant "all the best thoughts and ideas that make up the essence of the universe became flesh." English doesn't have one word for that.

So what about the *Son of God* and *Son of Man*? Both of those terms were developed in the Hebrew tradition to refer to that coming anointed leader that would restore Israel, defeat their oppressors, and set up a kingdom of justice and peace. Son of Man is a reference to "Adam." This leader would be the ideal version of a human being, thus a *Son of Man* (*Adam*). Part of the controversy surrounding Jesus in the first century was that his Jewish audience was expecting the Messiah to be a *Son of Man*, but Jesus also began to refer to himself as a *Son of God* (*divine*), much more than just an anointed human leader. The Jewish establishment was not exactly expecting this and it created problems for Jesus. Claiming to be God was a sin punishable by death. This was called *blasphemy*, offending the most holy practice or idea.[1]

▸ **Blasphemy** is when you offend the most holy of ideas or practices by word or action.

---

1. In the Hebrew cosmology, there are two distinct realms that overlap: the divine or heavenly realm and the earthly realm. Sons of God inhabit the divine realm, and Sons of Adam (man, humanity) inhabit the earthly realm. When God is at work in these various worlds, he often works in tandem with both human and divine creatures. Jesus fully embodies both worlds, sons of God and son of Adam.

Think back to our readings together in the TaNaKh (Hebrew Scriptures). The thing that distinguished the Jewish God from other religions was that God was nameless and a mystery, not some entity that could be defined and controlled. God was one God, not many Gods (see Deut. 6). The idea that God could be familiar and accessible in human form, separate from God yet the same as God at the same time, was simply ridiculous to any Jewish person at the time.

It took Jesus' followers nearly 300 years to work through what it meant for Jesus to be both the "Son of Man (Adam, human)" that was promised to the Jewish people and also the "Son of God (Divine)." The merging of these two ideas eventually became the concept of the Trinity: God, who is one, is revealed in three persons: God the Father (Creator), God the Son (anointed leader), and God the Holy Spirit (anointed Spirit). This is the traditional way of referring to these three aspects of God. There is a long and very complicated history of the complexity of the Trinity. Some additional ways of describing the Trinity could also be: Maker, Messiah, Spirit; Creator, Christ, Holy Spirit; or Creator, Redeemer, and Sustainer.

Back to the idea of rhetorical argument. Matthew's Gospel, like John's Gospel, had a target audience in mind. Matthew was writing to Jewish readers to convince them that Jesus was special and that he was the fulfillment of the promised messiah. He does this in a variety of ways. John, on the other hand, used the word "*logos*" because he was making an intellectual appeal to a Greek audience. *Logos* was understood as the collective rational ideas that held the universe together, and the *logos* was God and became flesh. Think about what you know about ancient Greek culture. Would it have been out of the question for God to take a human form? Certainly not. In the Jewish culture it was blasphemy; in the Greek culture it was a common mythos.

You've seen hints of this Jewish blasphemy in the reading you've done about Jesus forgiving sins. In the Jewish way of seeing the world, only God could forgive sins. So when Jesus forgives people he is making an indirect statement about his essence. And why indirect? Because in most instances a person who was claiming to be God would be stoned to death for blasphemy. Eventually, Jesus will be put to death for this crime, but you get the sense as you read that he is trying not to escalate things too quickly. More on that as we move forward.

There is a theological term for all of this: **incarnation**, or becoming embodied. The next chapter will build more on this important concept in Christianity, the divinity of Jesus. Why did God become human?

> ▸**Incarnation** is the theological term for God becoming human, being incarnate, enfleshed.

Questions for Reflection or Discussion

1. What rhetorical method do you think you favor? Pathos, ethos, or *logos*? Why? Which approach best wins you over to a new idea?
2. Pathos is appealing to one's emotions. Name a movie, TV commercial, or book that made you cry. Can you identify what that source was trying to convince you to think or feel?

71
Divinity Continued

Read Philippians chapter 2 and John chapter 14:1–14.

The theological word for the divinity of Jesus is **incarnation**. When God became human, he was embodied, incarnated, God-in-the-flesh. This complicated things.

Jews expected a messiah who would overthrow the foreign occupying powers. What they had zero expectation for was God showing up fully in human form. God working through a human, yes, but, when Jesus begins to vaguely refer to himself as having a divine essence and equality with God, it was considered blasphemy and was punishable by death. It is one reason that Jesus often admonishes his followers not to tell anyone about the miracles he performed. Jesus will eventually reveal who he is and why he has come, but will do so incrementally over time, when people are ready.

If one of the distinguishing traits of Judaism was that God was "one" (remember the foundational creed of Judaism, the *Shema*, that declared God is "one"), then why would God complicate that by being revealed in the human form of Jesus? Why make things difficult? This is what is often referred to as "the problem" within Christianity. How can God be one and also be three? Creator, Christ, Holy Spirit? The early followers of Jesus struggled with this obstacle, and the larger movement that emerged from his life has wrestled with this idea for centuries. The Christian tradition has never come up with an airtight explanation of how it works. So why complicate things?

Here are some traditional understandings about why God took human form; the reasons are limitless:

Earthly King. God wants to be our one true earthly king and regent. Remember in 1 Samuel when Israel rejected God as their king and demanded a leader they could see and touch?

> It seemed very bad to Samuel when they said, "Give us a king to judge us," so he prayed to the Lord. The Lord answered Samuel, "Comply with the people's request—everything they ask of you—because they haven't rejected you. No, they've rejected me as king over them. (1 Sam. 8:6–7)

In some ways the incarnation is an answer to that request. God was physically present among human beings and could be seen, heard, and touched. Jesus gives us a way to understand and comprehend God that was not possible when he was nameless and mysterious. It is a loving gesture on God's part to be revealed in this way. In doing so, God is also able to teach us a living law and demonstrate for us how to live. We get to hear and see God in action both as a teacher and example.

Divine Empathy. The writer of the book of Hebrews, an early church writer in the New Testament, wrote that "we don't have a high priest who can't sympathize with our weaknesses but instead one who was tempted in every way that we are, except without sin" (Heb. 4:15). Perhaps God doesn't need to become human to understand or sympathize with us, but God becoming human makes it easier for us to feel like he understands us. He has been through what we have been through.

Sacrifice for Sins. Jesus would make the ultimate sacrifice for sins. We will go into this in greater detail in later chapters, but it is important to mention this discussion as it is a big reason for the incarnation. Jesus will end the ancient practice of animal sacrifice for sins by offering himself as a final grand sacrifice. His death is an intentional act on behalf of humanity.

A Fuller Humanity. Jesus demonstrates what human beings are capable of if they will submit themselves to the guidance and empowerment of God. This idea is introduced and discussed in Philippians 2, and Jesus mentions it in John 14. This is where the delineation between Jesus the human and Jesus the divine becomes tricky. How can Jesus be fully human, limited in the way human beings are limited, and at the same time be fully divine, able to express limitless capacity as God?

▸An **epistle** is a transliteration of the Greek word for "letter," referring to the letters written to early followers of Jesus across Asia Minor and Italy.

The Same Mind as Christ

The *epistles* in the New Testament are letters written to the early followers of Jesus that formed across Asia Minor and the Mediterranean after the resurrection of Jesus. The apostle Paul tells the Christians in the city of Philippi that they should have the same mind as Jesus.

The same mind as Christ.

How is that possible? Can we think and act like God? Yes and no. Read carefully the words Jesus says to his disciples in John 14:8–14. Jesus is saying something tricky to his followers. He says that both his words and actions were not his own, but rather God working in him. Do you see the logical tail-chasing? If Jesus is God, then how can God work in him? Then Jesus tells them that they too can speak and act in extraordinary ways (teaching and healing); in fact they will do greater things than even Jesus did. If they will allow God to work through them, then these things can happen.

Think about a light bulb on a dimmer switch. Turned to full, it represents Jesus accessing his full divinity. But in the words of the letter to the Philippians, Jesus "emptied himself." He dialed down his divinity, intentionally, to the same level a human being has. Remember, in the Hebrew worldview human beings are created in the image of God, having the imprint of God within us. The chief sin of the Garden of Eden story was that we took it too far, wanting to claim full divinity for ourselves. So the trick is to delineate this carefully. We have the image of God within us, but we are not God. Again, to the Philippians 2:5–8:

Adopt the attitude that was in Christ Jesus:

> Though he was in the form of God,
>   he did not consider being equal with God something to exploit.
> But he emptied himself
>   by taking the form of a slave
>   and by becoming like human beings.
> When he found himself in the form of a human,
> he humbled himself by becoming obedient to the point of death,
>   even death on a cross.

The Greek word used for emptying is *kenosis*. Jesus emptied himself to connect with us, show what it looks like when God fills the human mind, and what we would be capable of when that occurs. Have the same mind as Christ? Yes, just as Jesus allowed God to work through his mind, so we too should allow God to work through us. Was the incarnation God's way of "playing human" so he could show us how to live a full humanity? This is one of the deeper reasons for the incarnation. God is potentially restoring us to our original humanity.

Again, there is some peculiar circular logic happening. This is often referred to as "the mystery of Christ." Jesus was fully God, yet fully human—a mystery that was an act of God's love for human beings, for our redemption and for us to reach our full capacity. But for these things to happen, we must fully surrender to God.

In the early chapters of the Acts of the Apostles, as the followers of Jesus are beginning to build a community of Jesus followers, you see Peter and John encounter a crippled beggar outside the temple (Acts 3). They tell the man that they don't have money to give him, but in the name of Jesus to stand and walk and be healed. Who healed the man? Peter and John? Or God? The traditional accepted answer is that God healed the beggar, but he did it in concert with John and Peter, two human beings who were united to God in a loving relationship. God healed a man through this connection.

Let's circle back around to two things Jesus did that are hard to comprehend. If he is God, as he suggests and the Christian tradition has affirmed, then why did he choose to be baptized? It wasn't for repentance. And if he *is* God, then why be subjected to temptation? A possible answer is he was modeling true humanity. Ritual bathing is important and he demonstrated how we human beings can resist temptation if we will depend on God in a similar way that he did. Jesus was modeling how humanity can work if we are connected to God.

Jesus was the incarnation of God. God wanted to have a close, loving connection to us, to be a tangible presence, to teach us, to be an example for us, to be the grand sacrifice that brings us closer to God, and show us the potential our lives would have if we empty ourselves and allow God to do loving acts through us. God blesses us so that we would be a blessing.

Questions for Reflection or Discussion

1. What are the advantages of God becoming human? Are there any disadvantages?
2. Have you ever wanted superpowers? In some sense, Jesus is teaching that we can heal and be wise in the same way he was, if we allow God's Spirit to work through our lives. What do you think about this?
3. Have you ever been tempted to do something you weren't supposed to? Do you think God gives people power to overcome temptation, if they depend on God?

72

Jesus the Rabbi

You are going to be reading Matthew chapters 5–7 and Luke 6:1–49. But don't do it yet.

These two collections of Jesus' teachings seem similar, but they have some subtle differences. These two sermons come with a host of questions that cannot be answered for sure. Is this the same sermon remembered differently? Did Jesus teach this sermon to different groups and change it a little for a different audience? As you read, look for the ways they are different.

In the previous two chapters when we were considering Jesus as a healer, we pondered what he did for a living. Most of us have a mental picture of him as a carpenter because that is what Joseph did. No doubt he was familiar with the craft, but it is most likely that Jesus chose to study to become a rabbi. Just like schools for young adults today, there were various levels of respected schools back then also. There were the "ivy league" type rabbinical schools that existed in Jerusalem and the larger urban centers. Jesus probably studied with a local rabbi in the rural synagogue near Nazareth or in the larger nearby town of Sepphoris. This is all speculation, as there is no record of what he did and there is no mention of his life from age twelve until he begins his ministry at thirty (that being the age when a rabbi's apprenticeship was over and he began his own "school").

The Gospels describe Jesus as a "different" kind of teacher, as one who taught with authority and not as the scribes and Pharisees who taught the teachings of Moses interpreting and applying them in a variety of ways. Rabbis argued about these interpretations to the degree that the argument became more important than the teaching. Jesus apparently cut through those games and got to the heart of the matter. People noticed.

Now go settle in and read these two sermons. The first is Matthew chapters 5 through 7, known as the Sermon on the Mount. The second is shorter but has some similarities: Luke 6:1–49. Then come back and finish this chapter.

The Sermon on the Mount is the most well-known teaching of Jesus, especially that first section, which is often called the *Beatitudes* because of the litany that repeats itself at the beginning of each line: *blessed are* (the poor in spirit, the meek, those who mourn, those who hunger and thirst for right-living, etc.). Each of these have the potential to generate important discussion. What does Jesus mean when he says that those who have a poor spirit are blessed? Shouldn't we have a rich spirit?

Did you notice that Jesus might be contradicting himself? He tells them to perform works of goodness so others can see and praise God, but then later berates those who practice their spirituality to be seen by others. Jesus wants us to work through the complexities. It is good to display acts of goodness, but it is also true that people might do those things for the wrong reasons.

Did you notice any differences between the Sermon on the Mount (Matthew 5–7) and the Sermon in the Valley (Luke 6:1–49)? The beatitude phrasing is slightly different, isn't it? In Matthew, he says the "poor in spirit" are blessed, whereas in Luke he says "the poor." What is the difference and why? In Matthew 5 he encourages those who are struggling with hardships. In Luke he denounces those who are rich and those who laugh. It seems harsher. Why?

Some think this is the same sermon remembered or written down differently. Some would say those who wrote the Gospels altered the story to fit a version of Jesus they preferred. This practice is called *redaction.* The Gospels are generally believed to be collections of stories that were passed around verbally and in scrolls to the different groups of followers that emerged after the resurrection of Jesus. When people write down a story, they typically have opinions as to why that story is important. Those opinions influence the way they tell the story.

Consider something else. Do you remember the four different cultural responses the Jews had to Roman occupation? Look at them again (see page 226).

When you read the teachings of Jesus, try to keep in mind these four different types of people in his audience. If you had been alive back then, you likely would have been sympathetic to one of these groups over the others. Even so, it wasn't a clear-cut sort of arrangement. You could be a Sadducee and hate that you were such a sell-out. You could be an Essene and have doubts about living your life so separate from the struggle of society. You could be a Pharisee and think maybe you were too over-the-top with your expression of your Jewish faith. It would be like being a Republican but disagree with some of their policies and viewpoints, or the same if you were a Democrat. Most people are a complicated mixture of practices and beliefs.

These two sermons seem to have different audiences. Jesus was a teacher who loved everybody: religious, secular, rich, poor, angry, cynical, sell-outs. His message penetrates to the heart of who people are, even in their complexity. When people say that Jesus "saves," they mean you are saved from hell after this life and get to go to heaven *and* it means you are saved from your own self-destructive tendencies to make yourself the God of your own life. Being a good teacher is about sensing how students are receiving (or not) what you are teaching and then making micro-adjustments in the moment. Surely Jesus, with the very mind of God, knew how to make such adjustments when he saw who was in his audience.

Your next reading will be a sample of Jesus' more well-known teachings: the Prodigal Son and the Sower and the Seed.

Questions for Reflection or Discussion

1. Name a part of Jesus' teaching from this chapter's reading that you find vague or difficult to understand. What you think he might mean?
2. Which sermon do you like better: the one on the mountain in Matthew or the one in the valley in Luke? Why?
3. Jesus told us that unless we forgive those who commit sin against us, then God will not forgive us the sins we have committed (Matt. 6:14). Do you think this is always true? Are there exceptions?

73
Temple Sacrifice and Synagogue Teaching

Every religious community has practices and rituals that shape its collective life more than others. When you go into a Baptist sanctuary, what is the focal point of the room? It is the pulpit, the podium where the preacher stands and teaches the scriptures. When you walk into a Roman Catholic church, what is the focal point? It is the altar, where the bread is broken and the wine is poured. In both of these churches, both practices are important, but at different levels. Baptists take communion, but preaching is more central. For Roman Catholics, preaching is important, but the remembrance of Christ's sacrifice is more central.

Teaching, as a religious practice, had fluctuating levels of importance in Jewish history leading up to the time of Jesus and afterward. Moses established "the law" as central, and it prescribed how they were to interact with each other. The Mosaic law also established the details of their worship and how people should interact with God. Remember those 613 guidelines that shaped every aspect of life and worship called the Halacha or "pathway"? Part of that path was the sacrificial rituals that thanked God and also paid for mistakes of the community. When Solomon built the permanent temple, he made the altar central to the outer court (sacrifice) and the Ark of the Covenant central to the inner temple (life guidelines).

Something happened in the sixth century BCE that forced them to rearrange those priorities. The Babylonians invaded Jerusalem and burned the temple to the ground. Those two aspects of their life and culture were crippled and their culture and religion had to adjust. One of the things that emerged was a greater emphasis on teaching and storytelling because sacrifices couldn't be made anymore. As a people in exile, they no longer had a temple. Again, it wasn't that teaching didn't exist before, but circumstances changed, creating a shift in what they were able to practice. Their emphasis shifted from sacrifice to preaching and teaching.

However, those practices resumed centuries later. Beginning in the fourth century BCE, the Persians allowed them to return and rebuild the temple in Jerusalem. Eventually a second version of the temple was completed—that was the building that existed when Jesus lived. Sacrifices were once again done on a regular basis and the law resumed its prominence in religious practice. Remember, the Pharisees desired to get back to what they remembered as the glory days of following the laws and the rituals. If they would do that, then the Messiah would come and defeat their oppressors (the Romans) and institute the golden age of Israel.

It was in those centuries after the destruction of the temple that teaching in the synagogue took a greater emphasis. Priests once again made sacrifices in the temple, but rabbis taught the law in the local synagogues. Jumping ahead to 70 CE, after Jesus' life, death, and resurrection, the Romans destroyed the temple once again. The Jews scattered, many of them resettling in Babylon and across Asia Minor. But it was this second destruction of the temple in Jerusalem that ended the ritual practice of sacrifice forever. Teaching became the new "sacrifice" of the Jewish culture. This would eventually be called the Talmudic tradition, the body of Jewish civil and ceremonial law (as well as some legends). All of this had its roots in the centuries before Jesus, but grew rapidly after the destruction of the temple by the Romans in 70 CE.

The focal point of their life and culture had been fluctuating, up and down like a roller coaster. During that evolution, teaching became central to the life and spirituality of the Jewish people.

Midrash

One of the practices of Talmud is called *midrash*. Midrash is the practice of taking a story, either from the Torah, the histories, the writings, or even "extra" biblical stories, and discussing all the different meanings they could possibly have. Those who practice midrash would even go as far as to literally place a story in the center of a blank page and then write different ways those stories could have meaning in margins all around the story.

Jesus tells a story to stimulate thinking about God, right living, forgiveness, responsibility, and mercy. He wants his listener to consider how these teachings shape their lives. Recall that the early Christians encouraged each other to "have the same mind as Christ." To do this, you need to grapple with what Jesus thinks and ask the Spirit of God to transform you. Part of this process is a form of midrash. Our classrooms and discussions are a kind of midrash. The table or circle that we sit around puts a story from the scriptures in the center, so to speak, and we talk through the various things it could mean.

▸**Midrash.** The practice of discussing the various interpretations, understandings, and applications of scripture.

Read Matthew chapter 13 and then Luke chapters 14, 15, and 16.

The readings assigned here give you just a sample of the stories Jesus told for this purpose. For those that follow Jesus and practice the Christian faith, reading and discussing the meaning of these stories is central to the spiritual life. In the Episcopal Church, one of my favorite parts of worship is the reading of the Gospel. We keep those stories in a special book and have an elaborate ritual of processing that book out into the middle of all the congregation, with a cross leading the way, followed by candles as the people sing. Some churches invite people to touch the book as it goes by or even kiss it. The music stops, all the people turn toward the book in a huge circle, and the reader lifts it high above their head and says, "The Gospel of our Lord Jesus Christ!" And then we read the story.

Why do we do all of this?

Because Jesus was God in human form and the stories he told were central to understanding who God is and what God wants for our lives. It is an invitation to a kind of midrash. Place the story in the center of a group of people and then discuss, "What does this mean for my life? What does God want from me?"

Midrash, as an abstract notion, is something we do all the time. Is there some big decision you need to make? You bring others to the situation and ask for their input. Is there something that has happened to you that you don't understand? You collaborate with friends, counselors, and mentors. *Help me understand what this means for my life.* We practice a kind of midrash. Wrestling with the teachings of Jesus is a valuable midrash.

Questions for Reflection or Discussion

1. Based on your experience of church and religion, what is more appealing to you, participating in rituals (baptism, communion, singing) or listening to a preacher or teacher work through an idea about God and life?
2. Who are the people in your life that you do a kind of "midrash" with? Whose wisdom do you seek to help you understand difficult ideas or events in life?
3. Do you have a teacher, mentor, or counselor in your life that helps frame what is of utmost importance?

74
The Parables of Jesus

Read Matthew chapters 22, 23, 24, and 25.

The teachings in Matthew chapters 22 and 23 are a sampling of Jesus' interaction with the Pharisees. He often challenged them and they often appeared to frustrate him. Some readers today consider Pharisees villains in the Gospels. Well intentioned, they just took things too far. Consider their historical context: The Pharisees sincerely thought that it was incumbent upon them to be faithful to God so that the Messiah would come and repair their broken culture. If someone wasn't faithful, then the Messiah wouldn't come. Their own history taught them what happened when you compromise your faith. Solomon allowed fertility religions to mingle with Judaism and it all fell apart.

▸ **Pharisee.** A person who belonged to a Jewish school of thought that followed the Torah strictly. The word is now often used to refer to any person whose strict adherence to Christianity seems exclusionary and unkind.

Matthew 24

Matthew 24 (also Mark 13 and Luke 21) is called the *Olivet Discourse* because Jesus gave this series of teachings sitting on Mount Olivet on the outskirts of Jerusalem. It is focused on the end of the age and a time when Jesus will return. As you may know, after Jesus' death he rose from the grave and taught his disciples about what his death and resurrection meant and what they were supposed to do next. But he also promised he would return for the end of this world and the beginning a new world. This is the Christian answer to the problem of Jesus not fitting exactly the Messianic expectations. He will, at a later time and era, return and be that conquering king. This is often referred to as "the second coming." There are many schools of thought about when and how this will happen. It's not something we go into any detail here, but it might interest you for further study. (See also 2 Thess. 2:1–10, Rev. 20–22, and Dan. 7–12).

The Jewish mystical tradition, *Kabbalah*, has a teaching that there will be not one Messiah, but actually two. Interestingly, this mystical teaching matches the Christian understanding of Jesus. The first Messiah will be a *messiah ben-David* (son of David), a wise and compassionate teacher and counselor who shows people how to walk in the pathway of Torah. The second one is *messiah ben-Joseph* (son of Joseph) who will be a loving but forceful warrior king. The Joseph it is associated with is from the end of Genesis, the one who rose to power in Egypt and rescued Israel from famine (see chapter 19). But isn't it interesting that the earthly father of Jesus was named Joseph? A coincidence? Who knows!

Matthew 25

Matthew 25 opens with a parable about the coming of Jesus and people not being ready. It then goes into a description of what judgement will look like when Jesus returns. It is the only time Jesus gives specifics as to the criteria of judgement. Christianity generally teaches that if you have faith in Christ and in his willingness to show you mercy, then when you die you will be with God. But Matthew 25 gives a description of what the life of someone who trusts in Jesus will look like: giving food to the hungry, clothes for those who have little, water for those in thirst, visiting the sick and those in prison. Those who do not do these things? That would be evidence they are not actually following Jesus.

▸**Second Coming.** The promise that Jesus will return one day to fully establish God's kingdom here on earth.

▸**Sheep and goats.** Jesus' teachings often describes God's judgment at the end of the age based on how one treated the weak and vulnerable, separating those who did and those who did not (the sheep and the goats).

Questions for Reflection or Discussion

1. Do you know anybody, friends or family, who follow a very strict version of their faith? Maybe your family is one of those. Do you ever have a sense that following it so strictly becomes more of a barrier to following God? What is good about people who are so faithful?
2. Can you think of ways that you or your family help those who are the most vulnerable in society?

75

The Practice of Abstraction

There are two things you are never supposed to discuss in polite society: religion and politics. Both have high potential for disagreement. People tend to be passionate about those areas of life and discussions about them can be emotionally fraught. Obviously, this applies to the Bible. There may even be people who read what is in this book and feel strongly that it is incorrect or at best is slightly off. You may even be one of them.

In this chapter is a practice that most readers of the Bible, even the ones who might disagree, all share in common. Anyone who wants to "get something" from the Bible does some version of this practice. I call it the *practice of abstraction.*

One definition of an *abstract idea* is something that is held separate from its original source. Here is an example: You are taking care of your younger brother who is sick by preparing chicken noodle soup, making a bed for him in the den where he can nap and watch TV, and bringing him water and medicine. Those are very concrete actions. But you can also say that you are *loving* your brother. *Love* is an abstraction drawn from those concrete actions. There are other abstractions that you could extract from that example: care, support, nurture, healing.

This practice is how most people, even folks who disagree about aspects of the Bible, use the scriptures. It isn't the only way the Bible is used. The Bible can also give readers ideas about who God is and what God is up to in the world. Often it is in those areas where the majority of disagreements about the Bible arise. But most everybody does some form of the practice of abstraction. Here are some examples from each of our units:

1. Story: God told Abram and Sarai to go to the land of Canaan.
   Abstraction: Take good risks and be vulnerable and venture out on a mission.

Application: When I had to move to Oklahoma, I was scared, but trusted God.

2. Story: God gave the Hebrews 613 guidelines to help them thrive.
   Abstraction: Certain *guidelines for life* help us thrive, some bring harm.
   Application: The guidelines I live by have God at the center and are wise.
3. Story: David sought to bring spiritual and cultural unity to the twelve tribes of Israel.
   Abstraction: *Unity* among a diverse group of people can strengthen them.
   Application: Name ways you build unity among diverse students at your school or in the United States.
4. Story: Jesus showed mercy to the woman caught in adultery.
   Abstraction: Though people make mistakes, *mercy* is a powerful response.
   Application: We show mercy to those who make mistakes.

See what we are doing here? We've been doing it all throughout this book and it is a common practice for people who read the Bible. The last example is actually the premise of this book's title:

> Story: Abraham and Sarah started a culture who will bless all the nations.
> Abstraction: The *blessings* we have been given should be paid forward.
> Application: I choose a career not just to make money, but to bless others.

Approaching the stories of the Bible this way opens us up to a world of possibilities, because almost always there are multiple abstract ideas that we can extract from our reading. The exciting and rich challenge is then deciding together as friends and in community how those abstract ideas become concrete in our lives. That is how God speaks to us through the scriptures and how our lives are enriched. It is a skill. The more you do it, the better you get at it, and the more beautifully complex the ideas and applications become. We call that the work of the Spirit. See? We just did it again.

Questions for Reflection or Discussion

1. Choose a story from those you have been reading together and do the three-step process of interpretation.

Unit Two

The Passion, Atonement, Resurrection, The Church, and Apostles

Genesis, Exodus, Leviticus, Jonah, Isaiah, Matthew, Luke, Acts of the Apostles, and Galatians

76

The Passion and Resurrection of Christ

Read Matthew chapter 26 through 28.

Jesus was a teacher and a healer for three years. In his third year of ministry, he went to Jerusalem and was arrested by the Sanhedrin (the religious council) and then was presented to the Romans for execution for sedition. We are going to read Matthew's account of these events.

This story is often referred to as "The Passion of the Christ." The word "passion" is derived from the Latin *passio*, which means to suffer. In Luke 9:51, after Jesus had spent years teaching and healing, it says that he "determined to go to Jerusalem." Each Gospel has its own version of why Jesus decided to return to Jerusalem at this point in his life and the events and consequences that followed. They are mostly the same, but vary somewhat in each Gospel. We are reading Matthew's version.

The Sanhedrin

The name of the high priest was Caiaphas; he was the leader of a governing body of Jewish priests and rabbis called the Sanhedrin. Those serving on this body were either sympathetic to the Pharisee or Sadducee understandings of Judaism. There are a few possible reasons why the Sanhedrin went to the Romans to have Jesus executed. Historical documents suggest that the Romans had taken the power of capital punishment away from local governments in their occupied territories. Others speculate that though Jesus was controversial, many of the Jewish leaders were intrigued by him and his reforms. And many of the Jewish people loved him. So the council may have been split and couldn't come up with enough votes to condemn him. Either way, the story recounts that Caiaphas sought to have him executed for treason against Rome.

The Arrest

Jesus was celebrating the Jewish Passover the night he was arrested. The symbolic connection with the blood protecting or saving the Hebrews from the Angel of Death to the blood of Jesus saving people from death and judgement is implied. (Go back to chapter 22 to refresh your memory of that story.)

Gethsemane was the name of the garden outside the walls of Jerusalem where Jesus went with his disciples to pray for strength. Jesus asked three that he was especially close with to go with him and watch while he prayed. They fell asleep and Jesus asks, "Couldn't you stay alert one hour with me?" (Matt. 26:40). There is kind of a typology to Jesus struggling with God in a garden; the "Son of Man" (like Adam, in a garden) is repairing what was broken in a garden.

When the authorities come to arrest Jesus, Peter takes out his knife and cuts the ear of a soldier off. Jesus tells them that those who live by the sword die by the sword, and then he heals the soldier's ear.

During their Passover supper, Jesus predicted Peter would deny him three times. After the arrest, Peter is recognized as a follower of Jesus and three times, before the rooster crows, Peter denies he even knows Jesus.

▸When Peter betrayed Jesus, **a rooster crowed three times.** This phrase is sometimes used to point to a betrayal.

The territorial Roman governor, Pontius Pilate, is ultimately the one who makes the decision to have Jesus crucified. Jesus would not be the first Jew to be executed for claiming to be the messiah. Pilate did not especially want to kill Jesus, but he probably did not care one way or the other.

▸**Pilate** was the Roman governor who sentenced Jesus to death. Sometimes this term is used to characterize someone who is pulled into some difficult political situation, often as one who is a scapegoat or betrayer. "What am I, Pontius Pilate?"

During the execution, the Roman soldiers mocked Jesus' claim to be king. They put a purple robe on him and a crown of thorns on his head. They eventually tried to give him some mild painkillers, but Jesus refused to ingest them.

▸**Crown of thorns.** The crown the Roman executioners mockingly made for Jesus.

Jesus' Death

At the moment of Jesus' death, it is said that the sky darkened, the earth shook, and the tall, thick curtain that separated the Holy of Holies from the inner court of the temple split, from the top to the bottom, signifying that the separation that existed between God and human beings was now reconnected. Jesus' death makes this possible, and he will now be the new temple (see John 2:13–25). Interestingly, thirty years later the Romans burned the temple to the ground. Judaism stopped the practice of animal sacrifice and the temple has never been rebuilt.

Do you remember when Ezekiel had a vision of a future temple that was thirty-six times the size of the Solomon's temple (Ezek. 40–47)? It was shaped like a man, the altar being his head, the sanctuary his heart, and the porticoes his arms and legs. Jesus alludes to this in John 2:13–22:

> It was nearly time for the Jewish Passover, and Jesus went up to Jerusalem. He found in the temple those who were selling cattle, sheep, and doves, as well as those involved in exchanging currency sitting there. He made a whip from ropes and chased them all out of the temple, including the cattle and the sheep. He scattered the coins and overturned the tables of those who exchanged currency. He said to the dove sellers, "Get these things out of here! Don't make my Father's house a place of business." His disciples remembered that it is written, *Passion for your house consumes me.*
>
> Then the Jewish leaders asked him, "By what authority are you doing these things? What miraculous sign will you show us?"
>
> Jesus answered, "Destroy this temple and in three days I'll raise it up."

The Jewish leaders replied, "It took forty-six years to build this temple, and you will raise it up in three days?" But the temple Jesus was talking about was his body. After he was raised from the dead, his disciples remembered what he had said, and they believed the scripture and the word that Jesus had spoken.

A wealthy man named Joseph, from Arimathea, asked if he could bury Jesus in his tomb. The members of the Sanhedrin agreed but asked to put guards at the entrance because of the rumors that Jesus predicted he would rise from the dead. They did not want the disciples to steal the body of Jesus and falsely claim he had risen from the dead.

The Resurrection

Sunday, after the Jewish Sabbath, some women followers of Jesus go the tomb to tend to Jesus' body. They encounter an angel who tells them that he is risen from the dead and is not there. We will spend some time in a later chapter on the significance of the final portion of Matthew.

Question for Reflection or Discussion

1. This story is somewhat familiar. Did you learn anything new in reading the entire account? Were you surprised by anything?

77
Atonement of the Cross

Read Genesis 22:1–19, Exodus 12:1–13, Leviticus 16:1–28, Isaiah chapters 1 and 53, and Matthew 25:31–46.

Why such a varied selection of readings? And why are some of them from back in the Hebrew Scriptures?

Jesus has been teaching and healing for what had been three years, and then, "As the time approached when Jesus was to be taken up into heaven, he determined to go to Jerusalem" (Luke 9:51). This is a pivotal point. Something different and unique is getting ready to occur. Jesus is going to Jerusalem to die.

There have been clues along the way. Jesus would often tell people to not say anything after he healed them or after they had proclaimed him Messiah. It was in part because that would increase the chances he would be arrested and put to death, as many of those who claimed to be a messiah in those times were. Jesus didn't want to die right away because he wanted to teach and heal people. He did that for three years. But now Jesus seems to be intentionally going to Jerusalem with the knowledge that he will be put to death.

The death of Jesus and what his death meant is central to understanding Christianity. His death was not just the logical consequence of political and religious conflict, though those things did contribute to his death. To say it plainly, Jesus died with purpose. He went to Jerusalem with the intention of being arrested and put to death. Why?

There are some phrases you may have heard before related to this:

- Are you washed in the blood?
- Are you covered in the blood of Jesus?
- Jesus died for your sins.
- Jesus died for you.

What do these phrases mean? The readings from Exodus and Leviticus give us the origins of blood atonement, how the sins of people were placed on a scapegoat that was then sent to die in the wilderness. This was also true for the blood sacrifices that atoned or paid for the sins of the people. Did you read Isaiah 1 closely? The prophet is questioning whether that is what God wants. He says that what God truly wants is justice and mercy toward vulnerable people. If those things are neglected, then those sacrifices to God are empty gestures.

Isaiah 53, however, makes a prediction about the promised super king, the Messiah, who would one day come to deliver them. He says that the king will be wounded and killed for his people and their sins will be placed upon him, even though he is innocent. This coming king will sacrifice himself for his people and for their sins. In some respects, the book of Isaiah is having an argument within itself. What is it that God requires from people for the sins they have committed? Does God require blood? Think of it in this manner:

> **Physical.** If you are driving and you accidently hit another car, most people agree that whoever is at fault is required to pay for damages. That is why we carry insurance. On a temporal, materialistic level we all generally agree on this notion. You pay for what you have damaged.
>
> **Emotional.** What if someone hurts your feelings? What do you require of that person then? Most of us would say we want an apology from that person, perhaps some kind of a gesture to show they are sincere, perhaps a promise and effort never to hurt us in that way again. Christian theology calls this an "amendment of life."
>
> **Metaphysical.** What if we hurt or offend God, what does God require to make it right? The first example is about the tangible world, things you can measure. The second example is harder to measure because it's about feelings. But this last one is called metaphysical, which means beyond or around the physical. This word is often used to talk about religious and philosophical ideas that are difficult to prove or measure. When people do something wrong, is the universe knocked out of balance? What needs to be done to bring it back? You could argue that

> like hurting another person's feelings, God requires an apology, perhaps some kind of gesture, and then an amendment of life. But is that all God wants?

These are the sorts of questions that arise when talking about atonement.

Foundational Christian doctrine accepts that God requires a sacrifice to pay for sins. In the old system it was an animal sacrifice. Jesus' death was intentional, on purpose, and had a metaphysical purpose. It will serve as a final sacrifice for the sins of human beings. In the Epistle to the Hebrews, you can hear a little bit of Isaiah's argument about whether or not God wants blood or compassion, but it also speaks to the final grand gesture of Jesus. The writer is trying to work this out in Hebrews 10:1–14:

> The Law is a shadow of the good things that are coming, not the real things themselves. It never can perfect the ones who are trying to draw near to God through the same sacrifices that are offered continually every year. Otherwise, wouldn't they have stopped being offered? If the people carrying out their religious duties had been completely cleansed once, no one would have been aware of sin anymore. Instead, these sacrifices are a reminder of sin every year, because it's impossible for the blood of bulls and goats to take away sins.
>
> Therefore, when he comes into the world he says,
>
> *You didn't want a sacrifice or an offering,*
> *but you prepared a body for me;*
> *you weren't pleased with entirely burned offerings or a sin offering.*
> *So then I said,*
> *"Look, I've come to do your will, God.*
> *This has been written about me in the scroll."*
>
> He says above, *You didn't want and you weren't pleased with a sacrifice or an offering or with entirely burned offerings or a purification offering, which are offered because the Law requires them. Then he said, Look, I've come to do your will.* He puts an end to the first to establish the second. We have been made holy by God's will through the offering of Jesus Christ's body once for all.

> Every priest stands every day serving and offering the same sacrifices over and over, sacrifices that can never take away sins. But when this priest offered one sacrifice for sins for all time, he sat down at the right side of God. Since then, he's waiting until his enemies are made into a footstool for his feet, because he perfected the people who are being made holy with one offering for all time.

Jesus' died purposefully, to be a grand sacrifice for the sins of all humanity. The animal sacrifices of old were a foreshadow of his one and last sacrifice. The universe, or God, requires blood for the harm people have caused. Jesus, the promised Messiah, takes the sins of his people on himself and sacrifices himself for them.

Some modern people are appalled at this idea. If you did not grow up in a church and are hearing this for the first time, it may sound odd. In the next chapter we will look at four ways of understanding Christ's death that add some nuance to the event.

Questions for Reflection or Discussion

1. Most of us think if someone damages our property they should pay to replace it. But what if someone hurts your feelings? What do you think they "owe" you then?
2. Do you think God requires anything from us when we sin or hurt others or ourselves?
3. What do you think about the idea that God requires blood to pay for the sins of people?

78
Blood and Nonblood Atonements

Read Psalm 50, reread Isaiah 1 and Matthew 25:31–46. Additional readings: Amos chapter 5 and Hebrews chapter 7.

If you grew up in a Christian church, then the idea that Jesus died on the cross with purpose may sound normal. But if you didn't, it may need some explanation. If Jesus died "on purpose," then why? Does God need blood to be okay with human beings? Here are four ways of understanding the meaning of Jesus' death on the cross.

> **Substitutionary Atonement.** This is the view that most Christians across the world have of what Jesus' death meant. God requires that there be some kind of payment for hurts that people cause themselves and other people (which hurts God). Such acts create an imbalance or deficit in the universe and need to be atoned or paid for. Because God loves us, God will come up with a substitute for this payment. The substitute is God's self in Jesus. This payment has the ability to cover all the sins of humanity: past, present, and future, because of who God is. This is God's grand gesture. God, in the form of Jesus, died in our place in order to pay for our sins. God was the substitute.
>
> **Ransom Theory.** This is similar to substitutionary atonement, but it adds some cosmic conflict to the scenario. The idea is that when human beings sinned, God gave them over to Satan, a cosmic adversary that had rebelled against God. Satan, then, in some sense, owned humanity and we needed to be purchased back. God purchased us by giving Jesus over to Satan in exchange for human beings. This language of being "ransomed" is found throughout the New Testament.

These two theories, *substitution* and *ransom*, are the two most commonly associated with Jesus' death on the cross. Both are considered expressions of God's love for human beings. Both theories are considered blood atonements in that they require blood for the relationship to be repaired. This is God's grand gesture on behalf of God's people. By Jesus advocating for people and making himself a sacrifice for them is considered a priestly act.

Some think this view of God needing blood is brutish. Are there other ways to assign meaning to Jesus' death that do not require God wanting blood to be forgiven of our sins? Yes, though it will not work the same way as blood atonements work.

> **Moral Exemplar.** This view suggests that God, incarnated as a human in Jesus, gave us the ultimate example to follow. If you follow in Jesus' pathway and commit to a life that seeks righteousness, a life that asks for and gives forgiveness, then you are participating in God's kingdom and will be included in the kingdom in the afterlife. Remember reading Matthew 25 when Jesus judges the nations, separating the sheep and goats? This is the *only time* Jesus gives specific criteria for what judgment will be based on: feed the hungry, clothe the naked, give water to the weary, give shelter to those who are homeless, and visit the sick and imprisoned. Also consider the opening passages of the prophet Isaiah when he questions whether it is blood God wants or rather the care and defense of the vulnerable.
>
> **Christ the Victor.** This view believes if you follow in the way that Jesus taught and modeled, it will cost you something. It could cost you wealth, societal advancement, popularity, friendships, and in many cases, it could cost you your life. Martin Luther King, Oscar Romero, and Dietrich Bonhoeffer are just a few examples of people who chose to follow in the way of Jesus and it cost them their life. This theory is called "Christ the Victor" because God's answer to those attacks was the resurrection. It may seem like evil is winning, but in the end Christ will be the victor. His death on the cross is an emblem of this final victory, and his followers will experience it also.

Moral Exemplar and **Christus Victor** are ways of seeing meaning in Jesus' life and death without God being the one who is calling for blood. And these views have been embraced by Christians who are uncomfortable with the blood-oriented atonement theories.

So which one is it?

Reading the overall arc of the Bible, both the Old and New Testaments, you can see all four of these ideas being presented. It is hard from a biblical point of view to explain away the need for blood atonement, but you also see the practice questioned. The scriptures ask the question: Isn't the pursuit of a compassionate and good life what God really wants?

Reread some of the key passages that lift up both sets of ideas again if you did need a reminder:

- Genesis 22:1–19
- Exodus 12:1–13
- Leviticus 16:1–28
- Isaiah 1 and 53
- Matthew 25:31–46

The truth of each of these understandings is held within the scriptures. Could it be that each are true in their own way and that they all work together to give a full picture of atonement and redemption? As much as my modern mind sometimes resists the notion that God requires blood for sin, I also know that blood is a powerful image and essential for life. The sacrifice of blood is a stark and powerful gesture of what it takes to love another person. Love requires sacrifice, and blood signifies that truth. When I approach Christ's communion table every week and eat the bread and drink the wine, I am reminded of that truth in compelling ways. Christ's death on the cross can be called God's poetry. Poetry is not "false language"; it is intensified language.

The pursuit of the fruits of the Spirit is also something God desires: love, joy, peace, patience, kindness, goodness, gentleness, faithfulness, and self-control (Gal. 5:22–23). This pursuit is in scripture also. It is why Jesus didn't announce his arrival and then immediately offer himself up for sacrifice. His teaching and healing were equally essential to who God is and what God wants for us. Care for the vulnerable, live self-aware, be forgiving, heal the brokenhearted. This is the life Jesus wants for us.

Atonement embodies all these things. It isn't one theory, it is all of them.

The word "messiah" means anointed leader. It was held for prophets, priests, and kings. Jesus' life and death was a priestly and prophetic work, advocating for humanity and teaching them what God desires for their daily living. A full and broad view of atonement captures both the priestly (sacrifice) and prophetic (righteous) lives together.

Questions for Reflection or Discussion

1. Which of the four theories of atonement do you identify with the most?
2. You might have heard the phrase, "Jesus died for our sins." Do you think Jesus died for your sins?

79

Jonah and Blessed to Bless

Read Genesis 12:1–4 and Genesis chapter 28. Then jump over to Exodus 19:1–6. Finally, go read the entire book of Jonah. It isn't long. Don't skip this, I want you to see something.

The book of Jonah is a fantastical story of a man being swallowed by a great fish. But there is so much more going on in that story that is often overshadowed by the fish bits. God asks Jonah to preach God's message of repentance and mercy to the Ninevites. They were not Israelites, they were Assyrians. Jonah does not want to do it and flees the opposite direction toward Spain. That is where the fish bits comes in. He begrudgingly goes to Nineveh and reluctantly does what God wants. When the people accept God's message, Jonah pouts. "I knew it! I knew you would show mercy to those people."

Then there is a strange episode about God giving Jonah some shade from the hot sun while he is pouting. Then God takes the shade away. It's there the story ends abruptly.

To truly understand the significance of Jonah, we need to go back all the way to Genesis and Exodus and consider the development of the ancient nation of Israel. This is why you were asked to go back and reread the call of Abraham and Sarah and then the recasting of that same Vision Quest to his grandson Jacob. It was Jacob who was first given the name Israel after wrestling with God. He craved God's blessing because he was anxious about fulfilling the family mission handed down to him by his grandfather Abraham. What was that mission? To take the blessing God has given their culture and bless all the nations of the earth. In order to do this, Jacob needs to start his family. He sets out to find a wife, but with this stern warning: *Do not* marry a Canaanite.

Anyone see the irony?

What is so bad about Canaanites? That is one of the serious challenges of reading the Bible clear-eyed and critically. Held within these stories are genuine tribal and cultural conflict. It is easy to say God loves all tribes and cultures. However, we should avoid a simple sentimental reading of culture. Is every practice and idea in every culture good and life-giving? Of course not. So was avoiding cultural mingling with Canaanites a good thing or not?

Think back to the first time we encountered the name *Canaan* in our reading together (see chapter 8). Noah curses his grandson Canaan for some unspoken shady dealings that occurred in Noah's tent after his nakedness was covered up in the wake of his drunken stupor. "Cursed be Canaan!" he screams. Noah cursed Canaan and all of his future descendants.

The cultural mistrust of Canaanites isn't all because of that story, but it is an ancient story attempting to explain the origins of a historic conflict. A big challenge for readers of the Bible is trying to understand what it was about the Canaanites (and numerous other tribes) that God did not like. It wasn't simply because they were not Hebrew. There are multiple tribes that the Israelites interacted and cooperated with along the way. The simple answer (and because of that probably not completely accurate) is that Canaanite culture was associated with fertility worship, which incorporated hedonistic sexual rituals and child sacrifice. These practices were a big reason why the Levitical laws on sex were so strict and why the demand for religious purity from the prophets was so intense. You can't mix your spiritual and cultural practice with others when their culture is so destructive and provocative.

So how do you bless all the families of the earth and at the same time protect and cultivate your own culture? Can you do both? Yes, but it becomes easy to start thinking of your life in terms of us-versus-them, insider and outsider. The technical word for this is *sectarian*, or a sect of people that maintain a closed community. Sectarianism has an upside and a downside.

Tracking the arc of the Hebrew Bible, from Moses to Solomon, you have the Israelites focusing a great deal on trying to be the people and culture God wants them to be. They do this by not getting tangled up with certain cultures and religions that would make that difficult. It seems that with David's reign they are finally growing into their own sense of themselves and their identity in God. But then Solomon falls into extreme syncretism (the mixing of his Hebrew religion with fertility cults) and the nation and culture falls apart spiritually.

The prophets emerge with their message calling people back to the original Vision Quest. Among them is the prophet Isaiah. He predicts that a future king will emerge and bring Israel back to God. But that is not all the king will do. For the first time, you hear another message: Not only will this future king bring health and strength to Israel, he will bring it to "all the nations." It isn't that such a notion didn't exist before, but Isaiah is the first time it is mentioned as a priority. Israel will be made whole again so they can fulfill their original Vision Quest—to bless all the nations on the earth.

Back to the Canaanite question. Can your life's purpose be to bless all the people on earth if you have a built-in prejudice against one of those "other" people groups? Perhaps, but only under very specific conditions and for the right reasons. It means not painting any person or group of people with a broad brush, all the while being able to identify what aspects of any culture are not healthy. Threading that needle is a very hard thing to do.

When you are raising kids, you want your children to be kind and respectful to everyone. You also don't want them to take abuse from anyone who wants to harm them. You want them to be friendly and respectful to all people, but you don't necessarily want them to be friends with everyone, especially those who are not helpful to them becoming who you are trying to raise them to be. There will come a time, after your kids have matured, that you want them to use their strength and identity to bless others, even those who may be living harmful lives. At that point, hopefully, they will be fully embracing their own sense of self and can differentiate from other people, especially from others who might harm them. Part of maturing is understanding how to navigate that terrain. It's about healthy self-identity and proper boundaries.

What we should not do is be so overly careful about living into our own religious and cultural identity that we never grow into the next step. That is one of the lessons of the book of Jonah.

"I will make of you a great nation and will bless you. I will make your name respected, and you will be a blessing. I will bless those who bless you, those who curse you I will curse; all the families of the earth will be blessed because of you." (Gen. 12:2–3). To be a "kingdom of priests for me and a holy nation" (Exod. 19:6) who will advocate for all the world you need a strong self-identity, but not so strong that you are exclusive and hurtfully sectarian.

Our next chapter will see how this tension was at work within Jesus and the early Christian movement.

Questions for Reflection or Discussion

1. Name a group of people that you enthusiastically consider yourself a part of.
2. Now name people who would not be able to be a part of that group. Is this a good or a bad thing?
3. Are there people you avoid because they might be a bad influence on you? What are ways you can love those people and not be hurt by them?

80

Jesus and the Canaanite Woman

Read Matthew 12:38–45 and then read Matthew 15:21–28. Then read Matthew 28:16–20. As you read, remember that Matthew was writing with a Jewish audience in mind.

In the previous chapter we read about Jonah refusing to go to a non-Jewish city to preach God's message of repentance and mercy and then pouting when the Assyrians end up accepting the message he quite reluctantly gives them. In Matthew 12, Jesus is comparing himself to Jonah.

What in the world for? There are some obvious parallels. Just as Jonah was in the belly of a fish for three days, so the Son of Man will be in the heart of the earth. Remember what we call these biblical allusions? A typology. Jesus is telling the Jewish authorities, who are demanding a sign of his authenticity, that he is a "type" of Jonah. So does that mean he is a reluctant, bitter, resentful, pouting preacher? No, in fact he is implying that he is a kind of inverse Jonah or a perfect version of the imperfect Jonah. Jonah went into the belly of a fish and came out reluctantly preaching to the world. Jesus, by contrast, went into the belly of the earth and comes out willingly proclaiming God's mercy to the world.

There are other pieces of the Matthew 12 passage that allude to this preaching outward. He references the Queen of Sheba's visit to Solomon, an outsider seeking out God's wisdom (1 Kings 10:1–13).

What of this very peculiar encounter Jesus has with the Canaanite woman in chapter 15? She is sometimes called a "Syrophoenician woman." Keep in mind the back-reading we did about the lingering prejudice against Canaanite people. This woman approaches Jesus and his disciples seeking healing for her daughter. Jesus ignores her. She persists and his disciples implore him to send her away because she is bothering them. Jesus finally tells her that he will not help her because he came to only help the lost sheep of Israel. He only came to help Jews and no one else. She pleads with him, and Jesus' answer is confounding. He basically calls her a dog. "It is not good to take the children's bread [Israel] and toss it to dogs [Canaanites]" (Matt 15:26). But she is unrelenting and insists that even the dogs end up eating some of the crumbs that fall from the master's table.

What in the world is Jesus up to?

Here are two theories about this encounter: The first tends to hold a more liberal view of Jesus. It suggests that Jesus was acting out a cultural bigotry that he was taught, one that was ingrained in the Jewish culture. It was ingrained because many at that time believed that it was the cultural diffusion that occurred after Solomon's syncretism that weakened Israel and led to their being occupied by foreign powers. It was religious (cultural) purity that would make it possible for the Messiah to return and bring Israel back to their glory. So Jesus was acting out of attitudes that he was taught growing up in that culture. If we strengthen Israel, then the Messiah will come. Helping others was a secondary concern. This theory suggests that the Canaanite woman's faith caught Jesus off guard and taught him about his own bigotry. He was so impressed with her tenacity that he healed her daughter and presented her as an example of great faith to his disciples.

However, there is a problem with this interpretation if you hold to a traditional view of the nature of Jesus. If Jesus is God incarnate, then that would mean he is perfect. You cannot be perfect and a bigot.

This leads us to an alternative theory about this exchange. Jesus, as a master teacher, was trying to see if he could wake his disciples up to a bigger idea. He pulls this sassy Canaanite woman unwittingly into his ploy. Suppose a teacher wanted to make a point about not excluding others by walking into class one day and treating one group of kids unfairly to see if the other kids would defend them. Was Jesus using situational satire to see if his disciples would come to the Canaanite woman's defense? Was Jesus doing a bit of prophetic street theater to wake his disciples up to their cultural and religious bigotry?

I think Jesus was doing the latter, playing chess on a three-level board, so-to-speak. And the last reading from Matthew 28 indicates that is what he was up to. Matthew 28:16–28 is called "The Great Commission." It is the last bit of instruction Jesus gives to his disciples after his resurrection before he makes his final ascent into heaven. Look closely: "Therefore go and make disciples of all nations" (Matt. 28:19).

Go where? To all the nations.

Make what? Make disciples (students) of what? Of the particular brand of Judaism that Jesus was teaching. What was the original vision quest of Abraham? God will bless you so that you can bless all the nations of the earth. Now go. Do it.

Do what? Baptize them in the name of the Father and of the Son and of the Holy Spirit. What are the origins of baptism? Jewish Mikvah. Why did Jews do ritual bathing? To make themselves ready to be in the presence of God, to repent of harmful behavior, and to convert to a life walking with God. This was a command to mikvah everyone in the world.

Teach them what? Teach them to obey everything I have commanded you: Teach people in all cultures the pathways (halacha) of God, so they too might be able to live as God created them to live and dwell in the presence of God like the Garden of Eden.

It is a long and winding, up and down, convoluted pathway, but the purpose of the life and ministry of Jesus, including his sacrificial death on the cross, was to open up the presence of God to all people. Jesus was telling his disciples that their culture need no longer hoard the blessing of God but instead was tasked with giving it away to all people. Jesus is the perfect Jonah. Jesus sends God's people outward to complete the task given to Abraham and Sarah, to bless all the families of the earth and repair what was broken in Eden.

Questions for Reflection or Discussion

1. Which interpretation of Jesus and the Canaanite woman do you think is better? Was she teaching him to love beyond what his Jewish

culture had taught him? Or was he testing his disciples to see if they would call him on his apparent bigotry?

2. What sort of prejudices do you have? Can you identify them? What would the correct reasons be for excluding someone, if any?

81
The Great Commission and Acts of the Apostles

Read Matthew 28:16-20 and then Acts of the Apostles chapters 1 through 4.

Jesus, the Jewish rabbi and healer, presented himself as the fulfillment of the promised Jewish Messiah. His claim to be the promised Jewish king would have been a threat to the Romans, and his claim to be God would have angered the Jewish authorities. He was arrested and put to death by the Roman Empire at the request of the Jewish religious authorities. According to the eyewitness accounts of his followers, he lay dead for three days and then rose from the dead.

What happened next?

Many who have a cursory knowledge of Christianity think that Jesus was a Christian. From our reading together, I hope you now have a profound sense of the Judaism of Jesus. How did Jesus' Jewish movement become a different religion entirely? At what point did it split off from Judaism and become Christianity? It was a slow process, taking forty years or more.

The book of the Acts of the Apostles tells the next part of the story.

If the four Gospels were "the movie" about the life of Jesus, then the book of Acts is the sequel. In fact, the author of Acts is generally understood to be Luke, the writer of the Gospel of Luke. There is some evidence that Luke and Acts were originally one book, but it was eventually divided. As we read portions of the first part of Acts, chapters 1–9, we will set the stage for the eventual transition of Judaism into Christianity.

The book starts by describing the ascension of Jesus into heaven. After Jesus' resurrection, he spent forty days with his disciples teaching and explaining what had happened and what they would need to do next. Among his teachings he promised them the gift of his Spirit, a sort of special dose of power they would need in order to do the work he was asking them to do. So after his departure they waited, and the Holy Spirit eventually arrived and overwhelmed them. Empowered by this gift, they went out and taught the crowds about Jesus.

It is important for you to notice that Peter's message is given at a Jewish festival called **Pentecost**, or the Feast of Weeks (Exod. 34:22), a kind of celebration of the first harvest of wheat. Jews from all over the expanded region came to Jerusalem to celebrate. Many different regions are listed as being present in Jerusalem, including Jews and the "God-fearing," which was a term for non-Jews who had converted to Judaism. At Pentecost, Peter was telling the story of Jesus' brand of Judaism to a larger Jewish audience. But notice the distinction, Peter is only preaching to Jews.

Read Acts chapters 5–7.

The followers of Jesus are forming new communities. The practice of healing has now been given to the disciples and the type of communities are pretty extraordinary. They are selling everything they have and redistributing resources to people as they had need. This would have been as strange then as it would be today. These groups were governed by immense love and generosity.

They held regular reenactments of the Last Supper that Jesus had the night of his arrest, which they called "Love Feasts." Rumors began to spread that they were eating flesh and drinking blood. This would have been expressly forbidden by Jewish practice and their reputation as a dangerous Jewish cult grew. A cult is a group of people who have split from an accepted religion because they have corrupted its accepted belief system. The teaching of Jesus was considered a corruption of Judaism. The Jewish authorities did not believe God would be human and the resurrection was a desperate attempt of his followers to keep their movement going. The religious authorities worked hard at trying to squelch it. The arrest of Peter and John and the stoning of Stephen capture this tension between the Jewish authorities and this rogue break-away Jewish group.

Take notice. When they were stoning Stephen for blasphemy, a young Pharisee named Saul was overseeing it while he held the coats of those who were throwing the rocks (Acts 7:58).

Questions for Reflection or Discussion

1. Some extraordinary things are happening to these followers of Jesus. What do you think is a bigger miracle: people being able to hear someone speak in their own language, healing the sick, or everybody selling all their possessions to give to other people's needs?
2. If you had the power to heal sick people, what would be your strategy to use it?

82
The Conversion of Paul for the Gentiles

Read Acts chapters 9–11.

The Bible, though many books written by a variety of authors over a period of 1,500 years, does have one central idea: *God wants to bless all the families of the earth through Abraham and Sarah's descendants.* Christians see the final emergence of Jesus as the last piece in that movement to bless all people. Jesus is God in human form, a living temple (where God dwells) that is now accessible to everyone. Jesus teaches all people the ways of God, a perfect version of what the Mosaic law called the Halacha or pathway, and when we fail to live up to that path, our sins are atoned for by the loving sacrifice of Jesus.

Paul

What you read in Acts chapters 9 through 11 is an important next step in this process of *all* people having access to God. Saul, a fiercely committed Pharisee, had been hunting the followers of Jesus, trying to stamp out their movement. This wasn't an uncommon practice. There were multiple "false messiahs" that made their Roman occupiers nervous and unsettled the Jewish authorities. Jesus was seen as a Jewish blasphemer and heretic and the authorities wanted his movement to fade away. Saul is traveling to Damascus to confront a group of Christians when the risen Jesus appears to him on the road in a bright light. Saul is knocked to the ground.

▸**Damascus Road experience.** Anytime someone has a life experience that changed them dramatically, or changed their thinking, this is sometimes referred to as a Damascus Road experience, after Saul's conversion to Paul.

> During the journey, as he approached Damascus, suddenly a light from heaven encircled him. He fell to the ground and heard a voice asking him, "Saul, Saul, why are you harassing me?"
>
> Saul asked, "Who are you, Lord?"
>
> "I am Jesus, whom you are harassing," came the reply. "Now get up and enter the city. You will be told what you must do." (Acts 9:3–6)

Saul is temporarily blinded and is taken in by a follower of Jesus named Ananias. Recovering at Ananias' house, flaky scabs that looked like fish scales formed over his eyes. God tells Saul that he chose him to share the story of Jesus with the Gentile world, to non-Jews. The "flakes fell from Saul's eyes" (Acts 9:18), and he is changed. Jesus has called him as an apostle, one who is sent out, to the Gentiles. Saul, who it just so happens was half Jewish and half Roman, begins to go by his Roman name, Paul. Paul will become one of the most influential leaders in the Jesus movement, sharing this brand of Jesus-Judaism with the entire world.

> ▸**Scales from my eyes.** Connected to Paul's conversion experience, this is used again to describe someone having a new perspective. I was blind, but now I see.

Meanwhile, a significant event important to this new task occurs.

Peter

Peter, the devout Jewish fisherman and follower of Jesus, had always tried as best he could to follow the guidelines of the Mosaic Halacha, or the pathway. This included following the food purity laws. At this point, a dramatic change is made. Peter has a vision on the roof of Cornelius, a Roman centurion, who was also a follower of Jesus. A blanket descends from above that holds all kinds of forbidden foods. A voice tells Peter he may now eat these foods. Peter refuses. The voice chastises him and commands him to eat: "Never consider unclean what God has made pure" (Acts 10:15).

To be fair to Peter, this would have been a very difficult command to obey. The food traditions had been in place for nearly1,500 years. Think about how much people hate change. When Peter went downstairs and announced to his Jewish friends that God had just told him that 1,500 years of religious tradition was now null and void, it would have caused quite a controversy. It was a new era in God's interactions with humanity. God wanted to expand the community of "chosen people" to include everyone. Food laws would limit that expansion.

For the next few decades, an argument ensued. If non-Jews were going to be allowed to be a part of God's community, would they be required to follow the same customs and traditions as Jewish followers of Jesus? Up to this point Jewish converts had been required to do that, so why not these converts also? Jesus was Jewish after all. Why was this any different?

It was different because God had announced it was now different. Not everybody would be convinced, and so they argued.

In some ways the remainder of the New Testament is working through a version of the following question: *What does being a follower of God in Christ Jesus look like exactly?* The New Testament books consisting of letters to the Christian communities of Rome, Galatia, Ephesus, Philippi, and portions of other books are all working through these questions specifically for non-Jewish followers.

In fact, many of the early churches (collections of people who were attracted to Jesus' teachings and believed him to be the Jewish Messiah and God in human form) were made up of two distinct groups: Jewish followers of Jesus and Gentile followers of Jesus.

In some instances these churches were divided into groups called the "circumcised" and the "uncircumcised." Now *that* is awkward.

The entire book of Romans is essentially Paul trying to resolve a squabble between Jewish and Gentile Christians in Rome. Apparently they had been arguing about which of them were God's true chosen people. Paul tells them that *both* of them are chosen and embraced by God. Neither group deserves God's grace. God's favor is a gift of God's love for both groups.

Why would this be so hard?

Again, think about it. It had been two thousand years of believing you are God's chosen culture, a kingdom of priests set aside for a special purpose. That is hard to unthink. But what did it mean to be a kingdom of priests? Recall the definition of a priest: someone who advocates to God on others' behalf. That was supposed to be the purpose of this special culture, to advocate for all the families of the earth, Jew and non-Jew alike. Jesus finally pushes them to go out into the world and advocate and embrace all people. That old self-perception of their special-ness was hard to reimagine. It's hard to unthink something you've been thinking for 1,500 years.

The early Christian communities argued about what parts of Judaism would need to be maintained by Gentile followers of Jesus. What they finally decided was that Gentile men would not need to be circumcised and would also not be required to follow the Jewish food laws (see Acts 15). But Paul did tell them not to "rub-it-in" with fellow Jewish Christians who still followed those parts of the Mosaic law. In other words, don't bring bacon to the church potluck. Be considerate of those around you and how that would make them feel.

Baptism, the Greek word for a ritual bath, called *mikvah* in the Jewish language, took on an added meaning. Since Greek converts would not need to be circumcised as a sign of their covenant with God, then baptism (or mikvah), a Jewish conversion ritual, soon came to serve as a replacement ritual for circumcision. Baptism was the sign of the covenant with Christ. Adults (along with infants and children) who would become a part of this movement were baptized. Remember, Jewish mikvah was a rite of both repentance and conversion.

This is truly where Judaism and Christianity begin to take on separate identities. At the time, Christianity was considered a Jewish cult, a corruption, or innovation of Judaism. When they dropped the requirement of circumcision and food laws, it began to become its own unique thing. I often say that Christianity is rogue Judaism, or Judaism stripped of a few of its distinctive rituals and then unleashed into the world.

Questions for Reflection or Discussion

1. Have you had anything close to a Damascus Road experience? Do you know anybody who has had something like that?
2. Can you name any traditions or practices that make you feel part of a group but that might make someone else feel excluded?
3. Would you have believed Peter when he told you God wanted to change a 1,500-year-old tradition?
4. Do you like change? When do you like it and when don't you?

83
Disciples and Apostles

Read Luke 6:10–16 and then Matthew chapters 13–14.

If the goal is now to give this reimagined, expansive version of Judaism to the entire world, someone has to lead it. The first to venture out were the disciples of Jesus.

Jesus was a rabbi. As rabbinic schools developed and were established in towns and villages, teachers would prepare students to eventually go and be teachers themselves. Jesus chose twelve rabbinic students to study with him. The word "disciple" comes from the Greek word for "student." Jesus chose twelve.

Twelve is one of those symbolic numbers, what we have called in past readings, a typological idea. That means the number holds a symbolic meaning and because of that it shows up repeatedly in different places, carrying with it that added meaning. Twelve is significant because it was the number of tribes that descended from Jacob, the grandson of Abraham, that made up the nation of Israel. Ten of them were Jacob's direct offspring, the other two were his grandsons through his son Joseph (Manasseh and Ephraim).

Because of that, it wouldn't be uncommon for a rabbi to have twelve students. Jesus does exactly that. After a night of prayer, Jesus called all those who were following him and chose twelve of them to be his inner circle. He narrowed it down. It reminds me of lining up to choose kickball teams during recess as a child. There were people who left everything to be students of Jesus and they didn't get picked for the final twelve! I wonder if I would have been picked?

Of course the word "disciple" has expanded to mean much more than student. If I started referring to my students as *my disciples,* no doubt I would receive calls from concerned parents. It would sound as though I was starting a cult. The word now is firmly enmeshed with religious meaning. Disciple is a loaded word.

▸**Disciple.** From the Greek, it means a student. Over time it has taken on more of a religious connotation.

The word "apostle" also became a loaded word. Derived from the Greek, it means one who is sent out on a mission. When Jesus sent his students out to teach and heal, he was giving them apostolic work. Like the word "disciple," it expanded and came to mean something specifically religious.

The word "apostle" for most Christians means only those original students (disciples) of Jesus that he sent out into the world to spread his teaching. It started with the original twelve, but then one of them, Judas, betrayed Jesus and ended up killing himself out of remorse. The other disciples replaced Judas with a man named Matthias (twelve was an important number for its symbolism). Eventually, Jesus appeared to another man named Saul, who changed his name to Paul, who also went on a mission to spread the teachings of Jesus. So Paul is also considered one of the original apostles.

▸**Apostle.** From the Greek, it means "one who is sent out." When Jesus sent his students out on missions to teach and heal, he made them apostles. Eventually the term came to refer specifically to the twelve (and only those twelve) students he sent out to start the Christian movement.

What is confusing about this is that there are millions of people over the centuries who consider themselves students of Jesus who have gone on missions to spread the teaching of Jesus. In fact, I am one of those people. I am a student of Jesus' teaching, and I spread it wherever I go. But I am not an "apostle" because I didn't walk with Jesus and learn from him firsthand. Only those who knew Jesus face-to-face can be described as apostles.

Take that a step further. Some Christian churches consider themselves "apostolic" churches. What they mean is that they are trying to follow the version of Jesus' teachings given to those original apostles. The thinking is that such a version of the faith must be the most accurate because those followers knew Jesus directly. Anyone who came after that may have some good ideas about Christianity, but what they teach needs to match the teaching of the original apostles.

Roman Catholics consider their version of Christianity to be *apostolic*. Orthodox churches also consider their beliefs and practices to be apostolic. The reformed churches from the fifteenth and sixteenth centuries broke away from the Roman Catholic tradition in great part because they thought the Catholic Church had departed too far from those teachings Jesus handed down to the original apostles. So they "protested" (protestant) and "reformed" the church to get it back in line to what they thought Jesus originally intended it to be. That is why we call it the *Protestant Reformation*. It was an argument about what original Christianity was supposed to be like.

▸**Apostolic.** An adjectival form of *apostle* that describes Christian churches who try to model their belief and practice after the version of Christianity the twelve apostles created.

As you can see, the definition of *apostle* grew complicated over time. Today there are so many different forms of Christianity. One way to understand all the various types of Christianity is this way: they tend to disagree on the original apostolic teachings or which of those apostolic teachings are okay to change. All of the apostles were men. Some churches now have women pastors. Is this okay or not? Knowledge and culture have shifted a great deal since the time of Jesus, and Christians disagree about the manner and degree the faith is allowed to change with it.

Questions for Reflection or Discussion

1. If you study the life and teachings of Jesus, you are in some sense a disciple, or student, of Jesus, just not one of the original disciples. Do you consider yourself a disciple of Jesus?
2. If you go on a mission to share the life and teachings of Jesus with others, you are doing apostolic work, but this does not make you one of the original apostles. Are you an apostle of Jesus? Why or why not?

84
The Twelve Apostles: Go Give God to Everybody

This chapter has a smattering of readings throughout. This is a quick look at the twelve students Jesus chose to send out on his mission. So there will be references you can look up as you read about each one.

Remember, the word "disciple" is derived from the Greek word for "student," and the word "apostle" is Greek for "one who is sent out." Both of these words took on added religious meaning unique to Christianity. But always keep their basic definitions in mind. These men were students of Jesus that were sent out on a mission to spread his teaching to others.

Andrew and Philip

The first two who followed Jesus were Andrew and Philip. They were first followers of John the Baptist, but he told them to stop following him and instead follow Jesus. Andrew was a fisherman and Philip was a biracial Jew with a Hellenistic (Greek) parent. Philip later spread Christianity to Phrygia (Turkey), where hostile Jews had him tortured and crucified. Andrew died preaching in Greece and was crucified on an X-shaped cross, which became his symbol. The X-shape you see in the flag of Scotland and the Union Jack of England are derived from various Brits adopting Andrew as a protective saint.

Simon, Called Peter

Andrew convinced his brash brother Simon to be a student of Jesus. You may have heard him referred to as Simon Peter. There is more written about Simon Peter than any other disciple. This is likely because of his temperament. He seems to be one who speaks before he thinks and is the first to charge into any given situation. But his brashness had a downside. He also seems to be the first to flame out. Regardless, he was given the name "rock (*Petrus*)" by Jesus because he would be the foundation upon which Jesus would build his Church, and Jesus said he would give him "the keys to the kingdom." In this sense Peter was the de facto head apostle.

After the resurrection, Peter migrated to Rome and became the chief pastor of the early Christian movement in that city. Because of this, and because of what Jesus said to him, the Roman wing of the Church believes that each of Peter's successors in Rome inherited that lead position and are to be considered the head pastor of the entire church, or the church Catholic, which means universal (think capital "C"). Because of this, the Roman Catholic Church today understands itself as the head church of all Christianity. But other Christian groups don't think this is what Jesus intended (Peter the head of the apostles, yes, but not his successors being head of the global church). Other branches of Christians developed around the same time in Constantinople in Turkey, another group in Alexandria in Egypt, and another group in Antioch in Syria. So in those early centuries there were multiple heads of different regional groups of Christians. And of course, Protestant Christians, who formed in the fifteenth and sixteenth centuries, don't recognize Rome as the head church.

If you really want a full picture of Peter, take the time and read the following passages:

- Matthew 14:22–33
- Matthew 16:13–28
- Luke 22
- John 21

Peter was eventually killed in Rome for spreading a false religion. He thought himself unworthy to be crucified in the same way as Jesus, so he asked to be crucified upside down.

Simon the Zealot

There was another lesser known apostle named Simon (the Zealot or Simon the Canaanite). This word "Canaanite" could be translated in two ways. You should have a sense by now that the designation "Canaanite" was derisive. Like Samaritans, Canaanites were seen as substandard Jews. (Remember "Cursed be Canaan!" from the Noah story?) But the word also might be derivative of a word meaning "rebel." Simon is called a Zealot, a political revolutionary faction committed to overthrowing the Roman government by any means necessary. Not much is written about him in the Gospels. Legend has Simon proclaiming the Good News in a variety of places: Egypt, Cyrene, Africa, Mauritania, Britain, Libya, and Persia.

Legend is that Simon was put to death by a governor in Syria, while another legend says he was killed in north Africa. Christian Ethiopians claim he was crucified in Samaria, while other traditions claim that he was sawn in half in Persia. You will often see paintings of the disciples with the instrument of their death in their hands. Simon the Zealot is often shown with a saw in his hand.

Matthew

Matthew was a tax collector that was despised by most of his fellow Jews. The Gospels never say that he was a Sadducee, but since they were the ruling class that was closely connected to the Romans, it is likely that Matthew moved in those circles. Initially, Peter hated him, that is clear. Read Matthew 9:9–13. Matthew is traditionally thought to be the author of the Gospel of Matthew, and it is a book that is oriented toward a Jewish audience. Legend has it that after the resurrection Matthew went to Ethiopia and spread the teachings of Jesus, and was beheaded there.

James and John

James and John were fishermen and brothers. Jesus gave them nicknames for their brashness, calling them the "Sons of Thunder." There is a story about their mother asking Jesus to make them second and third in command (Matt. 20:20–28) in Jesus' kingdom. John, believed to be the traditional writer of the Gospel of John (and of the epistles of 1, 2, 3 John and The Revelation to John), is sometimes called the "beloved disciple" because John's Gospel tells of a disciple "that Jesus loved" or one that he was close friends with, but never gives the name of who that disciple was exactly. It has been conjectured over time that John was referring to himself, anonymously for the sake of humility. We cannot be sure if it was him. John's Gospel was written oriented toward Greeks or the Hellenistic world. John is the only disciple believed not to be killed for preaching this new religion. He died of old age in prison on the Island of Patmos (The Revelation to John).

Thomas

Thomas was the disciple who was not present when Jesus first appeared to them after the resurrection. He told them he needed to put his fingers in the wounds in Jesus' hands and side in order to believe that he was alive. He later saw Jesus, who told Thomas to touch his wounds. Jesus told him, "Do you believe because you see me? Happy are those who don't see and yet believe" (John 20:29). Because of this he is called "Doubting Thomas." Thomas eventually went east to India and planted churches. If you travel to western India today, there are numerous Catholic churches named "St. Thomas." Legend has Thomas being thrust through with pine spears while in India, tormented with red-hot plates, and then burned alive.

> ▸**Doubting Thomas.** This name originally refers to the disciple of Jesus who could not believe Jesus rose from the grave until he saw and touched his wounds. It is often used to describe someone who is skeptical.

Judas Iscariot

Judas Iscariot (Judas from *Kerioth*, pronunciations have evolved over time) is known as the one who betrayed Jesus. He was paid thirty silver pieces by the religious authorities to give them the location of Jesus the night he was arrested. They didn't want to arrest him in open daylight and upset those who supported Jesus. Judas later regretted his actions and tried to give the money back. He bought a field with the money and committed suicide, hanging himself. Jesus knew that Judas would betray him and his role as a villain is complicated by the fact that Jesus died intentionally. If Jesus went to Jerusalem to die for the sins of humanity, in some ways Judas helped him accomplish that end.

Judas establishes a signal with the authorities when they go in the dark to arrest Jesus. He would be the one Judas gave a kiss. Jesus said to him, "Judas, would you betray the Human One with a kiss?" (Luke 22:48). The term "Judas's kiss" often means someone who betrays another.

▸**Judas's kiss.** The kiss Judas gave Jesus to show the temple guards who it was they should arrest in the Garden of Gethsemane. It now refers to someone who betrays a friend.

Judas (Not Iscariot) or Thaddeus, Bartholomew, and James the Lesser

In our count, that makes nine apostles. What about the other three? There was another named Judas and the writers of the Gospels distinguish him from Judas Iscariot by calling him "not Iscariot" so readers won't think he was the betrayer. He was also known as Thaddeus.

There is Bartholomew (also known as Nathaniel), a sarcastic fisherman that Jesus liked because he was honest and sassy (John 1:43–51). Legend is Bartholomew was flayed alive for spreading Christianity.

There is second disciple named James who later became the pastor of the Jerusalem church, distinguished from the other by the term "lesser" (which probably only meant he was younger). The Jewish authorities eventually had James killed for spreading what they deemed a false religion, throwing him off the top of the temple to make an example of him. James, unwilling to deny Jesus as the Messiah, was cast down from the temple and then beaten to death with a fuller's club. James is sometimes depicted holding a fuller's club in paintings and iconography. Strange, right?

The Twelve

There is an easy acrostic you can use to memorize these twelve disciples: Baptism of Jesus:

B artholomew
A ndrew
P hilip, Peter (2)
T homas
I scariot, Judas
S imon the Zealot
M atthew
J ohn, James the Greater, James the Lesser, Judas—not Iscariot (4)

Notice the variety of people Jesus chose to be his students and spread his teaching: tax collector, revolutionary, Hellenist, rationalist, sarcastic, true believer. There are a few people in this group who initially probably hated each other. Did Jesus do this intentionally? Jesus cared about all these different types of people, both their strengths and their weaknesses.

Because the number twelve was significant, the eleven apostles moved quickly to replace Judas after his suicide. Matthias was selected by the casting of lots under the guidance of the Holy Spirit. And as we have already discussed, Jesus appeared to Saul, a Pharisee, who was persecuting the early followers of Jesus and trying to stamp them out. He would become the "apostle to the Gentiles." God used a Pharisee, someone concerned with maintaining cultural and religious purity, to share the Jewish faith with non-Jewish cultures.

Questions for Reflection or Discussion

1. Having looked at each of the disciples, is there one of them that you relate to the most? How so?
2. Jesus gives Simon the nickname "Peter" because he will make him the foundation of the Church. Based on what you read about Peter, why do you think Jesus did this?

85

Paul Continued . . .

Read Galatians chapters 1 through 3.

I suggest reading this portion of Paul's letter to the Galatians in this chapter as sample of the struggle the early followers of Jesus had deciphering how to integrate non-Jewish people into this new Jewish movement. Peter has fully accepted the idea that God is available to all people, but when Paul visits the community in Galatia, he notices that Peter seems unwilling to sit and eat with the Gentiles. He publicly chastises him. Change is difficult.

Remember that the essence of the epistles (letters) written in the New Testament are working through two main issues: What does the Jesus-possessed life look like? What parts of the Jewish tradition must we hold onto as we open things up to Gentiles, and what do we let go? In most letters, one or both of those questions are in the background. God is for everybody; now what does that look like, in real time, in real life?

Questions for Reflection or Discussion

1. The ability to sit and talk with just about anybody is a rare skill. Are you able to be friends with most people?
2. Who would you find it hard to sit with at lunch and why?

86

The Epistles and The Revelation to John

The word *epistle* is derived from a Greek word that means letter. There is an entire library of letters in the New Testament that our biblical survey here does not have time to cover. However, now you have the larger historical, cultural, and religious context to understand the contents of those letters. They are:

- Romans
- 1 and 2 Corinthians
- Galatians
- Ephesians
- Philippians
- Colossians
- 1 and 2 Thessalonians
- 1 and 2 Timothy
- Titus
- Philemon
- Hebrew
- James
- 1 and 2 Peter
- 1, 2, and 3 John
- The Revelation to John

The content of the letters cover a variety of things, but one characteristic of them all is their attempt to work through the practical aspects of giving this reimagined Judaism to the entire world. They are love letters to new Christians across Asia Minor, the region where the apostles first began to spread the message of Jesus.

As you read the Epistles, look particularly for the tension between Jewish followers of Jesus and Gentile followers of Jesus. It was in that cultural tension, and the compromises made between the two, where the new and unique religion emerged out of Judaism. You may also want to turn to *The Bible Project* that has videos for each of these letters.

The Book of Revelation

The book of Revelation is one of the most notorious of the Bible's library and you may feel a bit cheated that we didn't read it. The authorship traditionally is attributed to John the apostle of Jesus, and was written as a letter to those new churches in Asia Minor (modern day Turkey). The word "revelation" is derived from the Greek word *apocalypse*, which means *to reveal*, and so the book is sometimes referred to as *The Apocalypse of John*. That word is a loaded word that most people think is always about the end of the world (zombie apocalypse?). This particular revelation does allude to the end of history, but an apocalypse may or may not include knowledge about the end of history.

The images and allusions in the book are starkly beautiful, sometimes encouraging, and at other times frightening. Many of them are confusing. They utilize highly symbolic imagery that is steeped in Hebrew and Mesopotamian poetic forms. The books of Daniel and Zechariah from the Old Testament use many of the same images. You'll recall that we did not go into any depth for those books either. The reason? Understanding the meaning of highly allusive apocalyptic imagery takes in-depth study that a survey like this does not have time to cover. (I would invite you to study them further.) Generally speaking, Revelation's strange imagery serves to be a kind of code language that wouldn't be immediately decipherable to the governments that were oppressing the letter's recipients. For Daniel it was the Babylonians; for John and his Revelation, it was the Roman Empire and the Emperor Domitian.

God's Pathway

At the beginning of this journey, I shared that Christian tradition understands the Bible, consisting of 66 books (or 82 if you include the Apocrypha) and written by over 40 different authors across the span of 1,500 years, is actually one unified story. God told Abraham and Sarah that through their descendants all the families of the earth will be blessed:

- The path of Moses at first was only for the Jews, the path of Jesus is now for all people.
- The animal atonement of Moses was only for the Jews, the atonement of Jesus on the cross is atonement for all people.
- The temple that Solomon built was only for the Jews, the temple of the body of Jesus is for all people.
- The Jews were to be a kingdom of priests who advocated for everyone. Their culture prepared the way for the great high priest, Jesus, who advocates for all people.

Do you see what God is doing?

The Bible is a long and convoluted journey. It takes the ancient people of Israel from religious and cultural insularity to an expansive inclusivity. There is still a pathway God wants all people to walk, a pathway that leads to a healthy and well-lived life. But when we fail, the blood of Jesus atones for those failures and his grace and love pulls us back onto the path. This is a journey for all people. Those who walk in the pathway of Jesus are included in this expanded kingdom of priests. Jews and Gentiles alike can be priests to the world, advocates for all the families of the earth. One way you could frame the entire Bible is with these two passages:

> "I will make of you a great nation and will bless you. I will make your name respected, and you will be a blessing.
> I will bless those who bless you,
> those who curse you I will curse;
> all the families of the earth
> will be blessed because of you." (Gen. 12:2–3)

> Jesus came near and spoke to them, "I've received all authority in heaven and on earth. Therefore, go and make disciples of all nations, baptizing them in the name of the Father and of the Son and of the Holy Spirit, teaching them to obey everything that I've commanded you. Look, I myself will be with you every day until the end of this present age." (Matt. 28:18–20)

God blesses us through the life, work, and presence of Jesus, a descendant of Abraham and Sarah, in the line of David, and the very presence of God. Now that we have this blessing of God in Jesus, we in turn give the blessing to everyone we meet. We have been blessed to bless.

Epilogue

Jesus Is the Way of Love

I fell in love with Jesus when I was a child, my young idealism drawing me toward faith. The idea that there was a man who once existed, and in some sense still exists, who was good and could be trusted, resonated with me. When my parents divorced and I felt somewhat lost and abandoned, Jesus became even more important to me. I remember walking out to the edge of town, sitting on a rusted barrel, taking out the pocket-sized photo of Jesus I was given by the American Baptist Church where we attended, and talking with Jesus. I prayed to God about my broken family. It brought me a sense of hope.

Because of that childhood experience I had some childhood thoughts about becoming a pastor when I grew up. In high school I had a tumultuous few years with my stepfather and my dependence on God was stirred up again. As I finished college I had to decide whether to go on to study English Literature in grad school or go to seminary. My adviser said to me, "When you read literature, you are always looking for God in it, even when God isn't there." I went to seminary.

A mentor once told me that if you aren't reading the Bible with a literary sensibility, then you probably aren't reading it correctly. The writers of the scriptures wrote their history with such poetic and artistic flair because they believed it could enrich the reader's life. God was revealed in history though this Hebrew culture and then fully in the person of Jesus. Anyone who hears that story could become a part of this interaction with God. Deep down this resonated with me. God created us, wants to be known by us, and is active in history—the world's history and my own. I think that can be true for you also. Remember, God is for everyone, even you.

Is God mysterious and known to us as if looking through a veil, obliquely? Yes, there seems to be little doubt as to the answer to that question. But I love that it is a mystery and at times a game of hide and seek. It seems playful to me, at times painfully so, but also lovingly.

As a liberally educated adult, raised by an intelligent and skeptical mother, I will confess that I have had moments of intellectual struggle with certain aspects of religion. But combined with other experiences and a community of smart, funny, and loving Episcopalians (and a goodly portion of smart, funny, and loving Baptists too), I am truly a believer. Jesus has encountered me and I have fallen in love with Jesus, our Creator in human form.

The prophet Isaiah said that when God's teaching goes forth into the world that it never comes back empty. Oh, that this might be true for all who have a chance to look for God in the pages of the Bible.

What You Didn't Get to Read

As a priest and biblical scholar, I have to confess that it pains me as you finish this book you only have part of the picture. It makes me feel like I failed as your guide. As I wrote in the introduction (and you may have noticed along the way), this book was shaped by a very specific context, a junior high religion class at Casady School in Oklahoma City. I have tried to shape the book so it could be more accessible generally to any audience. But there is also something valuable about admitting one's own circle of experience in relation to their work. This is my admission. I teach the Bible to preteen and early teens at an Episcopal school with an audience of students who have a wide range of religious experience (and none at all). That, along with our limitations of time in the humanities curriculum at Casady School, shaped this book. This is locally grown biblical theology.

So what have you *not* read? In many cases we have glossed over a few key stories that depict acts of rape. It is hard to avoid it completely in the account of Sodom and Gomorrah, that story being vague because the people in that city want to rape angels, which lends itself to ambiguity. And the way Lot's daughters ensure their heritage is very sketchy. The same is true for our reading of the book of Judges, which have some of the most horrific stories of violence, particularly toward women, within the scriptures. None of these acts are presented as normal or acceptable, but due to the ages of our students, we either handle them gingerly or hop over them altogether.

We maneuvered around some of the harsher, more brutish laws in the Torah, many of them related to sexual practice. I did convey that one way of understanding this context was the Hebrew tribes juxtaposition to the Canaanite tribes that were practicing all kinds of perversions, including child sacrifice. A deeper study of how Torah is understood within its context and then applied for modern use is not something we had the time to do in this survey. But you now have a basic context to read and think further.

We didn't delve into many of the writings of the prophets, only to make a nod to their context. I commend them to you, especially the books of Isaiah and Amos, as well as a slow and careful reading of Ezekiel (one of my favorites). These are beautiful literary works with fascinating images, ideas, and turns of thought and phrase.

Studying the apocalyptic writings of Daniel, Zechariah and the Revelation to John is fraught with complexity and potential pitfalls. It's hard to know that a given interpretation of them is accurate. Their ambiguity was intended, as they were written during a time when they needed to be careful about who understood them. There is a built-in challenge in studying this kind of "code-language." Because this is a survey, we did not do a deep dive into those books, but you have the foundation to take that venture up.

I also wish we could have done a closer reading of the Wisdom books in the Hebrew Scriptures, including the "Wisdom of Solomon" from the Apocrypha.

And lastly, we concluded our reading just as Christianity was getting its feet planted. There is a lot to read about the early church and the spread of Jesus' mission to the world.

You now have what I hope is a good introduction to the storyline and context of the Bible. What you read next is up to you.

Acknowledgments

I want to thank my friend and colleague Charles Blizzard, the former vicar at Casady School, for allowing me the freedom to create a comprehensive survey of the Bible. He, along with Elizabeth Larsen, the then director of the middle division at Casady School, gave me wide berth in considering what stories we could cover and how exactly to approach them. They were nonstop sounding boards all along the way.

I am deeply grateful to Sara Zedlitz, assistant director of the middle division at Casady School, who graciously agreed to proofread the first draft. Jake Staats, who at the time taught fifth grade geography, and David Braden, fifth grade math, occupied the rooms adjacent to "Bible Land" and learned quite a bit of biblical narrative simply by osmosis, as well as having to put up with hearing the *Books of the Bible* song through the walls some 300 times a year. They both are always so gracious.

Thank you to the good people at *The Bible Project* in Portland, Oregon. Reading the Bible through three times a year with middle school students was beginning to show me patterns in the scripture that your videos clarified and confirmed. And your beautiful artistic renderings—the "art of the chart"—helped our kids as they read also. All of us at Casady School are big fans of your work.

Heartfelt gratitude to my wife, Karen, who whether she knows it or not is probably the person I am always trying to win over when I am writing. Her approval means more to me than is probably healthy and all the reason why she should never give it to me completely. I'm chasing that dragon, Karen.

To my students at Casady School in all their wild varied religious (and nonreligious) backgrounds: You have never stopped asking the question, "So what?" about these stories. Attempting to answer that question for you (and for myself) has been a big part of this journey. For the most part, you have given me the room to say, "I don't know." This has made me a better teacher and preacher.

Finally, creating the class has changed me and drawn me closer to Jesus. For that I will be eternally grateful. Reading together with the students has brought me closer to God. I pray it is doing the same for them.

Fr. Tim Sean Youmans (PapaYou+)
Casady School, Oklahoma City, 2020

Appendix One

BVC: Bible Vocabulary Concepts

Genesis

Am I my brother's keeper? When God asked Cain where his brother was, Cain acted as if it wasn't his responsibility to take care of him. When used, the phrase implies that we are responsible for each other (Gen. 4:9).

antediluvian. Before the flood.

apocalypse. Typically associated with the end of the world, this actually means "to reveal." The coming of the end of the world might be part of an apocalypse that reveals that end. God revealed the planned destruction of the earth to Noah as part of that apocalypse.

circumcision. The physical mark Israelite boys would undergo to indicate they were a part of the Abrahamic tribe, ritualistically cutting off the foreskin of the penis, typically on the eighth day after birth (Gen. 17:10–13; Josh. 5:2–9).

cubit. First mentioned in the directions given to Noah to build the ark in Genesis, this is generally considered the length from a man's elbow to the tips of his fingers, about 18 inches.

deluge. Another word for flood.

dystopia. A world gone wrong and falling apart; the opposite of utopia.

east of Eden. God punished Cain by sending him "east of Eden." This is used to refer to someone who has been banished by a group of people or society (Gen. 3:24).

the **Garden** (or **Edenic**). A reference to a perfect world or utopia, before the "The Fall." We need to "get back to the Garden" (Gen. 2:15).

Her offspring will crush your head and the serpent will strike his heel. Christians believe this to be a foreshadowing (4,000 years in the future) of the death of Jesus (the serpent will strike his heel) and Jesus' victory over that death in the resurrection (her offspring will crush your head) (Gen. 3:15).

imago Dei. Latin for the "image of God;" often used to describe the larger Hebrew concept of human beings sharing aspects of God's nature.

mark of Cain. This was a mark God put on Cain to protect him from others harming him after he was banished for killing Abel. No one knows what the mark looked like (Gen. 4:15).

monotheism. The practice of worshiping one god. Abraham and Sarah were distinct from regional polytheistic practices. They followed one God, a foundational teaching for the Abrahamic faiths (Jewish, Christian, and Muslim) (Gen. 12:1–3).

mytho-poetic. Stories that show what is important to a group of people or a culture. These stories can be fiction, nonfiction, or a mixture of both.

olive branch. When the dove returned with an olive branch, it was a sign that there was land. Since the earth had been washed of violent people, the branch is now used as a symbol for peace (Gen. 8:11).

original sin. The belief that Adam and Eve introduced sin into the human race and every human is subsequently born sinful.

patriarch and **matriarch.** The head father and mother of a family or tribe. Abraham and Sarah are the chief patriarch and matriarch of the Hebrew culture.

polygamy. Having more than one wife, a practice not uncommon in the period of the biblical stories, especially in the Old Testament.

polytheism. The practice of worshiping more than one god.

sin. Sin is when human beings act or think against God's original intent.

the **snake.** A symbol for a dangerous temptation, and later conflated (mixed) with Satan because of a story from Jewish mythology about Satan being a fallen seraph (an angelic creature that is sometimes depicted as a serpent-like creature with wings) (Gen. 3).

Sodom and Gomorrah. The cities that Abram's nephew Lot moved to when they parted ways. God destroyed these cities for their inhospitality and wickedness. The term is now used to refer to a wicked place (Gen. 19:1–29).

young earth. The idea that the biblical creation accounts are literal descriptions of the earth's origins, and if you track human history using this primeval text, the earth is approximately 6,000 years old.

Exodus

genocide. Killing the entire population or generation in order to demoralize your enemy.

God's chosen people. God chooses Israel for a specific task, to be advocates (priests) to God on behalf of the entire world (Exod. 19:1–8).

infanticide. Killing infants to demoralize your enemy or to control their population.

kingdom of priests. Israel is given the task of being advocates (priests) to God on behalf of the entire world (Exod. 19:1–8).

manna. The name for the flaky bread was a similar sounding word for the question, "What-is-it?" The answer is *miraculous bread from heaven.* (Exod. 16:4–5).

water from the rock. The idea that God will provide out of nothing (Exod. 17:1–7).

Leviticus

aliens. People who are not native to a country. Biblically, one should treat foreigners with kindness because you yourselves were once strangers in a strange land. Contrast this with the earlier command in Exodus to not intermarry and to smash the altars of other religious cultures they might encounter. This is a tension within the scriptures that is often hard to resolve (Deut. 25:5; Eph. 2:12).

gleanings. Don't harvest everything from your fields, but leave some on the ground for the poor, disabled, foreigners, and those abandoned by their providers. Also, don't harvest the corners of your fields at all. Leave that for the needy also. They can come in at the end of the day and "glean" (take, gather, reap) from what is left over.

sabbath year. A year which occurs every seven years when the people were to let the land stand fallow (not plant) to recoup its nutrients (Lev. 25:1–7).

scapegoat. The priest symbolically places all the sins of the people onto a goat and then it is driven into the wilderness to die. Today the term is used to describe someone who has been blamed for someone else's mistakes (Lev. 16:20–22).

Year of Jubilee. Every seven sets of sabbath years, on the fiftieth year, the community was required to do an economic reset: forgive debt, return property taken as interest, and set slaves free (Lev. 25:8–17).

Joshua and Judges

antihero. A protagonist that is ethically challenged but accomplishes good outcomes in spite of, and sometimes because of, their moral ineptitude.

laying out a fleece. The sign Gideon asked from God to ensure that God would be with him in a battle against the Moabites. Today it is used to refer to someone looking for a sign from God (Judg. 6:36–40).

The patience of Job is a common saying today that refers to Job enduring his suffering without knowing exactly why it was happening to him.

Rahab and the red cord. This was the signal to the Israelite army not to harm Rahab and her family in return for helping the Israelite spies. This is a typology of the blood over the doorposts in the Passover (Josh. 2:1–22).

shibboleth. The word that the Gileadites used to determine who were Ephraimite traitors because they could not pronounce the "sh" sound. It is now used to refer to insider, code language (Judg. 12:6).

theodicy. Generally the study of why bad things happen to good people. It's root meaning is God justifying God's ways to human beings.

typology. When stories, ideas, or images repeat across time periods to recall important stories of the past and show a connection across time. The first story is the type, the repeating story is the antitype.

Samuel

concubine. A female servant, essentially a slave, who serves in the household of a powerful man, often includes serving in a romantic function as a mistress.

lament or **lamentation.** A statement, song, or poem grieving the loss of something or someone important. See Job or Psalms.

mikvah. A ritualistic bathing done in the Jewish tradition, later adapted by the followers of Jesus as an initiation rite for converts to the Jesus movement. Early on, it served as a substitute for circumcision for Gentile converts to the Jesus movement.

speaking truth to power. Saying things to powerful people that they need to hear, but do not want to hear. This can be difficult because they can hurt you or kill you in retaliation.

1 and 2 Kings

chariots of fire. A movie that was based on a committed Christian Olympic runner, which was a reference to the story of Elijah in 2 Kings 2:11, 6:17, and Josiah in 23:11. (It is also a well-known theme song from that movie.)

cut the baby in two. A reference to the story that demonstrates Solomon's wisdom and is used to describe a difficult situation that needs an unconventional and wise solution (1 Kings 3:16–28).

Jezebel. Since Queen Jezebel rebelled against God by promoting fertility worship, the name is often associated with a woman who has loose morals or has indiscriminate sex with lots of people (1 Kings 18:17–19).

misogyny. The belief and practice that men have a higher intrinsic value than women, which leads to the mistreatment of women.

passing the mantel. Elijah placed his cloak onto Elisha's shoulders as a way of passing his role onto him. The phrase is now used when a position is passed from one person to another (2 Kings 2:1–15).

syncretism. When you mix two or more religions into one, adapting practices from both. It is not practicing different religions separately, but rather a conflation of the two.

Wisdom of Solomon. Solomon was known for asking God for wisdom and creating the collection of wisdom sayings in the scriptures, so this phrase often is used to describe someone who is wise (1 Kings 3:1–5).

Prophets

"All along the Watchtower." A song written by Bob Dylan that was inspired by the imagery in Ezekiel, to speak the message of people's self-destructive behavior to them even if they do not want to hear it (Ezek. 33; Isa. 21:5–9; Rev. 6:1–8).

prophetic voice. Speaking to people about things they would rather not hear, but need to hear.

valley of dry bones. Ezekiel's vision of human bones coming back to life (Ezek. 37:1–14).

"Wheels in the Sky." The title of a song by the band Journey of a sad dystopic landscape. It offers imagery similar to Ezekiel's vision of a fiery chariot (Ezek. 1:1–29).

The New Testament

apostle: From the Greek, it means "one who is sent out." When Jesus sent his students out on missions to teach and heal, he made them apostles. Eventually the term came to refer specifically to the twelve (and only those twelve) students he sent out to start the Christian movement (Matt. 28:16–20).

apostolic: An adjectival form that describes Christian churches who try to model their belief and practice after the version of Christianity the twelve apostles created.

blasphemy. When you offend the most holy of ideas or practices by word or action.

Crown of thorns. The crown the Roman executioners mockingly made for Jesus.

Damascus Road experience. Anytime someone has a life experience that changes them dramatically or changes their thinking, it is sometimes referred to as their "Damascus Road experience" after Saul's conversion to Paul (Acts 9:1–22).

disciple. From the Greek, it means a follower or student. Over time it has taken on more of a religious connotation as a personal follower of Jesus.

Doubting Thomas. Refers originally to the disciple of Jesus who could not believe he rose from the grave until he saw it and touched his wounds; it is often used to describe someone who is skeptical (John 20:24–29).

epistle. A transliteration of the Greek word for letter, referring to the letters written to early follower of Jesus across Asia Minor and the Mediterranean Sea.

Gospel comes from the Greek word for "good news" or "good tidings." The term was commonly used for the declaration of a political victory or change in leadership. It is now most commonly used to describe these four accounts of Jesus' life, who brought good news of God. The four Gospels in the New Testament are Matthew, Mark, Luke, and John.

incarnation. The theological term for God becoming human, being incarnate, enfleshed.

Judas's kiss. The kiss Judas gave Jesus to show the temple guards who they should arrest in the Garden of Gethsemane. "Judas, do you betray me with a kiss?" Jesus asked him. It now refers to someone who betrays a friend (Luke 22:47–48).

Messiah complex. Usually meant in a derisive way, this description implies that someone is arrogant enough to think they can help or rescue someone or a group of people.

midrash. The practice of discussing the various interpretations, understandings, and applications of scripture.

Pharisee. A member of an ancient Jewish sect (school of thought) that followed the Torah strictly. Today it is often used to refer to any person whose strict adherence to Christianity seems exclusionary and unkind (Matt. 23:1–36).

Pilate. Sometimes used to characterize someone who is pulled into some difficult political situation, often as one who is a scapegoat or betrayer. It is based on the actions of Pontius Pilate, the Roman governor who oversaw the trial of Jesus and ordered his crucifixion (Matt. 27:1–26).

rooster (cock) crowed three times. This is sometimes used to point to a betrayal, stemming from the time that Peter denied knowing Jesus (Luke 22:54–62).

scales from my eyes. Connected to Paul's conversion experience, this is used again to describe someone having a new perspective. I was blind, but now I see (Acts 9:17–19).

Second Coming. The teaching of Jesus that promises he will return one day to fully establish God's kingdom here on earth (Matt. 16:27–28; 24:29–31).

sheep and goats. The teaching of Jesus that describes God's judgment at the end of the age based on how you treated the weak and vulnerable, separating those who did and did not into sheep and goats (Matt. 25:31–46).

Appendix Two

Books of the Bible Songs (with Chords)

To listen to these songs go to: *www.blessedtobless.us*

Books of the Bible

(G) Genesis, Exodus, Leviticus, Numbers, Deuteronomy (D)

Joshua, Judges, Ruth and 1st and 2nd Samuel (G)

1st and 2nd Kings and 1st and 2nd Chronicles (D)

Ezra, Nehemiah, Esther, Job, and 150 Psalms (G)

Proverbs, Ecclesiastes, Song of Solomon (D)

Isaiah, Jeremiah, Lamentations, Ezekiel, Daniel, Hosea (G)

Joel, Amos, Obadiah, Jonah, Micah, Nahum, Habakkuk (D)

Zephaniah, Haggai, Zechariah, and last comes Malachi (G)

Refrain: (C) *Abraham and* (D) *Sarah were blessed by* (G) *G-d*

to (C) *bless all the* (D) *people of the earth* (Em)

Apocrypha (Hidden or Esoteric)

Tobit, Judith, additions to Esther, Wisdom of Solomon (D)

Sirach, Baruch, letter to Jeremiah

Song of the Three Holy Children (G)

Susanna, Bell and the Dragon, 1st and 2nd Maccabees (D)

Esdra, Manasseh, more Maccabees

and then a few more Psalms (G)

Refrain: (C) *Abraham and* (D) *Sarah were blessed by* (G) *G-d*

to (C) *bless all the* (D) *people of the earth* (Em)

Christianity Emerges Out of Judaism

(Em) Matthew, Mark, Luke, John, Acts, Romans,

(C) 1st and 2nd Corinthians (Em)

(D) Galatians, Ephesians, Philippians

Colossians, 1st and 2nd Thessalo(Em)nians

1st & 2nd Timothy, (C) Titus, Philemon, Hebrew, (Em) James

(D) 1st and 2nd Peter, 1, 2, 3 John, Jude and the Reve(Em)lation

(C) *Yeshua,* (D)*anointed the Lamb of* (Em) *God*

who (C) *takes away the* (D) *sins of the* (Em) *world*

(C) *Yeshua,* (D) *anointed the Lamb of* (Em) *God*

(C) *prophet, priest and* (D) *king to bless the earth* (Em)

The Entire Bible

(D) Creation, the (Em) Garden, the Fall, the (C) Flood, the Tower of (D) Babel

(D) Mytho-Poetic (Em) tales that (C) show us who we are

(D) Conceives of a (Em) culture that will (C) one day bless all (D) people

(D) Abram and (Em) Sarai wait for (C) years to have a son

(D) Isaac and Re(Em)bekcah pass this (C) Vision Quest to (D) Jacob

(D) Fighting for (Em) blessing, wrestles (C) God, Israel wins

(D) The family (Em) grows until it (C) follows Joseph (D) southward

(D) Living in (Em) Egypt 'til the (C) slavery settles in

(C) Four hundred years (G) later (Em) Moses draws them (D) homeward

(C) Back to (G) Canaan land after (Em) forty years (D) at bay

(C) Given the (G) pathway, the hala(Em)cha, to build this (D) culture:

(C) A kingdom of (G) priests that will (Em) bless the world one (D) day

(D) Joshua, the (Em) savior, leads them (C) back into land of (D) Canaan

(D) Keep yourself (Em) separate from the (C) Canaanite melee

(D) The up and down (Em) spiral of the (C) Judges (worst book ever) (D)

(D) Gideon, (Em) Samson, and (C) Deborah's faithful days

(D) The people (Em) ask for a king, want to (C) look like the other (D) nations

(D) Saul is (Em) chosen, but he (C) goes around the bend

(D) David the (Em) shepherd boy, (C) anointed to replace him (D)

(D) He will unite (Em) the tribes, and (C) build Jerusalem

(C) David is the (G) archetype for a (Em) king who will reign (D) forever

(C) Prophet, (G) priest, and king for the (Em) nations held at (D) bay

(C) David's (G) house will be (Em) established now and (D) forever

(C) A kingdom of (G) priests that will (Em) bless the world one (D) day

(D) Solomon (Em) starts off wise but (C) power and money corrupt (D) him

(D) Building temples (Em) for his wives, that old (C) Canaanite melee

(D) The kingdom (Em) splits, corruption (C) reigns both north and (D) southward

(D) The prophets (Em) raise their voice for (C) justice in their day

(C) Assyria, then (G) Babylon, then (Em) Persia have (D) dominion

(C) From the House of (G) David a child (Em) will be born some (D) day

(C) Wonderful (G) counselor, (Em) suffering servant (D) coming

(C) Messiah of all (G) Messiahs: (Em) prophet, priest, and (D) king

(C) Born in a (G) stable to Mother (Em) Mary and Father (D) Joseph

(C) Rabbi, (G) healer, lamb who (Em) takes on all our (D) sins

(C) The final (G) sacrifice to (Em) finish all the (D) trouble
(C) Incarnate in (G) Jesus, God's (Em) Presence 'til the (D) end
(C) In Jesus, the (G) blessing of (Em) Abraham, is (D) met